Please Touch

How to Stimulate
Your Child's Creative Development

Susan Striker

A FIRESIDE BOOK
PUBLISHED BY SIMON & SCHUSTER, INC.
NEW YORK

The author is grateful for permission to reprint material from the following:

Creative Art for Learning by Merle B. Karnes, page 11. Copyright 1979 by The Council for Exceptional Children. Reprinted with permission.

"The Family Circus"®, reprinted with permission of Bill Keane and The Register Tribune Syndicate.

"How" by Lois Libien and Margaret Strong, reprinted by permission of the Tribune Company Syndicate, Inc.

"Machine Sounds Around the House," from *Resources for Creative Teaching in Early Childhood Education* by Bonnie Mack Fleming et al., © 1977 by Harcourt Brace Jovanovich, Inc. Reprinted by permission of the publisher.

"Marvin" by Tom Armstrong, © 1983, 1984 Field Enterprises, Inc. Courtesy of Field Newspaper Syndicate.

Simon and Schuster/Fireside Books,
Published by Simon & Schuster, Inc.
Simon & Schuster Building
Rockefeller Center
1230 Avenue of the Americas
New York, New York 10020
SIMON AND SCHUSTER, FIRESIDE and colophons are
registered trademarks of Simon & Schuster, Inc.

Designed by Barbara Marks

Manufactured in the United States of America

1   3   5   7   9   10   8   6   4   2
1   3   5   7   9   10   8   6   4   2 Pbk.

Library of Congress Cataloging in Publication Data
Striker, Susan.
Please touch.
Bibliography: p.
1. Child rearing.   2. Creative activities and
seat work.   3. Children—Recreation.   I. Title.
HQ769.S8866   1986   649'.51   85-26107

ISBN: 0-671-60593-3
0-671-49648-4 Pbk.

Acknowledgments

Thanks to my friends Pat Feller and Dana Wyles and my agent Chris Tomasino for assistance, inspiration, and input, and to Doug Wyles for introducing me to the art of Frank Post, who did the illustrations for this book.

Thanks to musicologists Ann Russell and Nancy Sheridan Montgomery for generous contributions to the music chapters of this book and to my dear friend, music teacher Maryann Craven, who donated so much of her time, information, and experience to the music chapters.

For generous contribution of time and expertise in the area of movement I wish to thank Patty Caplan and Cynthia Olivera. Thanks also to Jack Wiener of The School for Creative Movement in the Arts, who generously provided information about movement and dance.

Thanks to Leslie Day of the Association for Infant Massage, who contributed the section on massage.

Special thanks to my husband, Michael, for his patience, support, and help. Thanks to Suzanne Kolodziej and Janet Liff for their assistance in compiling the list of children's museums.

I would especially like to give my thanks to all of the children who contributed to this book, and who generously agreed to be photographed or who donated art work.

Thanks also to their parents, for their cooperation.

Oren Abeles   Jesse Conan
Tally Kristen Brolin   Elizabeth Craven

Pat Feller
Sarah Feller
Paul Gnellery
Miguel Gomez
George Gumpert
Dennis Holland
Nicholas Krohley
Russell Lambright
Jeffrey Lane
Amanda Miller

Elizabeth Newman
Jonathan Nickerson
Peg Nickerson
Rachel Perschetz
Katherine Severs
Jesse Sneddon
Jason Striker
Laura Wigmore
Gregory Wyles
Evan Zeisel

Special thanks to my son Jason, whose curiosity and creativity inspired the book, and who cheerfully allowed his every move to be photographed, documented, and dated.

Illustrations by Frank Post from photographs by Susan Striker

Music Copyist: Christine Buck Kissel

*Dedicated to all of the children
whose parents and teachers have so carefully
taught them all the things they must
not touch or do in this world.*

Contents

Imagination gives wings to the intellect.

Frank and Teresa Caplan
The Second Twelve Months of Life

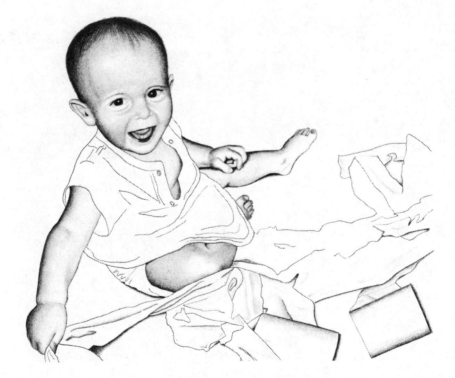

PLEASE TOUCH is about helping your child to explore his or her surroundings in an adventurous manner, but with sensitivity.

Introduction

If you want your child to "fit in" at school, to understand that he or she is "no better" than other children, and to never take risks, this book is not for you. If it's important to you that your home and your child's clothes *always* be neat and tidy, then this book will make you uncomfortable. On the other hand, I'm not promising to turn your child into Michelangelo. This book is not about drawing or painting well. It is about encouraging your child to think independently and confidently. It is about helping your child to explore his or her surroundings in an adventurous manner, but with sensitivity. It is about helping your child maintain the level of curiosity all children are born with, but most lose by the time they are ready for school. It's about being a special kind of parent, one who is willing to supervise closely when it would be easier to say "no, too dangerous," and one who doesn't mind the extra clean-up chores invariably created by active, exploring, adventurous, and curious children. I believe that most people who have special, talented children really have normal children and a special talent for parenting.

As an art teacher and an author, I have found it necessary to direct a great deal of my own creative energy toward combatting the inhibiting actions of well-meaning parents and teachers, stifling misnamed "art" activities, and discouraging toys and games that prevent children from thinking for themselves and developing curious minds. Although I am an art specialist, I work with children, and children's brains do not have little pigeonholes in them. It became increasingly clear to me that one reason children are unable to express themselves through art is that they are systematically programmed not to express themselves in other areas, such as music, dance, words, or physical activities. Restrictive environments mean that parents are saying "Don't touch" all day, and to a child that is the same as saying "Don't learn." "Please touch" and "Try it if you want to" are the two phrases that best sum up the philosophy of this book. Of course, it is easy for a teacher to criticize parents. But I'm a parent too, and here I suggest some of the alternatives that I tried with my own child, as well as with my students at Young at Art.

Babies have traditionally been thought of as gifts to their parents from the stork or from God. But babies really are gifts which their parents present to the world. How will your baby grow up? What contributions will be made to the world because of the thoughtful, sensitive way you raise your child? We all have great hopes and expectations for our offspring, but it's easy to forget our long-range goals while caught up in the day-to-day living with an infant and toddler.

Your child is special—different not only from all other children, but even quite different from your other children. And yet certain behavior and patterns of development are quite predictable. He or she will surely sit at around six months, hold things easily between thumb and forefinger at eight months, walk at twelve months, and talk at twenty-four months. Just as certainly, that same baby will tear books, draw on walls, spill innumerable cups of juice, break things, have some trouble sharing at times, and use tantrums to express frustration. How you react to the accomplishments and handle the behavior which you find unacceptable is a great influence on the child's future behavior. The toys, books, and play experiences you provide, and the way you express love for your child, also will have an influence on the kind of human being your child becomes.

As a parent it is *not* my goal that my child become an artist. I do want him to have confidence in his own ability to solve problems, to develop a sense of fantasy, and, above all, to think for himself. A creative thought process will carry over into any area he later becomes interested in. It is unfortunate that the word *creativity* has become so closely linked to art activities. I have seen the word plastered across a so-called art kit that also had the words *trace* and *color* on it; both activities leave no room for actual creativity. Art ideally *should* be a creative endeavor, involving original ideas and experimental thinking, but it isn't always. It is possible to produce something that looks quite artistic without having a creative thought in your head. At the same time, it is possible to be a creative banker, attorney, teacher, scientist, and housekeeper. Someone said to me: "Wouldn't it be terrible if, after all of your hard work, your son decided to be an investment banker?" "Emphatically no!" was my response. I am trying to raise my child to be free enough to become anything at all. More importantly, I don't want his life's choices to be governed by what *I* would like, but rather by what *he* would like. The art projects we do are *not* designed to program him into choosing a career in art. They are emphasized in our lives because I feel that they are one of many forms of play that, when presented properly, encourage children to get into the habit of using their own minds. They are equally valuable for future investment bankers, doctors, lawyers, and accountants as they are for future artists.

I combined my studies in art education and my experience as an art teacher and the director of Young at Art (where children aged one through twelve are taught to think creatively through participation in art, music, and play activities) with the realities of motherhood in preparing this book. After all, it's one thing to say "Don't punish your child for drawing on the walls!" It is quite another to say, "This is what I did, and why, when my child drew on the walls!"

We know that children develop approximately half of their intelligence by the age of four, so the preschool years, when your child is with you instead of with professional teachers, are the key period in his or her intellectual life. Many have misinterpreted this information to mean that babies can read, do math, and draw like adults. In fact, there are many preliminary activities that serve as preparation which children need to experience in order to be able to do these more sophisticated things. Before they can concern themselves with reading, writing, math, and drawing, they must learn about light, air, water, hard, soft, day, night, language, moving, walking, eating, love, and fear, just for starters. The activities you chose for your baby and toddler to participate in should be chosen with care. They not only lay the groundwork for future learning, but they help to shape the child's approach to life and attitude toward learning. From the simplest of nursery rhymes the child is introduced to a love of words. Finger games can prepare a child for math, and scribbling lays a groundwork for writing.

Research studies show that a child develops approximately 50 percent of his or her intelligence by the age of four, another 30 percent by eight, and the final 20 percent by seventeen. Thus it is clearly up to Mother and Dad, and not some art teacher who may be expert at it ten years later, to start your child firmly on the road to creativity and sensitivity. While you may not be the person who teaches your child the difference between Picasso and Braque, you must be the only one who can teach your child what life is all about and whether imaginative thinking, an appreciation of beauty, and problem-solving skills are to be a part of it.

All parents are only human and despite our best intentions, we are doomed to make mistakes along the way as we raise our children. If you must err, do so on the side of overindulgence. Give your child too much love, too much of your time, too many toys, too much interest, too much trust, and too much freedom. I believe that in order to free your child to be a creative and independent thinker you first need to give your child three major gifts:

1. A confident feeling of being thoroughly loved, liked, and respected.

2. The freedom to satisfy curiosity as much as possible, safe in the knowledge that his or her accomplishment is valued despite inevitable messes and inconvenience to the parents.

3. License to perform as many tasks as possible that he or she expresses interest in, without having to live up to preconceived expectations of right or wrong.

Children are all very different and develop at varying rates of speed, but the following chart shows approximate times of readiness for development of several aspects of creativity:

DRAWING

6-12 Months	12-18 Months	18-24 Months
Holds, looks at, mouths crayon.	Does tentative scribbles.	Draws vertical, horizontal, diagonal lines, experiments with scribbles, interested in textures.

24-30 Months	30-36 Months	36-42 Months
Does freer, circular scribbles and begins to include a variety of scribble shapes in drawing.	Names shapes after drawing them. Lines are often connected to enclose shapes.	Tells stories about pictures. Begins mandala experiments; may draw humans.

CLAY OR PLAY DOUGH WORK

6-12 Months	12-18 Months	18-24 Months
Tastes and eats clay.	Pinches, squeezes, and pounds on clay.	Rolls snakelike coils.
24-30 Months	**30-36 Months**	**36-42 Months**
Will make clay balls. Names objects made and plays with them. (Trains, snakes, pancakes are favorites.)	Incises decoration on clay and sticks things into it.	Produces flat designs with clay. Adds on, builds.

PAINTING

6-12 Months	12-18 Months	18-24 Months
Smears paint with hands and tastes it.	Does body decorations, makes dabbing movements with brush.	Paints lines similar to scribbles.

24-30 Months	30-36 Months	36-42 Months
Continues scribbling development through paint.	Paints whole areas of paper.	Does paintings of lines and shapes even after realism has commenced in drawing.

MOVEMENT

6-12 Months	12-18 Months	18-24 Months
Lies on back and kicks legs. Crawls. Pulls self upright.	Begins walking. Sways rhythmically to music; loves to perform for audience.	Runs, stands on tiptoe.

24-30 Months	30-36 Months	36-42 Months
Jumps in place; walks on tiptoe.	Stands on either foot but cannot alternate as in skipping; marches.	Hops in place. Starts to skip. Is very well coordinated and can begin experimenting in organized dances, sports.

MUSIC

6-12 Months	12-18 Months	18-24 Months
Enjoys listening to music and is interested in producing sound with instruments. Can make mouth sounds: cluck, gurgle, babble, etc.	Bangs on drum, cymbals, xylophone. Starts blowing. Loves to sing. Sways, dances rhythmically.	Can blow horn, harmonica. Manipulates fingers on piano.

24-30 Months	30-36 Months	36-42 Months
Hums, but no particular tune. Enjoys making music.	Listens to tapes, records. Enjoys observing musicians.	Sings in tune. Makes up songs. Enjoys singing in groups. Can play instrument, though not a melody.

BLOCK BUILDING

6-12 Months	12-18 Months	18-24 Months
Enjoys knocking down structures completed by others.	Carries blocks around; puts them down in specific places.	Builds vertical or horizontal rows.
24-30 Months	**30-36 Months**	**36-42 Months**
Connects two blocks with a third.	Builds enclosures.	Labels constructions and plays around them.

IMAGINATIVE PLAY

6-12 Months	12-18 Months	18-24 Months
Enjoys peek-a-boo and watching adults pretend. Imitates animal sounds. Can substitute one object for another.	Initiates games such as peek-a-boo; pretends doing something such as feeding doll. Will do things to elicit response from parents. Understands difference between pretend and truth. Uses toys to act out adult roles.	Likes to pretend adult roles; solitary dramatic play with props (dolls, cars).

24-30 Months	30-36 Months	36-42 Months
Enjoys hearing stories and being read to.	Involved role playing, story telling, dress up.	Extensive pretending and sustained role playing take up most play time. Enjoys cooperative play with other children joining in pretending.

PART I

The Child: Age 0-1

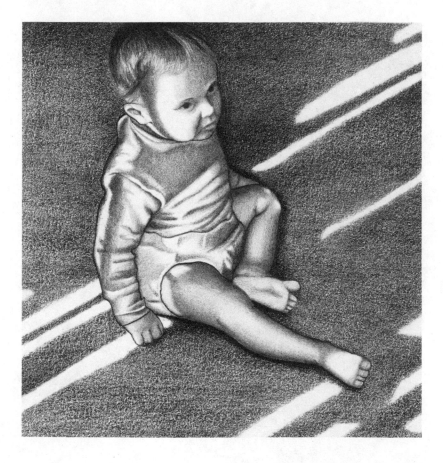

ONE

The
First Year

Parents hardly ever have to "teach" their children anything. All they really have to do is provide opportunities for learning and an atmosphere that is conducive to free exploration. Keeping children, and their homes, clean and germ-free can have the negative effect of inhibiting independent thinking and curiosity. You can help your child appreciate the world through all of the five senses by pointing things out, providing exposure, and showing appreciation for the child's personal reaction to things. Show your baby everything, and give everything a name, from day one. Put an infant's hand on the bark of a tree, a screen, velvet, carpet, and anything else in proximity, and describe it. Talk about the changing effects of light, shadows on the wall, the honking horn, and the scent of flowers. Don't be surprised when the baby sees and hears things you no longer notice.

Respect the child's preferences and encourage him or her to participate in decision-making. Of course, "What would you like to wear today?" is too difficult a decision for a baby, but "Which of these two items would you like to wear?" is a good beginning. When you are dressing the baby you can say, "Would you like to wear the soft blue dress or the stretchy pink one?" Well before the first birthday you will get an answer. Listen! Being a decision-maker starts with very small decisions.

New mothers and fathers generally worry about breast feeding, formulas, rashes, diapers, baths, and fevers, if not in that order. Your primary role as a parent, however, is to help your child be-

You can help your child appreciate the world through all of the five senses by pointing things out, providing exposure, and showing how much you value the child's personal reaction to things.

come a self-sufficient adult. I knew as little as any new parent about diapers, formulas, and infants' illnesses when my baby was born. But, after teaching college, high school, junior high school, elementary school, and nursery school, with each new job seeking younger and younger children, I became increasingly convinced that the preschool years are the most important ones in establishing a creative mentality—those years when, too often, the child's only teachers are parents whose estimation of their own art ability is that it is nonexistent, and who rarely rely on their creative thinking powers in their daily lives. As soon as school does start, the child's first teacher invariably has never even taken an art course and her goals for the children stress reading and number skills. Socialization emphasizes conformity and "learning the rules." Music is usually limited to learning the words to some songs, never making up songs. It is many years before an art teacher comes along who (hopefully) stresses creativity. By then, it is too late and the whole class sits politely, hands folded, waiting for directions on precisely what to make and how to make it. By then, too many teacher-made pictures have been colored-in, all childlike art has met with the question "What is it?", too many maps have been traced, and too many shamrocks and triangular Christmas trees have been cut out and painted according to specific adult directions. The most important problem facing a parent is: How, with no experience as a teacher of creativity and while in the course of daily routines that are frequently in competition with your own needs, can your baby be given the strong sense of confidence in him- or herself that will provide an ability to face the world independently? It's a serious business and very hard work to raise an intelligent, sensitive human being. Your baby thrives on love, attention, visual and intellectual stimulation and freedom to explore.

Security

You must not only communicate to the baby that you can be trusted, but also that you trust the baby. Let your baby know with certainty that you really care when he or she cries by responding immediately. Your trust in the baby is communicated when you allow your child to explore the environment without unnecessary adult-imposed restrictions. Sometimes you need to relax and let the baby decide on his or her own personal schedule of growth. Each generation has new experts advising parents. One pediatrician tells parents to feed on a rigid schedule while another recommends feeding on demand. One expert tells us to put a stop to thumb sucking while another warns us that it fulfills an important psychological function. Who is right? While the experts come and go, children's needs remain precisely the same, generation after generation. What we, as parents, need to do more of is listen to our children. Your baby can't talk, but he or she can communicate very well. He or she will let you know when it's time to eat, when it's time to be held, and when it is time to move on to a new stage of development. When the baby decides to stop sucking his or her thumb, or give up breast, bottle, blanket, or pacifier, that is the right time to do so—even if babyhood seems long over to you. When my baby made it very clear that he wanted to sleep in our bed, I read books that counseled strongly against it and books that touted it as being the best thing for a child's emotional well-being. Then I ignored the books and listened to my baby. I took my baby into bed with me, and we all got some sleep.

Forcing a child into his or her own room when the real need is to be in mommy's arms, making a child who still needs diapers feel "naughty," taking away a breast, bottle, or pacifier when it is such a source of comfort, all add up to feelings of rejection and inadequacy. Every child eventually wants privacy, controls the bladder and bowel, and outgrows the need to constantly suck. Whether this growth was self-determined or forced by parents has a lot to do with a child's feelings of confidence and self-esteem.

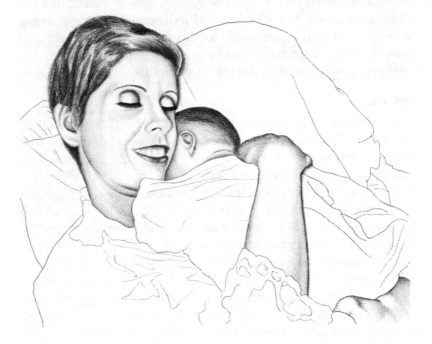

If your baby wants to sleep in your bed, listen to your baby instead of "the experts."

During those early months of helplessness, your child learns to feel secure or insecure. These feelings remain buried deep inside forever. Insecurity blocks creativity and happiness, while neuroses stop so many people from developing their full potential.

> A negative self-image is one of the most powerful brakes on brilliance that exists.*

Many people look at artists such as Van Gogh and think that their neuroses helped them to become great artists. I think that is a fallacy. Truly creative people in all fields, not only the fine arts, need a lot of confidence and a strong sense of personal freedom.

There are two common practices among parents which I feel strongly are detrimental to a child's development, and my own son provided the ultimate test of my beliefs in both cases. My child refused, from his first month, to sleep alone. He cried until he was held, and then he slept immediately; he drank from a bottle until shortly before his fifth birthday when he simply gave it up. . . . He asked me if I would buy him a train if he gave up his bottle. I said "yes" and he gave up his bottle. It was completely his idea.

Responding positively and affectionately to your child's expressed needs, whatever they are, can be difficult, but it pays dividends. At this age the baby may need to be carried a lot, or taken along even on your trips to the bathroom, provided with a lot of visual stimulation, rocked, or sung to. Take the time to do it now. A secure, loved infant soon outgrows these needs and becomes independent. One who is taught, or forced, to behave in a way less inconvenient to the parents can replace these needs with more neurotic behavior.

> The evidence simply suggests that there are good reasons why parents should not be afraid to take their cues from the insistent demands which ordinary babies make, and should not stifle their natural inclination to treat babies as sensitive and responsive individuals with needs and feelings similar to their own.†

---

* David Lewis, *How to Be a Gifted Parent* (New York: Berkeley Publishing Co., 1982), p. 172.

† John and Elizabeth Newson, *Toys & Playthings* (New York: Random House), p. 31.

When I was a new mother, a very elderly woman came up to my son and me on the street to admire him. "Enjoy him now," she said sadly. "When he grows up he won't belong to you anymore." The fact is that children's needs are not balanced out for the convenience of their parents. They need you *totally* when they are young, and seem to need you not at all after they grow up. You will relate to your grown children far better if you meet their needs now, and willingly let them go later. You will have plenty of time to yourself when you are old—perhaps more than you want. For the next three years, you won't have any! Parents have been bucking that simple fact of life for ages. One mother told me that she locked her bedroom door so that her baby couldn't bother her if he climbed out of his crib. He was expected to play alone from the time he awoke at sunrise until her alarm clock went off at 8 a.m. She got up in time to drive him to his daycare center, where he stayed until 6 p.m. After dinner, bedtime was set at 7:30, and she insisted on it "even if he wasn't tired." She needed "time to herself," she explained. That child will probably be doing things to get his parents' attention long after other children are breaking away. There is always danger that the attention-getting devices children use can be self-destructive. With daycare centers by day and separate bedrooms at night, it's no wonder that there is such a tremendous emotional and psychological distance between children and their parents. By adolescence the rift is so great that communication becomes impossible. Parents have to respond to their babies' babbles and listen to their two- and three-year-old offspring's endless chatter if they want to be a part of the significant discussions that take place in the later years.

To My Grown-up Son

My hands were busy through the day
I didn't have much time to play
The little games you asked me to.
I didn't have much time for you.
I'd wash your clothes, I'd sew and cook,
But when you'd bring your picture book
And ask me please to share your fun,
I'd say: "A little later, son."
I'd tuck you in all safe at night
And hear your prayers, turn out the light,

Then tiptoe softly to the door . . .
I wish I'd stayed a minute more.
For life is short, the years rush past . . .
A little boy grows up so fast.
No longer is he at your side,
His precious secrets to confide.
The picture books are put away,
No good-night kiss, no prayers to hear . . .
That all belongs to yesteryear.
My hands, once busy, now are still
The days are long and hard to fill.
I wish I could go back and do
The little things you asked me to.

—Author unknown

Take the extra time now, and your child will be secure and feel loved. In the long run, your child will be far less demanding than one who has to fight, whine, wait endlessly, or bargain for Mama's or Daddy's time.

Children never become truly independent unless they feel secure and loved during the dependent stage. Children begin communicating the moment they are born. If you respond immediately

to your baby's expressed needs, the baby will become relaxed and feel secure. Children learn early on just how important they really are by how much their caretakers respond to their requests. Responding to the whimpers at this stage quickly progresses to responding to grunts and then to words.

The most important aspect of the new baby's physical well-being is comfort. A full belly is the obvious solution. The newborn is used to the 98.6 degree temperature of mother's body and will be most comfortable the first ten days if kept warm. After that, your own comfort should be your guide in dressing your baby, except that your hair keeps your head warm, and your baby is probably bald, so a light cotton hat should be considered even when you are hatless.

Communication Through Touch

Another important way to communicate love is through close physical contact. Holding the newborn child in your arms or in a baby carrier a good deal of the time will ease tension and help create a secure baby. Talking to your baby, showing him or her things, and

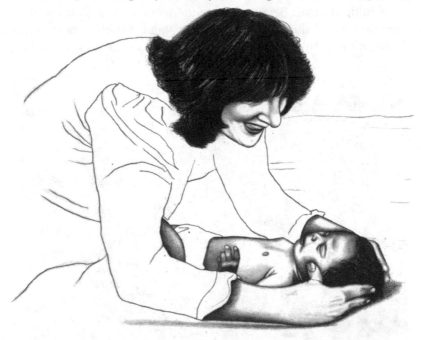

If you feel that you do not communicate well with your baby through the sense of touch, you may be interested in learning about infant massage.

holding and touching him or her are the highest priorities for a new parent.

Touching has been shown to contribute greatly to a baby's physical and emotional well-being. Massage is one way to communicate with your baby through touch. If you feel that you need encouragement communicating with your baby through touching you may want to try it. *Loving Hands: The Traditional Indian Art of Baby Massage* by Frederick LeBoyer (New York: Alfred A. Knopf, 1976) is an excellent book about the subject, as is *Baby Massage: Parent-Child Bonding Through Touching* by Amelia D. Auckett (New York: Newmarket Press, 1981).

Leslie Day, massage therapist, mother, and director of the Association for Infant Massage, says:

> Give the massage in a warm quiet room. Undress the baby and put the baby on his or her back in front of you or right on your lap. Start the massage on the head with slow, circular strokes using all your fingers. Apply vegetable oil to the face. Using your fingers, massage from the center of the face out to the ears, working your way down from the top of the forehead to the chin. Apply oil to the chest with hand movements similar to flattening the open pages of a book. Use your palms and starting from the center of the chest, fan upwards to the shoulders and down the sides of the baby.
>
> Apply oil to the arms and work on one arm and then the other. Glide your palm and fingers up the outside from the wrist to the shoulders and back down again. Glide up from the inside of the wrist to the armpit and back down. Making circles with your thumbs, knead the upper and lower arms outside and inside down to the wrist. Knead the wrist, the top of the hand, and then the palm. Using your thumb and forefinger massage each finger.
>
> An hour after the baby has eaten apply oil and massage the abdomen clockwise in a circle. If the

baby is colicky use the outer edge of your hand and, starting at the top of the abdomen, slowly and with some pressure bring your hand down and gas will be eliminated.

Apply oil to the legs and glide your palm and fingers up the outside from the ankle to the hip and back down. Glide up from the inside of the ankle all the way up and back down. Knead the thigh, lower leg, ankle, top of the foot, the sole of the foot and then massage each toe. Massage one leg fully before beginning the other.

Turn your baby on his or her belly with the head turned to the side and massage the back of the head.

Apply oil to the back, buttocks and legs. Glide your palms and fingers up from the ankles to the tops of the shoulders and then back down. First do one leg and then the other, and repeat several times. Using your thumbs, knead the back from the shoulders down over the buttocks. Do not use pressure on any bones, just on the soft muscle tissue. Continue to knead, moving down the thighs and calves. End the massage by using long, loving strokes up and down the entire back of the baby's body.

Contraindication: Do not massage if the baby has a fever. Do not massage a baby who seems not to enjoy it.

Celebrating Your Child's Accomplishments

You need not only to love your baby but to be able to let your baby know that you love him or her and to make him or her feel loved always. So many people whose parents genuinely love them never really know it. I've heard many parents say that they didn't bother doing anything special for the child's first birthday or Christmas because the child was "too young to understand." It is, however, enough if the baby feels like the center of attention, knows that something exciting is happening, and feels special. What better way is there to do that than to invite friends who come bearing

A child is never "too young to understand" what it feels like to be the center of attention.

gifts, light candles, serve cake, and sing to the child? Birthdays come only once a year, hardly often enough for a child to feel like the center of the universe. But, other milestones occur that provide opportunities for you to make your child feel special and important. This family gathering was turned into a celebration of Jason's very first tooth.

Parties for babies, especially when other guests are very young, can either be chaotic or delightful. The difference has to do with preparation and planning. Some foolproof tips for giving a party for a very young child follow:

A baby's milestones and accomplishments can be turned into excuses for celebrations.

1. *Young children should be invited to come with their primary caretaker.* Not until the fourth birthday can you invite children by themselves.

2. *Buy or bake two cakes,* one for the young guests to eat which is precut and put on plates in the kitchen before the party begins, and another smaller one that is elaborately decorated to be brought out, complete with candles, for the birthday song and then promptly put away to be enjoyed later when the family has dinner. This prevents a lot of squirming children from ruining your party while they wait for their slice of cake.

3. *Include some planned entertainment.* Have someone who plays guitar, harmonica, or accordian come for a thirty-minute sing-along. Give him or her a list of your child's favorite songs to be included in the repertoire. "Old MacDonald Had a Farm," "The Bus Song," "Ring Around the Rosy," "The Hokey Pokey," and "Shoo Fly" are favorites the first few years. The entertainer should wear no clown makeup or other frightening disguise this year. Keep in mind that active participation, rather than passively watching an entertainer, is more fun for any child under the age of four. Other good party entertainment includes movement games, rented films or videotapes, puppet shows, and (if the children aren't wearing party clothes) group art projects such as murals, chalk sidewalk drawing (which keeps your house clean), or cake decorating (which doesn't). Remember that the children are very easy to please, and the birthday child's Dad wearing a top hat and clumsily pulling a stuffed rabbit out of it will probably enchant them. You don't need Houdini; you need someone who likes and understands kids.

4. *If you plan to socialize with other parents, you will need to arrange for someone to stay with the children and supervise their play.* Or you can alternate with your spouse so that one of you is with the children and another with the adults at all times.

5. *Buy and address the thank-you notes at the same time you do the party invitations.* Keep a pencil and the envelopes in your pocket so that when your child opens a gift you can lightly write what it is on the flap of the envelope. This will greatly facilitate thank-you-note writing. After age two, I had my son do a drawing inside notepaper that was printed commercially with the words "thank you" on the outside. After he played with or wore each gift, we stopped to "write" notes.

6. *Give every child a name tag to wear,* so that you and any visiting adults can more effectively supervise the children by calling them by their names.

7. *Clearly state the time the party will end, and hand out the party bags and coats then.* One and a half hours is plenty for the first four birthday parties. Do not serve alcoholic beverages to the parents or they will stay too long and the children will become overtired.

8. *Put the exact same toys in each party bag.* Giving cars to boys and dolls to girls can cause great unhappiness. You may want

to include both a small car and a small doll in the child's first party bag, so everyone will be happy. If you include books, the children will all want to climb up on their parent's lap to be read to, and will most likely be refused this request at this time and place, resulting in several simultaneous tantrums. For the first and second birthdays, don't include anything in the party bag that you don't want played with at the party, such as crayons or water guns. At Young at Art, all of the party favors are made by the children during the party. They include drawings, paintings, collage, and crafts. If you used balloons as decorations, be sure that there are enough to give one to each child and that they are all the same color balloon with the same color string to avoid tears and jealousy. The new foil balloons don't pop as easily as the old-fashioned rubber ones do (although they cost a bit more).

9. *Don't expect the birthday child to wait until the party ends to open presents*. Let her or him rip them open immediately, and wait to teach party etiquette on the third birthday, when gift opening can be postponed until after the party is over.

For decades we have been warned against "spoiling" our children, but more children are spoiled by lack of love than by too much. In addition to giving birthday parties that were major celebrations, other events we used as excuses for celebration included the first time Jason crawled, his first scribble, his first word, step, haircut, swimming lesson, painting, and countless other things. Until the child has a family of his or her own, perhaps no one will love him or her as much as you do. You have the tremendous responsibility of setting the pattern of expectations the child will follow for life. Children whose parents treat them like royalty don't wind up marrying spouses that treat them like dirt, and children whose parents give more attention to their offspring's minor accomplishments than to their major infractions of rules are the ones who go on to make even greater accomplishments throughout their lives. Don't let your children feel that you judge them by their tantrums or spills, but by the little steps forward that they make each day. And keep in mind that all steps forward will, of necessity, be accompanied by some steps back. Teach children that they are "no better" than anyone else, and they won't be!

Investing Time in Your Child

We've come almost full circle as far as I'm concerned on the matter of career versus motherhood. Up until the fifties, mothers had no choice; they stayed home. Then, stay-at-home mothers were ridiculed and supermom myths abounded. Although I still believe in being a supermom, I don't think it's possible with a child younger than two and a half or three (depending on the child).

I am from the generation that postponed childbearing for a career. Like all of life's important choices, it involved compromise. And, before the fact, the problem of child care seemed simple enough. I believed all the clichés about quality of time being more important than quantity, and I was sure that in no time I would be back to work. No one, least of all my own full-time mother, could have prepared me for the strong bond that develops in time between a mother and her baby. The only way to build that bond is with time—time to play with, read to, swim with, visit museums with, and grow with. Your child doesn't just need quality time; he or she also needs to see you tired, angry, bored, sad, and distracted, in order to really know you. Children who are raised on the "quality" time theory will never be able to understand true intimacy.

No matter how feminist your ideals are, this problem arises. If you stay home for the three years most psychologists recommend, your career will suffer. If you go back to work right away, your relationship with your child will suffer. Babies need as much time as careers do. Men's careers haven't suffered from the mandatory time so many of them spent in the service, and mothers can take time to care for their babies without feeling that life will pass them by. Servicemen are frequently rewarded with higher starting salaries upon leaving military service. Child care has its own rewards.

Investing time in your child doesn't have to mean not working; it does mean that your work schedule must change. Since many bosses are inflexible, you may have to become your own boss! Phyllis Gillis's book *Entrepreneurial Mothers* ($16.95, Rawson Associates) offers guidance to mothers who want to start a business. She has said that starting one "offers a mother income and uninterrupted work experience—a stop-gap measure until she returns to her previous job. Or it can be an end in itself."* For help in finding out how to fit work in with mothering, consult: CATALYST, 14 East 60th Street, New York, NY 10022 (212-759-9700), for a list of career-counseling services that help women find career options.

I reluctantly quit the full-time job I had invested fifeen years in, after my maternity leave ended and my boss refused to take me back on a part-time basis. But, I knew that Jason was worth more than the yearly salary and job fulfillment combined. This book would never have been written if I hadn't. Until society changes, part-time work, working out of your home, or self-employment are the best alternatives to a full-time job for mothers. You'll never become the president of General Motors while working part-time, but it does provide some income, keeps you feeling purposeful, and helps you keep up your skills while getting the baby accustomed from the beginning to trusting a secondary caretaker. You can never make up this lost time with your child, but you can catch up with your career later on. My baby-sitter inevitably got sick the week before a deadline, and there were many days when the inspiration to work was high, but I spent the day in the playground. (I must share with you that this short paragraph was interrupted by a "Mommy" from the next room. I stopped work, repaired a car the baby-sitter wasn't allowed to touch, and was sidetracked setting up a special art project at the kitchen table with three children. It was twenty minutes before I got back to work.) My own child

* ". . . and a business," Judy Linscott, *New York Daily News,* Jan. 25, 1984.

has spent a lot of time "helping" me work and playing in my home office. Although he usually slowed down my work considerably during his first four years, he also inspired two books and came up with many original art-project ideas that I used in my work. He suggested that I write *The Superpowers™ Anti-Coloring Book* before he was four, and it was in the bookstores by his fifth birthday. When I taught a college class about art for young children, he came to proudly demonstrate his skills. My students learned more from that class than they could have from a lecture from me.

Working mothers are not new. Mothers have always had work to do. We have done something unnatural by doing all of our work away from the home, but we must find a way to prevent this fact from interfering with our children's development. Children learn by participating. If you exclude your child from most of your day, you also eliminate many opportunities for growth and learning.

I was very impressed with the way many resourceful mothers I know managed to continue working. One was a freelance editor who got up two hours before her daughter did each morning to work, worked through the child's long afternoon naps, and again in the evening. Another woman spent every morning doing interesting things with her daughter and left for work when the child had her nap. She taught a college class, did the necessary paper work, and was home before the child woke up. My secretary only worked mornings in order to be with her child afternoons. After the child's bedtime she did typing in her home to make ends meet. Another woman I know worked two days a week while her husband cared for the child, and then he went off to work and she cared for the child. That little girl had two "good mothers" and thrived. When a full-time job is essential, there are enough evening and night jobs to allow you to work after your husband comes home from work or vice versa. After all, it's no accident that children have two parents. If you are a single mother, or even if you're not, sometimes it's possible to find another mother with a child who is the same age as yours and split the work and mothering with her.

Many bright, educated mothers I know have children who are being raised by underpaid, uneducated childcare workers. These intelligent, creative well-educated people went back to work full-time shortly after their babies were born, although economically it was not a dire necessity. They left their children with nice, fairly competent but usually totally uneducated people. Each time the growing child had a question, it was more likely to be answered unsatisfactorily by the baby-sitter than by the parent. I recently saw one wheel her charge, whose mother is an attorney, into a bar instead of the playground on a lovely spring day. Even if you are fortunate enough to find excellent help, your baby will want and need affirmation of your love, not an affectionate stranger's. It is a rare housekeeper who will stand by while your child "expresses" himself or herself if it means mopping the floor afterward.

You and your child will also both need some time away from each other and with others, but being away full-time is not the alternative. Even the best daycare centers cannot provide the one-to-one relationship your child needs. Caring for several children, rather than one, makes it necessary to impose rules that benefit the group as a whole but do not necessarily meet an individual's needs. You can let your child engage in behavior at home that would create bedlam in a daycare center. Your child will probably be in school by age three, and will have a strong sense of security by then, as well as the adventurous spirit no daycare center can encourage. By this age he or she will probably be toilet-trained, able to dress himself or herself, quite proficient at verbal self-expression, and anxious to socialize. The baby who screamed at the sight of a baby-sitter will have turned into a three-year-old who is happy to stay with an interesting new friend or go off on a school adventure, and hardly bids you adieu. But before that, no child is substantial enough to go it on his or her own. A three-hour separation can be refreshing, an eight-hour separation stressful.

Although the child does best with one primary caretaker, it is of course necessary for you to have some time to yourself or to pursue your work. I found that the ideal arrangement for this all-important first year is for you to spend at least half of the day really with your child, and find one responsive baby-sitter who your child can learn to trust for the other half. In the first few months your baby will not care whether you or another caretaker meets his or her needs. Toward the end of the first year, you will have to invest more time with your child and use ingenuity when you do leave him or her. *Never* leave a screaming child with a baby-sitter, in a daycare center, or at school. And never sneak away without saying good-bye. If you need to go out, your baby-sitter can tempt your child with talk of visiting the firehouse, playground, or other favorite place. After the child is happily off on an excursion, then you can get away. It takes extra time and planning, but adds to the child's sense of security.

It's so much easier for the baby to leave you than for you to "abandon" the baby. Between nine and fourteen months, babies are establishing very close ties with the mother and panic if she leaves—even for only a few moments. Although many mothers feel stress at not even being able to go to the bathroom alone, children need this experience of closeness. This is the very worst time for you to have a full-time job that requires long hours away from your child. I'm not against working mothers; I published two books a year and continued part-time teaching during my son's first four years. But I am against making yourself unavailable to your child on a full-time basis.

> Although the baby may crawl away from the mother to explore, the separation is her choice. When separation is forced on her by the mother the infant may become upset. She still needs her mother, but not so constantly. She is building her independence by using her mother as a secure base. Part of her courage comes from knowing she can rely on her mother to help her when she needs her.*

* Frank Caplan, ed., The Parenting Advisor (Garden City, N.Y.: Doubleday/Anchor Press, 1978), p. 408.

TWO

Home Environment

Your home is the first environment your child will explore. Before the baby is even born, you will probably shop for the nursery furniture and decorations which will provide opportunities for his or her observation and help to shape his or her taste. Since you are the one who will decide what the very first thing your child looks at will be, why not make it a Picasso instead of Mickey Mouse? Faces are what babies like most to look at; hang brightly colored reproductions of close-up portraits as well as the favorite unbreakable mirror in the crib, for those moments when baby isn't looking at your face. Photographs of art work are no substitute for looking into a real face and seeing it change expressions, but they are a nice addition to the human interaction babies need so much. By presenting aesthetically interesting pictures at this early age, you are providing the exposure your child needs to be able to appreciate art later on.

Sheets with patterns on them may provide something for a baby to look at, but I much prefer plain white because they don't hide shadows as patterns do. Solid colors are the best background for studying the effects of changing light. Babies are fascinated with shadows. If you have a solid white wall, place a light behind your hand and hold it up to create moving shadow puppet shows on the wall. A light behind a white sheet will work also. Busy prints or patterns on floor, walls, or furniture interfere with observations of the effects of light and shade.

Hang pictures over the changing table and vary them periodi-

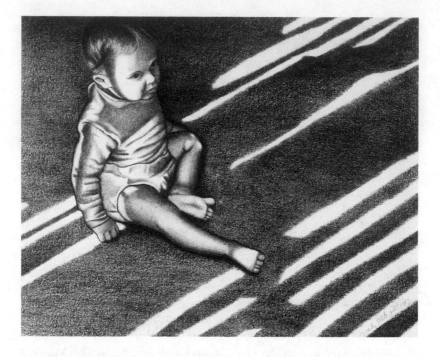

Solid colors provide the best background for studying the effects of changing light.

cally. When the child becomes too active to willingly lie still for a diaper change, this ever-changing art gallery will distract him or her, and provide you with the opportunity of expanding your child's horizons while tending to the more mundane aspects of parenting. Choose from prints of great art, photos of family members, animals, or other babies, and paintings and drawings by children. Babies love art produced by other children, so if your new baby has no big brothers or sisters, you can recruit friends and neighbors to lend you masterpieces by their young children. If you follow the suggestions in this book, by the time your baby is a year old, you will have plenty of your own child's masterpieces to choose from, and the borrowed ones can be returned to the artists. As children begin to express interest in certain things, display the finest illustrations you can find of them. Wherever possible, use prints of great paintings or fine art photographs. Great artists painted many more pictures of animals than did the mediocre illustrators of most available children's books. When I wrote *The Anti-*

Babies are as interested in looking at great art as they are in looking at pictures designed for children.

Coloring Book® of Masterpieces, which included color prints of great art, my mother pointed out to me that a very large percentage of the pictures that I chose for the book had hung over the bed in my room when I was young. Although I hadn't remembered that, I did have an affinity for those works of art that seemed like old friends.

I also filled my automatic slide carousel with slides of some of the great paintings of the world. I set the timer at ten seconds and let my baby look at great art. And, he did look at it, with interest, as early as two months of age and throughout his infancy. I believe

THE FAMILY CIRCUS®   By Bil Keane

10-21

Copyright 1982
The Register and Tribune
Syndicate, Inc.

"We've been in this part already, Mommy. I remember this vent."

this exposure creates a preference for good art, while exposure to the cartoons on television and in prints and wallpaper designed for children creates a preference for that. When the child begins crawling, tear prints out of old art books and hang them in the baby's room—at child's eye level, not yours. Change them weekly to maintain interest. The crawler finds so little of interest, with only vents, electrical sockets, and telephone wires down there.

I have never understood the custom of installing electric outlets at crawler's eye level, while except for an occasional floor lamp, most electrical appliances sit on tabletops anyway. The reverse makes much more sense; light switches should be low and the outlets out of reach. Outlets are so dangerous for curious crawlers, while light switches, normally out of reach, provide the perfect opportunity for observing cause and effect. Unless you are designing and building a new home now, you'll need lots of outlet covers

Ideally, light switches should be in reach for studying cause and effect, and electrical outlets should be out of reach for safety.

and attractive distractions. When Young at Art was renovated, all electrical outlets were installed five feet off the floor for the safety of my students. Perhaps now that fathers are more involved in parenting and mothers are more likely to become architects, home design in the future will take children's needs more into consideration.

All mothers know that their children look at and react to things in their environment from the beginning. Just as newborns are quite capable of expressing unhappiness when they are hungry or in need of love, parents recognize that their children also communicate pleasure, boredom, and interest. It is never too early for mental and visual stimulation. It is now that your child is being introduced to a new world. Impressions of it and information about it are being sopped up the way a sponge sops up water.

> Experts feel that few geniuses are born, but that many are literally made at home.*

At my son's birth, unlike the stereotype of a screaming newborn, he made his appearance with his eyes wide open and alert, began looking around, and was clearly aware of his surroundings. His expression, like mine, seemed to say "Who are you anyway?" Many other mothers I have spoken to said their children were also clearly interested in the world around them immediately! Therefore, you want to pay attention to what is in the newborn's line of vision when planning placement of a crib and baby seat. An infant whose head is propped up while awake sees more than does a child lying down in a crib, so you might want to put a pillow under the baby's mattress at wakeful times (putting one under the head can be dangerous).

> It seems fairly clear that babies well under six months can be expected to become bored and discontented if they are left on their backs with sideways vision obscured and nothing but a ceiling to stare at. Some researchers have suggested that not only a baby's immediate performance but his developmental progress is in fact accelerated by the upright position.†

If your newborn spends many wakeful hours in a crib, you will want to provide many stimulating and interesting things for him or her to observe. Carriages make wonderful beds, since they are movable and can be parked to provide a new show regularly. In addition to the slide show, you will want a collection of several mobiles. Keep in mind that the first mobile was invented by the artist Alexander Calder when you choose—Little Bo Peep and

---

* Frank Caplan, ed., *The Parenting Advisor* (Garden City, N.Y.: Doubleday/Anchor Press, 1978), p. 329.

† John and Elizabeth Newson, *Toys & Playthings* (New York: Pantheon Books, 1979), pp. 27–28.

Many new mothers are surprised to discover that their newborn infants are alert and interested in their surroundings.

Since you're going to vacuum anyway, your house may as well be dirty!

Mickey Mouse are not your only choices. Alternate several mobiles, not just one, to prevent boredom. Before even Calder, nature
surely provided the most effective mobiles of all! Remember that a
tree, with its leaves moving against the light of the sky, passing
clouds, and birds will fascinate all newborns. During my son's first
autumn he loved to feel the leaves and throw them in the air and
watch them fall around him. When Jason caught a cold and was
housebound, I brought some autumn leaves in and let him play
with them on the floor. This kind of play doesn't make for impec-
cable housekeeping, but the rewards come in other ways, and
probably won't really be noticeable until much later. If you are
serious about encouraging creative play and sensitivity to the world
around us you must be willing to do the extra clean-up chores that
come with it. After all, since you are going to vacuum anyway,
your house may as well be dirty!

Despite the traditional insipid pink and baby-blue nurseries we
are accustomed to seeing, your infant will much prefer one of the
bright primary colors. Bright red, vivid blue, or shiny yellow
touches against a softening white background are much more stimulating to look at than pastels. Infants aren't infants very long, so
designing a room that is aesthetically pleasing should be as high a
priority for the nursery as it is in the rest of your home. Instead of
investing in expensive wallpaper with pictures, choose washable
paint and regularly change the pictures and decorations to stimulate the child's interest. Even adults stop looking at a picture if they
pass the same one a hundred times a day. "Nesting" is an observable syndrome. Sometime during pregnancy every woman seems
to feel compelled to decorate the nursery, and often other portions
of her home as well. Since a good portion of a child's first three
years involves so much touching, taking apart, and drawing on,
this redecoration seems poorly timed. Because of it, Mom spends
far too much time discouraging exploration in order to protect her
beautiful new environment, when the priority should be exposing
her baby to as many new, first-hand experiences as possible. If you
can, postpone redecoration of your home until your child is about
three; if you can't do that, then remember that washable walls are
an absolute necessity throughout your home. Later on, your child
will surely "crayon" on them and it's best to be able to demon-

An obliging pet may teach your child the meaning of "furry."

strate to the child that the work of art is more important to you than clean walls are. Floors, too, should be easy to clean and difficult to destroy. Open shelves, within the child's reach, encourage independence and are therefore the ideal place for toys. Buy a crib that converts to a bed. With the money you save by not having to replace the crib with a bed in two years, you can buy:

- A child-sized plastic laminate work table and two chairs for early art work and social activities
- A large chalkboard to hang at child's eye level
- A sturdy two-sided easel
- Six or so inexpensive, standard-sized picture frames for hanging the child's first scribbles in

- An unbreakable mirror to hang just above floor level which can be looked in as well as painted on
- Lots of prints and postcards of great art

In addition to providing your child with an environment that will encourage your child to use his or her eyes, you will also want to encourage maximum use of all of the senses. Your home surely includes many different colors, textures, smells, and perspectives on the world. Take the time to help your child observe them and offer the descriptions that provide for the quickly increasing understanding of words that helps your child assimilate information. If you don't have an obliging pet to teach your child about "furry," a teddy bear or a piece of furry fabric feels nice on a child's face. Try sensitizing your newborn child to the way things feel by holding things to his or her face, hand, or tummy and saying things like: "Doesn't that feel furry?" "Does the soft furry teddy bear remind you of Fido?" "Feel this scratchy emery board."

In addition to providing a safe environment for your child, your home should include mental and physical challenges as well. Eight-month-olds need free space to crawl around in, even if that means temporarily putting some of your furniture in storage, as I did. Nine-month-olds need steps, and to the city apartment dweller, or even the homeowner with too large a staircase, that sometimes means a jungle gym in the living room. Thoughtful design of your home will provide climbing areas, quiet corners, hiding places, jumping ledges, and a place that can get dirty. Windows on the world need bars for safety; they should never be a forbidden area. Vary tactile experiences through the use of smooth, rough, bumpy, and furry materials in the decor. Keep areas loosely labeled so that the child's imagination can decide what it will be today, and what it will become tomorrow. Don't let that cute designer bed that looks like a locomotive tempt you. It can only be a train, while a plain one can be a car, a horse, or a desert island, all in the same afternoon. Mirrors make a lot more sense than murals. They reflect changing views and encourage dramatic play, while murals depict the same picture day after day and can get so

boring that we stop seeing them at all. Since your child will most likely want to have a view of you no matter what kind of play he or she is engaging in, whatever room you spend the most time in will be the child's playroom. Low dividers can provide toy storage without obstructing the view of you.

Nothing is more unsettling than disorganization. A young child who is looking for a toy will learn, by finding it easily, that life is predictable and secure. Years before a child can read, pictures can be recognized as labels for things, and these labels become a kind of prereading activity. Keeping all dolls together on a shelf or in a box with a picture of a doll on it, all vehicles in the "car box," etc., sets a pattern for thought organization that will serve your child well in later school work. Plastic milk crates, attractive trash cans, rubber dish pans, clear Lucite storage boxes, and even cardboard boxes, which can be painted or covered with adhesive paper, all work well. The key to staying organized is to get ten times as many storage containers as you think you will need.

Finally, I realize it's a matter of personal taste, but I don't think you have a chance of helping your child develop good taste if you choose baby room accessories, or even clothes, full of cutesy characters. Children begin to form their preferences early—one who has never been exposed to nice things or never seen great art will never prefer them. Before long, television, movies, and tremendous ad campaigns will try to convince your child that these characters are essential to the decor of his or her room, but now, during this short time, your influence prevails. You don't have to be knowledgeable about art or music to expose your baby to it. Anyone can visit or write to a museum gift shop to buy prints for a child's room or turn on a radio occasionally to a classical music station.

THREE

Excursions

In their first year, too many children are left to play in their nurseries instead of being taken everywhere. How much a child is exposed to during these all-important months is up to the parents. The interest evidenced even by a child only six months of age upon seeing a parrot, or any other bird or animal, for the first time should be enough to convince all parents that traveling with an infant to the zoo or to a local pet shop is well worth it. The more excursions your baby goes on now, the more adaptable he or she will be to new situations later. A trip to a shoemaker is as new and interesting for a baby as a planned entertainment. Disposable diapers, baby washcloths, and clothing with snap closures in the crotch mean that you can unobtrusively change a diaper anywhere. If you are nursing, a large shawl will provide modesty, and if the baby is on milk or formula, you can carry a clean empty bottle and a thermos, or the new screw-cap bottles of formula that need only the addition of a nipple and do not require refrigeration before opening. A lightweight stroller or a carrying pack is essential, and consider a backpack, like school children carry, for yourself to keep your hands free while carrying all those essentials plus a baby. Every new mother will tell you that it is other mothers, and not gallant gentlemen, who gladly hold doors open and help you fold your stroller when the bus or train arrives. If no one offers, overcome your shyness and ask. Remember, these important outings are going to benefit your child if you enjoy them together, not if they become a hassle for you.

An infant's interest in discovering new creatures should be enough to convince all parents that excursions to a zoo or local pet shop are well worth the trouble.

It's important to talk now. Tell the baby where you are going and don't forget to include the information on when you will be back. *You* may know that you always return home after a trip to the supermarket, but your baby hasn't learned that yet. It doesn't matter if he or she has no idea of what you are saying. The sooner you talk to the baby, the sooner the baby learns to understand. Always remember that everything is a learning experience. Introduce your baby to neighborhood shopkeepers and talk about the reason for your visit.

I never understood why parents buy a baby carriage with a hood and wrap the newborn up against the elements under mounds of blankets. Every time I peek under one of those awesome hoods to admire a baby, I find them staring wide-eyed at the solid-color ceiling of the hood. It is your job to expose the baby to the world and its wonders, not just to protect against the dangers. You can put a pillow under the carriage mattress so that the baby is propped up enough to look around. Or, buy one of the new car-

It is your job to expose the baby to the world and its wonders, not just to protect against the dangers.

riages that have clear plastic windows. Unless there is a hurricane, an airing should include visual stimulation as much as, if not more than, fresh air.

Once I saw a family come to a beautiful beach in Puerto Rico with an infant. At great inconvenience to themselves they carried a playpen. As they placed the baby out of "harm's way," they also deprived him of learning about sand, one of the earth's most fascinating properties. His movement was restricted, he was prevented from seeing the effects of changing light, he had no opportunity to find a sea shell or other object from the sea to play with. He could just as well have stayed home, since overprotection rendered the excursion quite useless.

Museums

People think of art as something sophisticated and for adults only. During the first few years, children are fascinated with everything, and will look at great and ghastly pictures with equal interest. Why show them junk? I was doing research for another book after Jason was born and museums became his second home. Some don't permit strollers on weekends or at all, so it's important to check ahead. It is fun to point things out to infants. As you enjoy the exhibit yourself, talk about the pictures. Comments like "Oh, look! A painting of a baby just like you" or "That's a big house. It's even bigger than Grandma's house" will elicit a response that might surprise you. But don't let the fact that you receive no response stop you from talking. I got plenty of strange looks from museum visitors as I consulted eight-month-old Jason on his feelings about a picture. About one I asked, "Jason, how do you like those clouds?" And as Jason looked up at the ceiling instead of at the picture, I realized how much he understood what I was saying. I was delighted to discover that this exhibit also had pictures of clouds hung on the ceiling, so my credibility was not shaken and Jason's notion of clouds being in the sky was not confused. This kind of enriching experience will make your child quite different from one who spends long hours alone, imprisoned in a crib or playpen. Your comments about paintings in museums or art galleries do not have to be insightful or crammed full of knowledge of art history. Just focus on one aspect of the picture that might inter-

"Oh look! A picture of a baby just like you."

est the child and try to personalize the experience for him or her. If it's an abstract painting, simply focus on one of its characteristics, for example: "Look at all of those squares, some are big and some are little." Or, "That picture has a lot of yellow in it just like your room at home does."

Restaurants

My husband and I began early to take Jason to restaurants. We never went without a bag of books and toys. Later, when his table manners became uncivilized, we added a large sheet of newspaper to place under his chair. We frequented a restaurant that covered the table with white butcher paper instead of cloth and invited patrons to draw by placing a cup of crayons next to the salt and pepper. We frequently played "musical chairs," all of us moving to a new seat as Jason completely covered all of the paper within reach and needed more room for his drawing. Another favorite of ours was a gaily decorated Italian restaurant usually shunned by sophisticated New Yorkers who consider it a "tourist attraction." Nevertheless, clowns, magicians, and strolling musicians entertained at no extra charge and while our son was thus distracted, my husband and I could relax over dinner far longer than in most other restaurants. When the infant turns into an active toddler who can't sit through a long dinner, place your order and then take an exploration walk, either in the restaurant or around the block. When the food comes, the baby will be ready to sit for a while and won't disturb other diners.

Vacations

Plan a vacation in an area very different from where you live. City kids need to visit farms and farm children will be fascinated with cities. Don't postpone this year's vacation until the child is older. Just because your child won't remember the specifics of a trip later on doesn't mean that it didn't have an enormous impact on his or her development. After all, few of us can recall anything about learning to walk and talk, but we can still do it!

The three of us went on our first vacation together when Jason was eight months old. Before Jason was born, my husband and I enjoyed dressing up and having dinner in elegant restaurants. With Jason, we spent long days exploring the beach and then returned to our room messy and exhausted at 6 p.m. One evening as we headed back to our rooms looking like slobs, with the baby in my arms, we passed a beautifully dressed, sophisticated-looking couple. They were heading for the formal dining room and we were about to call room service. As we approached them the woman sighed wistfully. "Oh, you make me miss my baby. She's ten months old and we didn't bring her." They went on to tell us that they were staying a week. While their poor child was home for a week that must have felt like a year, perhaps developing lifelong insecurities because she had no idea why her mother and father had abandoned her, Jason had our undivided attention twenty-four hours a day and was absorbing new sights, sounds, and experiences by the minute. I know that I got a lot less sleep than that other woman and I ate second-hand raisins while she ate chocolate mousse, but I came away from our encounter certain that we were having a much better time than they were. Believe it or not, mothers of grown children tell me that the day when their children were glad to see them go came too soon. During the first early months, your child learns to feel secure or insecure. These feelings remain buried deep inside forever. Trips together help form the foundation of a happy family and provide incomparable stimuli for an infant. Parents too discover new pleasures as they find themselves doing and enjoying things they would never plan on an "adult" vacation. Too many people worry about how a child threatens the ties between husbands and wives and ignore the importance of working to restructure the family to include the child.

Even if you are not planning a trip, a visit to the airport, train station, or bus depot makes a great outing. You don't have to be going anywhere special to plan a trip on a train. The ride on the train can be one stop with a return home. When the activity is followed by reading a book about trains and giving the child a gift of a gaily wrapped toy train, you will have generated interest in a whole new area. Follow up with bus, taxi, trolley, boat, and plane rides. On Jason's many excursions during his first eighteen months, a friendly pilot invited him into the cockpit, a conductor thrilled him by giving him a used ticket, and many patient bus drivers waited while he put tokens in the coin box. Such experiences provide education for children that no toys possibly can. The fire house, greenhouse, post office, zoo, aquarium, auto repair shop, and pet shop make exciting trips for a baby. Babies will also love going to the playground long before they can play.

Excursions provide a storehouse of experiences the child can draw on forever.

Visiting Friends

Taking your child with you when you visit friends, and taking your child to visit children of his or her own age, provide new areas of exploration and important opportunities for increased social interaction. A family event, such as a wedding, should make provisions for including even the youngest family members. I always included children in invitations to my home, and hired a baby-sitter to keep them safe and happy in Jason's room. If a teenager was among the invited guests, I made arrangements to see that he or she had the job. So many parents have to leave their children during the work day that they don't want to leave them evenings as well. Stay-at-home parents who are looking for a respite from young people don't have to bring their children if they don't want to, but the choice is theirs.

If you wait until the "books" say babies are ready to play with other children, you've missed a lot of time. Take some time each day to visit a friendly shop, a playground, or a neighbor's home with your baby. The more you do at the beginning, the more comfortable your baby will be with other adults and babies and new settings later on. If you keep your baby home every day, going to nursery school will become a wrenching trauma that negates many of its good effects.

Play Dates

Play dates and play groups are an important predecessor to school. If you start early, your child will adjust better to school. Find one or two other children whom your child seems to get along with, have regular weekly meetings, and set up a predictable play routine. You can begin well before the child is one year old. This is especially important for only children, who aren't getting the experience of playing with siblings, but children who have brothers and sisters shouldn't be deprived of the experience of an independent social life. Don't expect your child to like and play with all children in the same way. Even at this tender age, children develop "special" friends. Do encourage friendships between boys and girls.

Don't let the fact that the children look as if they are ignoring each other discourage you from setting up play dates.

Children are much more natural about their social encounters than adults are. When an adult has a social engagement with someone, it is usually imperative that the two people talk and interact for the duration of their time together. Babies and toddlers are happy to turn their backs on one another for long periods of time while something else is of interest to them. However, don't let the fact that the children look as if they are ignoring each other discourage you from setting up play dates. See pages 163–67 for information on how to organize play dates. During the parallel play they are very much aware of each other's presence and are learning from each other even if they appear to be ignoring each other.

FOUR

Toys, Playthings, and Playmates

Perhaps a baby's best toy is, potentially, her own mother. Watch the baby stare at her eyes, play with her finger, become alert at her voice, finger her face, explore her mouth.*

You are the only "toy" your child will be interested in for many months. Looking at your face, listening to your voice, having close physical contact with you, and being introduced to the world by being shown things by you, are all he or she wants and needs. Many toys reflect this need. Keep in mind, however, that it is you, not a bear, doll, or crib with a simulated "beating heart," that your baby needs. Just how physically exhausting and emotionally draining this job of being a new mother can be is underestimated greatly in our society. Hopefully, the baby's father is an active parent and, if you are really lucky, a grandmother, baby-sitter, or nanny is also available—and there will be days when all of the above don't seem like enough! Alternate a few mobiles over the crib for variety, provide lots of chewable toys, and save your toy budget for next year when you'll really need it. The best gift of all is your time and your own patience. Take your baby to museums, shops, restaurants, and even the office, instead of going alone and leaving Baby with a baby-sitter. Stop to look at construction workers at work,

---

* John and Elizabeth Newson, *Toys & Playthings* (New York: Pantheon Books, 1979), p. 42.

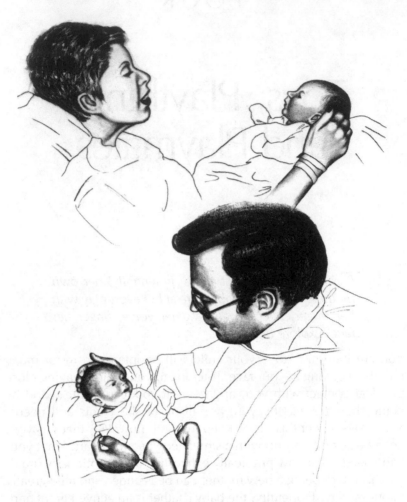

You are the only "toy" your child will be interested in for many months.

birds building a nest, or a tow truck towing a car. Interact with the child and allow freedom to explore.

For many months, examination of new objects is done with the eyes, hands, and mouth—not necessarily in that order. Saying "no" every time your baby mouths something is as harmful to the intellectual curiosity of the infant as the potential germs can be to physical well-being. Dirty sponges may be unhealthy, but a brand-new one feels wonderful in the hands and in the mouth. Wear clothes with roomy pockets to keep a variety of clean items handy and offer them as substitutes when your baby picks up dangerous

Saying "no" every time your baby mouths something is as harmful to the intellectual curiosity of the infant as the potential germs can be to physical well-being.

or unsanitary objects and sticks them in his or her mouth.

> During the first year or so, the mouth is the main
> mirror by which the world is reflected to the child.
> Let it be a pleasant reflection.*

Your drawers, shelves, handbag, and closets hold an endless array of nontoys that will fascinate your child. Real objects will always be more interesting than toys. Pots, empty film boxes, baskets of harmless household tools such as strainers, wooden spoons, spatulas, plastic cups, plastic bowls, a clean hairbrush, a box filled with Band-Aid boxes, egg beaters, containers with lids, bags, fabrics, and old telephone books can provide more entertainment and information than commercial toys often do. Since children of this age spend more time playing with the wrapping and boxes that toys come in than they do with the toys, consider giving your child a wrapped box full of other wrapped boxes for an afternoon's

---

* Haim G. Ginott, M.D., *Between Parent and Child* (New York: Avon Books, 1965), p. 179.

You may think of a roll of film only as something to put in a camera and take pictures with, but free exploration of one provides a child with enough information to make its cost well worth it.

entertainment. You may think of a roll of film only as something to put in a camera and take pictures with, but freely exploring one provides a child with enough information to make its cost well worth it. Open-ended exploration of materials provides more varied kinds of learning than many "toys" do, and you will find that your child is happier and better off receiving your permission to raid the premises than receiving an expensive toy.

Children are fascinated with water, sand, and the sun streaming in through a window. Just looking will never do. There is

Open-ended exploration of materials provides more varied kinds of learning than many toys do, and you will find that your child is happier and better off receiving your permission to raid the premises than an expensive toy.

something so endearing about watching a child catch a ray of sunshine. Providing one object that will block the sun and another that is transparent is an example of using a "toy" in a way that will take advantage of the child's momentary interest and expand it into a meaningful educational experience. That "transparent thing" may be your best nightgown instead of a toy, but at the moment it is the best plaything for your child. Children find catching the sun, the moon, and running water far more compelling than playing with most toys.

Children find catching the sun, running water, and the moon far more compelling than playing with most toys.

No one needs to teach a child to explore his environment. As soon as babies crawl or roll over or move their bodies in space, they harbor the strongest desire to touch, taste, and investigate the physical objects and mechanisms of their motion. On the way to the supermarket, crawlers are the most behaved observers of cars, trucks, buses, trains, and construction sites. At home, they will spend endless amounts of time watching the flight of birds at the feeder or barking dogs in the backyard.*

When your child unrolls the entire roll of toilet paper, use it as an opportunity to talk about "roll" and "unroll," "tear," "wrinkle," "soft," "long," instead of right and wrong. The cost of the

---

* Frank and Theresa Caplan, *The Second Twelve Months of Life* (New York: Grosset and Dunlap, 1977), p. 88.

Since neither anger nor punishment can put Humpty Dumpty together again, a flexible parent can look at it as an unplanned lesson in texture exploration. Wait until the exploration is finished and then enrich the experience through verbalization.

roll will be less than that of a toy, but the experience is far more valuable for the child.

Here is a child getting into the kind of situation not at all uncommon if you live with a toddler. Since neither anger nor punishment would have put Humpty Dumpty together again, a flexible parent can look at it as an unplanned lesson in texture exploration, wait until the exploration is finished, and enrich the experience through verbalization. It can be a time of learning, when you teach a child how to handle a mop, make an omelet, and recite Humpty Dumpty, or it can be a time for punishment and tears. Mopping the floor is inevitable no matter how you respond to the behavior, so you might as well do so in a positive, rather than a negative way. The first way is pleasurable and filled with discovery; the second is filled with guilt, squelches curiosity, and inhibits future behavior. I am absolutely certain that your child will *not* still be doing this kind of thing into adulthood, so stop worrying —and let your child enjoy childhood and learn as much as he or she can. It is impossible for adults always to know what children are ready to learn, but the children always know. You and your family will have some great laughs and a very fulfilled child if you look at the first eighteen months this way. Your role as a parent does not translate into teaching your child not to touch, take apart, and squish everything in sight. With or without your words of "wisdom," your child will very soon outgrow this stage. As a matter of fact, when I misplaced the previous photo, I tried to "stage" the egg situation again, just to get a good picture. After some coaxing, Jason very tentatively touched an egg yolk and left the room. I was reminded of the situation two years later when Jason, while helping me prepare breakfast, stopped with a "*Yuk,* I got egg on my hand," and wouldn't continue until his hands were clean. He really had a need to feel the egg at one precise time in his life. No matter how you handle it, this time will not last very long at all. Parents need most of all to put these experiences into perspective. They are necessary to basic learning about the physical properties of the world. It's so important not to call the child "bad," when what he or she is doing is so innately good. The sad fact is that children do much more learning sitting on the kitchen floor squishing eggs for fifteen minutes when they are ten months old than they do sitting in neat rows taking tests in classrooms in the years to come.

> As they wipe up the fifteenth congealing glob of puree from the floor and pursue soggy lumps of toast up the baby's sleeve, parents can be forgiven if words like "discovery" and "creativity" are not uppermost in their minds. Nonetheless, this is what it's all about. From about six months onward, children begin to make a most determined onslaught on their environment, and the curiosity play of this period is both a stimulus to, and evidence of, their developing understanding. Now the baby wants to find out what happens when you squeeze, punch, pound and bite objects; that some things tear or break, others stretch and bend, still others clatter or bounce. Through endless experimentation, children begin to discover the nature and properties of all the different materials

which they encounter in the world . . . sometimes
a baby will seem destructive at this age: certainly
if she comes upon a heavy book or magazine, she
is likely to pick it up by one page . . . and once
the page has come out in her hand, she will screw
it up, bite it, wave it, and throw it down, and come
back to it for another try at tearing.*

I set a goal for myself when my child was born. I would not
say "no" to him until he was two. Not that I let him do everything
he wanted to do. I diverted his attention with something more
interesting or I described what would happen when he did touch
something. The only slip-up I made was when, as a new walker,
he started to step off the curb into traffic. I screamed "No!" and he
didn't go. The word was very effective since it wasn't overused. As
soon as I calmed down, I showed him the oncoming cars and told
him about red and green lights. After that, he wouldn't allow me
to cross against the light.

I don't want to sound as if you should be letting your child set
the rules in your home. When your child reaches for a hot stove
you will, without advice from anyone, remove the child as quickly
as possible and say "Hot!" There will be so many other opportunities when you will have to set firm rules for the safety of your
child and the convenience of other family members, that it is important to stop what you are doing and say "Yes, let's look at this
together" as much as possible. If you decide to bring your child up
this way, you won't say "no" to your child just because it means
extra work for you. You will not permit unacceptable or inconsiderate behavior, and you will not be permissive in all areas. You
will, however, try never to stifle your child's curiosity. The key is
to make as few rules as possible, and to be sure that the ones you
do make are absolutely final. Freedom can be effective only within
safe boundaries; otherwise it becomes chaos.

Nevertheless, there naturally are times when it is
necessary to scold; and then, instead of merely
scolding the child for bad behavior, it is better to
show him an alternative or to reason with him. If

* John and Elizabeth Newson, *Toys & Playthings* (New York: Pantheon Books, 1979),
  p. 49.

the child should start tearing up a newspaper that you have not yet finished reading, for instance, instead of merely slapping his hand and taking the paper away from him, you could give him another newspaper to play with.*

When the child empties your handbag, puts your car keys into the cat's dish, or unravels the string you were just about to use—that is not mischief. This normal curiosity is the most effective motivation to learn and should never be discouraged. In most cases, these acts won't be repeated, since your child's curiosity will have been satisfied.

Children are learning something every waking moment. The term "educational toy" is meaningless, since children learn from every play experience. The question of what they learn has to do with the experiences and toys you provide for them. If the toy permits only one kind of play, the child soon stops expanding his or her approach to new things; if the toy plays by itself, the child soon expects everything to work without any human intervention; if the toy requires adult control, the child soon learns dependency responses.

Toddlerhood is a dangerous time. Nature provides the toddler with such overwhelming curiosity, despite the obvious risks, for very good reasons. To be good parents we should preserve the curiosity while protecting from harm. To do so takes a lot more time, energy, and hard work than squelching curiosity does. It is that investment you make now that will pay off later. The payoff is a happy, healthy, curious individual with a solid background of firsthand experience behind him or her.

Some time before a child's first birthday, he or she will become fascinated with the toilet. This fascination will last for several weeks, *whether you permit it or not*. Yes, I know toilets are "disgusting." I'm sure they contain many different kinds of germs. I'm also sure that your pediatrician will be appalled by my example. I simply cleaned the toilet with strong soap and a brush and flushed it several times after each use. My son played in the toilet to his heart's content and moved on to more "interesting" things after about two weeks. His health was not affected. Saying "No, dirty"

---

* Masaru Ibuka, *Kindergarten Is Too Late!* (New York: Simon and Schuster, 1977), p. 98.

I'm sure that your pediatrician will be appalled by my example.

won't cure the fascination. It will only extend the length of time interest persists and will merely create unnecessary dependence on adult approval next time an object interests the child. Children can topple into a toilet and drown, so the key ingredient in parental supervision becomes not saying "no," but being close at hand for safety's sake. I read in the newspaper of a baby who drowned in a toilet upstairs while her parents chatted with friends downstairs. I feel that it is better to allow a baby to play, under your supervision, in a freshly cleaned toilet than to risk the possibility that the child will seek it out as soon as your back is turned.

Of course, I am not trying to tell you that you must let your child play in the toilet. I am saying that, as a parent, you will set limits for your child constantly. Only you can decide how many risks you are willing to take and how many sacrifices you can make to encourage independence and a sense of adventure about learning. It is sometimes tempting to be overcautious. Many of our rules are not really helpful to the growing child's long-term development, even if they seem to simplify the immediate moment. Too many rules are for our own convenience rather than the child's needs. You can surely persuade your baby to stop touching everything in sight—but if you do that, you are stifling curiosity and blocking learning. Your child's performance in school and life will forever reflect this.

Even Dr. Spock, whose advice in the area of psychology tends, in my opinion, to be old-fashioned and authoritarian, talks about the advantages of distracting a child.

> They're very distractable, and that's a big help. Year-old babies are so eager to find out about the world that they aren't particular where they begin or where they stop. Even if they're all absorbed in a ring of keys, you can make them drop it by giving them an egg beater. Their distractibility is one of the handles by which wise parents guide them.*

There must be, at some point, a conscious decision on your part to raise an independent, curious child and not one who always waits for direction and approval from you. You need to train yourself to stop saying "no" and to point out some more interesting objects to a child who is about to touch something you don't want him or her to touch. Permit the child to satisfy curiosity if at all possible; divert attention when it's not.

Taking time to let a child look at and touch and try things will certainly make the child more relaxed than one who constantly hears "no" and "don't touch." I saw one mother wheel her baby's stroller right up to a tree in a doctor's waiting room and, as the child reached up to touch a leaf, say exactly that to her. I felt sorry for that four-month-old child who might never know what a plant

* Benjamin Spock, M.D., *Baby and Child Care* (New York: Pocket Books, 1976), p. 306.

A child reaching out to touch a leaf is not being destructive.

or flower feels like. By the time she is old enough to responsibly touch a plant, she certainly will not have any interest in doing so. I know that mother meant well and was trying to teach her child to respect another's property, and I have no doubt that the little girl will grow up to be well-mannered. But, I feel that children who are helped to appreciate beautiful things also learn to respect the property of others. That mother could have looked at, talked about, and touched that plant with her child.

Each "no" or "don't touch" that we say to a child should be weighed. Say it only if it's really important, although I think it's better, if you have the patience, to offer the child something distracting instead. Every "no" limits a child and communicates an attitude that will carry over to the next experience. A child reaching out to touch a leaf is not being destructive. At this age a child is learning what leaves, wood, sand, skin, hair, and a multitude of other materials look like, feel like, smell like, and do. I met one child whose very first word was "no." He was not all that unusual, unfortunately. As the parent of an infant and toddler, I think you have an obligation to say "yes" to your child more often than "no." "Yes, touch," "Yes, let's slow down on our walk to the store so that you can climb up and down that step 500 times," "Yes, I'll stop cooking dinner and hold you because that's what you need now."

Before you have gotten used to the idea that you are a parent, your child will have grown up. You'll have decades to rush to the store, cook gourmet meals, and tend to your own needs, but only these two or three short years to meet your baby's needs. Take the extra time now, and your child will be a curious individual, as well as one who feels secure and loved.

In his first few months, Jason was always grabbing at eyeglasses. I let him pull mine off whenever he wanted to, but my husband, who can't see without his and who doesn't have an extra pair, always said "no!" By twelve months, he never pulled at mine and was still torturing his father. Daddy decided there must be a

Your home is full of exciting toys for your child to explore.

lesson in that somewhere, and he benefited from it quickly. When Jason discovered his valuable videotape machine, Daddy's new theory was really put to the test. Those little hands really can't do any damage to the sophisticated machine and after sufficient exploration, Jason moved on to bigger and better things and Daddy breathed a sigh of relief.

I was put to the test when Jason found me working with my very sharp, nine-inch scissors and wanted them. Even a dangerous item like that can be looked at, touched, talked about, and explored under extremely close supervision. As soon as he picked the scissors up, I picked him up. I held him on my lap and, with my arms around him, held his hands and showed him how the scissors can open and close. We played the "open-close-open-close" game, and I showed him how sharp the point was. I sang the song "Open-Shut Them," as I did so with the scissors. In no time he felt comfortable with scissors, and by age two he could cut

Even the most dangerous items can be looked at, touched, talked about, and explored under extremely close supervision.

paper, holding the scissors in two hands while I held the paper. In my "toddler art" classes I give scissors to one-year-olds and together we sing "Open-Shut Them." In this way the children learn something about scissors before they learn how to cut. Many students start school at age five or six with no idea either of how scissors work or of the potential danger. I'm not suggesting that you hand your child a pair of nine-inch scissors to play with, but when the child becomes interested in a potentially dangerous item, that is the ideal moment for the child to learn about it. Saying "no" accomplishes two things: It postpones the exploration to a time when you are not there to supervise, and gives the child a feeling of inadequacy. With you holding the child, he or she can learn a lot, as long as you are not too uncomfortable with the idea. What it takes is more time than some parents are willing to give.

Here is Jason discovering that cars go around and around on a record player. His friend Pat encourages him in this new and creative use of a phonograph rather than saying "No, don't touch." Of course, it is an electrical appliance, so this is a toy that is saved

A creative child discovers that a phonograph can be for cars as well as records.

for supervised play time only.

At this age it is safest to make all play time supervised play time. It can be tempting to always show a child the "correct" way to use toys and tools, but more often their own discoveries are of more use to them and filled with innovative thinking. Essentially, what you want to develop here is a new attitude, emphasizing and reinforcing a child's curiosity rather than teaching, too early, good safety habits, fear, or good manners. This means encouraging your child to examine everything that interests him or her. You can remove real safety hazards by using quick thinking yourself, to locate a more interesting item when possible.

Water play is of endless fascination for babies. All water activities must be closely supervised, but some steps can be taken to give your child a feeling of independence, even if it is an illusion. An inexpensive plastic bath seat with suction cups on the bottom of it permits your child to sit in the bath when he or she is still new to sitting. Since you don't have to strain your back bending over the bath holding him or her, you'll be more inclined to permit

longer water play time and your baby will enjoy the feeling of independence, even while you hover nearby for safety.

There are so many things to learn from water: full, empty, sinking, floating, hot, and cold are just some of them. Early water play is the best teacher of many concepts. Sprayers, shallow pools, hoses, watering cans, assorted-sized containers, and hopefully a lovely summer's day will add immeasurably to your child's experience. But if it is snowing, that doesn't change the fact that your child needs to experiment with the properties of water. So turn on the faucet and play indoors. The ten minutes you spend mopping up afterward will be well worth it.

You will find that a short step stool at the bathroom sink is far more effective than a playpen. Needless to say, that activity should be saved for when you want to spend time in the bathroom. It is one way to have a long, leisurely bath, wash and dry your hair, put on a wide array of makeup, or clean the bathroom with your child close at hand—learning, safe, busy, and happy. There is now a toy sink that attaches to the side of the bathtub.*

* Sinkadink, #1242, *Just for Kids*, $19.95. Also available at a discount ($16.95) through Parents' Guide Network Corp., P.O. Box 1084, Lenox Hill Station, New York, N.Y. 10021.

Water play is of endless fascination for babies.

Toys to Make

I know that new parents usually don't have time to be constantly building toys, but unfortunately toy manufacturers often build toys that are not so much educational as they are designed to attract adult purchasers. It is possible for you to make some interesting playthings for your child without investing a great deal of time or money. The toy pictured here was made from all of the discarded hardware our building superintendent could find in the basement.

This toy was made from discarded hardware.

Another toy included all of the different locks we could find. Each opened a door to reveal a reproduction of a great painting. Both toys take advantage of a child's natural curiosity about the environment. A stuffed alphabet provides endless enjoyable games with letters separately and together. They also help a child learn to recognize letters and can make a game, rather than grueling work, out of learning to read. Brightly colored plastic keys, available in most toy stores, are nice to have, but are no substitute for the real ones. My locksmith didn't even charge for three blank keys when I told him why I needed them. We put them on a safety ring, washed and boiled them, and never again had to worry about Jason's playing with our germ-ridden and very necessary set.

Tests for Toys

Before giving them to a child, all toys, whether they are store-bought, homemade toys, or household objects, should be studied in two ways:

1. *Are they safe?* One relative, a highly talented and well-known artist, made a puppet for Jason's first birthday. It was a work of art, but the hands were cut of balloon pieces, one of the most frequent causes of choking deaths in young children, and it was decorated with buttons, sequins, and other items that are quite dangerous for a one-year-old. The puppet was admired under parental supervision and then hidden away—out of the child's sight as well as out of the possible sight of an unknowing baby-sitter or visitor. However, just because a plaything is potentially dangerous doesn't mean that your child can't play with it. It means that you must closely supervise the play. I saw a man grab plastic wrap from a child who was sitting in the center of a circle of doting relatives while he opened gifts. Of course, plastic wrap can be very dangerous and babies can suffocate with it, but there is no way that the child would have been allowed to choke while surrounded by these closely watching adults. Learning about what plastic wrap feels like during this supervised situation may discourage exploration at a later time, when the child may be unsupervised.

2. *Do they allow your child freedom for various kinds of interpretations?* Toys that can be used in different ways at different times are the best investment. They stimulate imaginative thinking and encourage creative play.

Television

There is a backlash of conscientious people, who, in an overreaction to the bad quality of some children's television, don't permit their children to watch television at all. There are bad books as well as bad television shows, but no one ever suggested that this is a good reason to stop reading to children. I can't imagine a parent with the time, energy, or multimedia effects to provide his or her child with the learning a show like *Sesame Street* can provide. I put Jason in front of it, in an infant seat, for five minutes when he was three months old, and sat and watched the show with him and pointed things out to him. His attention span for this show quickly increased and I encouraged him to make watching *Sesame Street* part of the daily routine. The result of all this was that he could, at eighteen months, repeat all of the letters of the alphabet; he accurately recognized and spoke several letters and numbers; he knew and said the names of many characters on the show, and he genuinely enjoyed watching it.

At the same time, I was outraged by the theme of cruelty and violence that is commonly an integral part of other shows, and shocked to find that adultery was regularly behind the "humor" in one popular cartoon. The fact is that children are always learning, even when they watch television. From *Sesame Street* they learn letters, numbers, and sound moral values. From Tom and Jerry and other animated characters, including some of Walt Disney's and Jim Henson's more commercial ventures, they learn that torturing and maiming animals by means of fire, explosion, crushing, tarring and feathering, and throwing off of great heights is both amusing and acceptable. Conscientious parents can boycott the sponsors or networks of these programs. Since there is now enough good, entertaining, educational television, and given the availability of videotape machines, it has become easier to avoid poor shows. The fact is that young children find *Sesame Street* as entertaining as the cartoons. The recent trend in publishing toward books derived from licensed television characters suggests that it is time to reevaluate the issue.

Television viewing is often compared unfavorably to reading. It can be tempting for busy parents to use the television as a mechanical baby-sitter, while it is necessary to take time to hold your child on your lap and read to him or her. If, however, a good portion of your child's time in front of a television is spent with you, enjoying shows together and discussing their positive and negative aspects, the value of that time is increased immeasurably. The two of you increase your mutual interests by watching shows together. In fact, I know many thirty-year-old Kermit or Miss Piggy fans! You won't be able to permit viewing some of the awful shows after viewing them yourself. When the child learns early enough that there are specific times each day set aside for television viewing, you should not have trouble setting limits now. Despite the emphasis on independence in our home, the television was built into a piece of furniture six feet high, giving me total control over the amount of time and the quality of shows viewed by my child.

A videotape machine allows you to tape a show and view it at your convenience. It is an expensive "toy," but if you can afford it, I think it is a very worthwhile investment. It allows you to monitor and control your child's exposure to television, and an added attraction is that with the camera attachment you can film your child's most precious moments. Occasionally, televised concerts, family movies, or specials can be very worthwhile, but often they run after your child's bedtime. This is when a videotape machine will be appreciated.

Books

> Books may sometimes be used to make a tunnel, sometimes as drawing paper, and sometimes utilized as something to tear apart. Insisting that a child use books for reading, which is a one-sided adult notion, might produce effects worse than not giving him any books at all. The small child will gradually find out for himself that books are most interesting when read when he takes an interest in reading itself.*

Washable, simple books are available and children enjoy looking at them, particularly while sitting on your lap, as early as three months of age. A child this age can't ask you to do this, as he or she frequently will in coming years. You need to initiate it and repeat it frequently, stopping as soon as the child loses interest. A precursor to reading is looking at pictures. As you look at pictures together, and identify the objects in them, your child quickly learns that abstract picture symbols represent real things. In a few years the transition will be made to understanding abstract letter symbols. Rather than reading the text, try pointing out all of the things you see on the page. "See the child wearing a hat? You have a hat, don't you? It keeps your head warm. What else is a hat good for?" You can then act out these ideas: "Does it make you look different? Can you hide behind it? Can you put this key in it? Will it hold water?" etc. "See the dog? Would you kiss it?" (Kiss the child.) "Would you crawl after it?" (Chase the child.) Continuing this game after the child begins talking and can answer your questions helps build the notion that there is rarely only one answer to a question, and thinking of far-fetched, ridiculous answers can be

* Masaru Ibuka, *Kindergarten Is Too Late!* (New York: Simon and Schuster, 1977), p. 146.

fun and will be rewarded. Too many children learn that there is only one answer to a question that will please adults and they hold back ideas rather than risk being wrong.

Since your child will be looking at pictures, why not look at the best? Many great masters have painted pictures of the subjects that most interest young children. Far better to look at these than at the often mediocre illustrations in most children's books. Children begin to form their preferences early. Children who are exposed only to cutesy characters and cartoon art will prefer that. Only children who have seen great art can possibly prefer it. When Jason became fascinated with trucks I "wrote a book just for him," while my friend did the same for her little girl who was fascinated with babies. Our books consisted of pictures of cars and babies on postcards found in a museum gift shop. Simply paste them on white cardboard, punch holes in the margin, and clip rings through the holes. You can, if you like, cover them with washable clear Con-Tact paper. Buy a lot of postcards next time you visit a museum gift shop to "write" your own art books. Just separate them into logical categories such as babies, animals, men, women, houses, flowers, etc. These books are more elegant than other books for babies, and are doubly effective since they teach the child words and concepts as well as providing early exposure to great art. Some of the books I made for my son were eventually published.

We also made our own texture books. To encourage an interest in furry textures, I went to a nearby furrier and asked if I could buy any old unusable scraps he had for my baby to play with. The furrier presented Jason with a whole envelope of different types of fur and didn't charge anything for them. I drew some pictures of animals on cardboard (you could cut pictures out of a magazine as well) and pasted a square of the appropriate fur on each animal. As we looked at the book Jason could touch the animal and really get a sense of what it feels like. This idea became *Touch, Pat, Feel,* an exhibit at Young at Art and soon to be published as a book.

Very young children can be introduced to some art concepts through books. I have reviewed books about various categories of the visual arts, music, and dance in Appendix III. I was critical of some books which appeared to be geared to this age group but, in fact, offered far too much information at one time to be absorbed by a young child. Most books for young children about color try to teach all of the colors at one time, which is too confusing. They further confuse by showing illustrations of objects such as "blue shirts" or "green cars" when these are objects which remain "shirts" or "cars" even when they are different colors. You can make your own books about color by cutting out magazine photos illustrating one color at a time, sticking only to objects which are always the same color, such as green grass, lettuce, "go" signals, etc. You can also find examples of fine paintings to illustrate one color while providing exposure to art. At Young at Art we wrote a book to teach each concept, including each of the colors and shapes.

As you shop for books, keep in mind that bad books can be as mindless, harmful, and desensitizing as bad television can be!

The Influence of Other Adults

Human beings are the most significant "playthings" for any child. From people, not toys, books, or television, children learn the most. Parents are surely the major influence in their children's lives, but other adults also influence them. If Grandpa always entertains your child by drawing pictures for him or her, and Grandma has a house full of breakable heirlooms, much of your hard work will be wasted. If a well-meaning baby-sitter says "no" to all the activities you have been encouraging, the effects of your hard work will be diminished. Older siblings who have themselves just mastered difficult tasks may proudly show a baby the "only correct way" to do something and frustrate the baby's efforts to explore on his or her own. It is up to you to see to it that other influential adults who will have close relationships with your child understand and respect what you are trying to accomplish.

On the other hand, friends and relatives can often help your child in ways you cannot. Some people can read a story over and over to a baby long after your patience has expired. Others can demonstrate skills and promote interest in areas that are outside your expertise. There may be an adult in your baby's life who will sing like a bird in comparison to your off-key concerts, speak to your child in a foreign language, or share some other skill or talent that you do not possess. If we passed the local bakery without stopping to make a purchase, the clerk ran after us to give Jason a free cookie. All of these people and many others were special to Jason and made him feel special.

Older siblings, who have themselves just mastered difficult tasks, may proudly show a baby the "only correct way to do something" and frustrate the baby's efforts to explore on his or her own.

Your child's life will be greatly enriched and your influence and love for your child are in no way diminished when you encourage him or her to love others. There are some who admonish their children "never to talk to strangers." This warning is meaningless, since every day we must talk to shopkeepers, tradesmen, and others we have never met or do not know very well. Jason's dentist always greeted him with a big hug and kiss. They had a lovely relationship which, I felt, was an important factor in dental hygiene. Permitting hugs from Dr. Ken but not from the local child molester means not letting your child out to play alone. Our favorite doorman gave Jason occasional gifts, always under my watchful eye and with my approval. I always encouraged my son to be warm and friendly *with these people*—but I never let him out of my sight! Even in rural areas children go outside to play unsupervised and are hurt, killed, or kidnapped. You cannot rely on young children to understand and follow directions that have to do with protecting themselves. Constant supervision is the key.

FIVE

Art Experiences

Experts agree that the kind and quality of art experiences you give your preschool child will have a deep and lasting effect on his abilities, perceptions, and personality. They affect his powers of observation, his emotional health, his confidence, and his ability to express himself.*

Finger Painting with Food

A child will do his or her first "finger painting" with applesauce, not finger paint, on a high chair tray as early as six months of age. A plastic tablecloth under the high chair means you don't have to be a martyr to allow this kind of food play. "Don't play with your food" doesn't make any sense for a child this age. It will be a goal later on, but now your child should be doing as much touching, as much squishing of food as he or she wants. This is all part of exploring surroundings, and the finger painting movements are all helpful in making your baby become well coordinated. This coordination provides readiness for scribbling, which in turn provides readiness for reading and writing. One spoonful of applesauce on a clean high chair tray is all you need.

You probably already permit this kind of experimentation, but it is helpful if you realize that this kind of play is both a kind of pre-

* Frank Caplan, ed., *The Parenting Advisor* (Garden City, N.Y.: Doubleday/Anchor Press, 1978), p. 535.

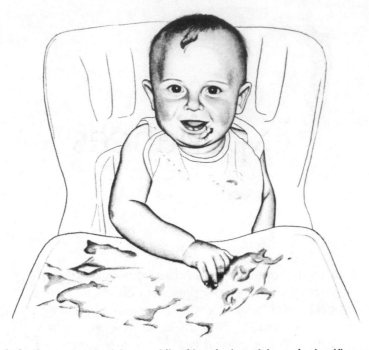

Food play is a pre-art activity providing kinesthetic activity and scientific exploration.

art activity and scientific exploration of the physical world. The early kinesthetic activity and adventurous satisfaction of curiosity work together as catalysts, developing your child's intellect. You can help by providing a corner of your home that doesn't have to remain clean or which can be lined with plastic or vinyl, by never dressing your child in clothes that should be kept clean through a meal, and by encouraging the activity when it spontaneously occurs. It's almost impossible to plan it; the child will do it when he or she is ready. Invariably, this happens on the one day you decide to skip a bath or shampoo, or are having important guests. Nevertheless, learning can't be postponed. Good parenting, like good teaching, requires flexibility and a sense of humor. Despite frequent scrubbing, I never was able to remove the chocolate pudding from my living room wall. I had moved my son's high chair there in order to be able to watch him at work finger painting with his food while I answered the phone. We moved when Jason was two and a half—a tactic which I recommend highly! I often wonder what the people who took over our apartment thought about the indelible brown goop that dripped down the living room wall. It is helpful if you can talk about what the child is doing, how the hand or arm is moving (going back and forth, up and down, or 'round and 'round, etc.), and what the food feels like (squishy, mushy, cold, lumpy, etc.). Applesauce, chocolate pudding, whipped cream, mashed peas, and other baby foods provide a wide variety of textural experiences. You can also mix your own edible "finger paint" with:

> 1 egg yolk
> 2 tablespoons water
> 1-2 drops food coloring

Children do so much learning in a kinesthetic way. This activity will be beneficial to your infant only if you carry it over to the time when he or she reaches out to touch something you would prefer not touched, such as a recently cleaned mirror. I do not wish to sound as if I condone keeping a dirty home. A clean, tidy home provides safety and a sense of continuity for your child. But it is not more important than your child's need, in the early months, to explore. At this age, children are learning about what different foods, wood, glass, sand, mud, plastic, various fabrics, hair, skin, dirty leaves, and a zillion other things look and feel like. Every new mother will tell you that infancy goes by in the blink of an eye. Knowing that, it is helpful if you take a casual approach to your child's fingerprints and be prepared when you see them everywhere to know your child's exploration of your home is the beginning of a sense of adventure about the rest of the world.

A friend told me of her experience with her two-year-old daughter who woke early, reached into her diaper, and painted the wall next to the crib with her own feces. My reaction was to ask my friend if she had been doing finger painting with her daughter, and her response was, "Oh, I know I should, but it's so messy." Needless to say, the child's bedroom was now a lot dirtier than a properly supervised finger or food painting experience could have ever made it. I have read some very advanced, serious studies saying that children have a need to play with their own feces. I don't believe a child who is given enough other items to squish and paint with has any such need. This need will more than likely manifest itself in the child who always hears "don't touch" and who is never permitted to play with food, finger paint, mud, or anything else that is "messy" or "dirty." I believe the overwhelming need children have is to touch everything they can and explore every aspect of the world with all of their senses. To a baby, feces are nothing more than one of a multitude of interesting textures to explore.

Play Dough

Since a child who is not yet a year old is still exploring things through the mouth, nontoxic play dough or an edible homemade recipe consisting of:

　　　　　1 8-ounce jar peanut butter
　　　　　6 tablespoons honey
　　　　　3 cups powdered milk

is the best modeling material to use for introductory sculpture projects.

　　　Edible play dough is fun to pound on, roll, and pull apart.

Finger Painting

The finger paint that I bought said "age three and up," but I'm afraid that if you wait until age three, a lot of the curiosity and joy

Children under three derive great satisfaction from finger painting.

in finger painting is long since gone.

After your child has had some experience with manipulating foods and appears to be using the mouth less for exploring everything, you can try offering real finger paint instead of applesauce. Presenting this activity after mealtime also may help minimize the amount of paint the child may eat. A child who is confined to a high chair that has a plastic drop cloth beneath it will do minimal damage to your home.

Another way to confine finger paints in order to simplify housekeeping is to tape a piece of paper in the empty bathtub. Plan the activity for right before bath time. Strip the baby and let him or her have fun. Demonstrate how to manipulate the material, then remove your own paper from his or her line of vision and encourage your child to try it. Never paint or draw realistic pictures when demonstrating to a child in this stage of development. It can be confusing and may stifle normal exploration of a new material. Finger painting is a very valuable activity which should be offered to a child fairly regularly for the next few years. After a few initial, introductory experiences, which may be messy, your child (and

After a few initial introductory experiences which may be messy, your child and you will learn how to control the material neatly and can concentrate on the more important aspects of finger painting.

you) will learn how to control the material neatly and can concentrate on the more important aspects of finger painting.

The manipulation of the material is what is important at this stage, so one color is all the child needs. You will save money if you buy quart jars of finger and tempera paint, since your child will be using large amounts of them for the next few years.

Be careful to buy only nontoxic finger paint so there will be no reason to be concerned when the child tastes it, as he or she invariably will.

Tasting finger paint is part of a child's introduction to it. Don't worry—it tastes awful and your youngster will soon figure out that there are better things to do with it.

Body painting is essential in the early introduction of paint. Every child does it, and it is an important part of the learning process and will be outgrown by age 2½. Freud called this the anal-erotic stage. It is not done to aggravate you! Since the baby is

Since you will be careful to buy only nontoxic fingerpaint there is no reason to be concerned when the child tastes it, as she or he invariably will.

already in the bathtub, let him or her relax and have fun. When interest in the activity wanes, simply turn on the water and it's bath time!

Bathtub finger paint has a soap base and can be a perfect compromise for parents who really can't bear the idea of real finger paint in their beautiful homes, but it is better as a supplementary art and water-play experience than as a substitute for the real thing. It is sold already prepared or you can make your own. See page 161 for recipe.

Body painting is an essential aspect of the early introductory exploration of paint.

The mouth is the first way a child explores a crayon.

Scribbling

I recommend giving a child a nontoxic, unwrapped, easy-to-hold crayon at about the age of ten months. Demonstrate how to use it by scribbling, never by drawing pictures. The child will at first mouth the crayon, which is harmless, and may not be ready to draw with it for a few months. Offer it anyway, and lavishly praise its first use as a drawing tool.

Some children may scribble as early as eight months, others won't start until after the first birthday.

Scribbling includes all of the hand and arm movements needed in later writing and drawing and is an essential learning activity for all children. The more free scribbling a child does, the easier writing will be later on. In fact, scribbling is more helpful in preparing a child to write than is early letter formation.

Early drawings may be done while attention is focused elsewhere.

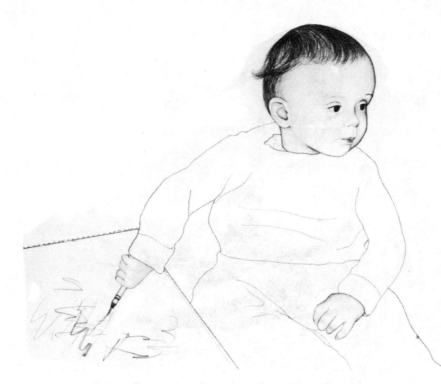

First drawings may be done quite accidentally.

Soon the child will scribble more purposefully, slowly learning what hand movements can produce.

You can help by making comments such as: "Oh, look, your arm goes 'round and 'round and so do the lines on your paper!" "It seems that when you press hard on the crayon the lines get darker." "You have made a long line and a short line." "Your line goes up and then it comes down." Point to or touch the lines you are referring to and repeat the child's hand movement with your own for emphasis.

This random activity is followed by controlled linear scribbles, twenty of which have been isolated and identified as part of the scribbling process.

Your child's first attempt at scribbling should be met with a round of applause and a big hug that clearly says "Mama and Daddy love to see you draw!" Saying things like "I love it," or "It's very pretty!" are not helpful unless you can say why. Saying "I

Soon the child will begin to scribble more purposefully.

love that curvy line,'' is much more helpful than saying ''It's pretty.'' Praise is not as useful or significant as your expression of interest, which gives the experience a sense of importance. ''Pretty'' is a value judgment which teaches the child a premature concept of art as decoration. Banish ''What is it?'' from your vocabulary. Children learn the value of scribbling from their parents, so it is up to you to communicate how valuable these simple drawings are. No child who thinks of his or her scribbles as being babyish or bad can grow up to have confidence in his or her art ability.

Scribbling is something like babbling—it doesn't sound like much, but children need to do it before they can express themselves eloquently. Scribbling doesn't look like drawing or writing as we know it, but it is the most significant activity your child will engage in in preparation for it. Just as you repeat sounds to a babbling baby and respond lovingly to his or her efforts, so too you must be a springboard for a child's attempts at scribbling. Scribbles contain all the secrets of later decoding, and if you look carefully

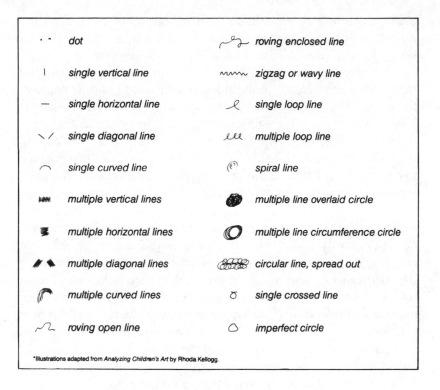

· ⌃	dot		roving enclosed line
ǀ	single vertical line		zigzag or wavy line
—	single horizontal line		single loop line
\ /	single diagonal line		multiple loop line
⌒	single curved line		spiral line
	multiple vertical lines		multiple line overlaid circle
	multiple horizontal lines		multiple line circumference circle
	multiple diagonal lines		circular line, spread out
	multiple curved lines		single crossed line
	roving open line		imperfect circle

*Illustrations adapted from *Analyzing Children's Art* by Rhoda Kellogg.

you will see the foundations for later words and pictures. Your encouragement frees the child to further explore the world of lines and shapes. The child who senses your disinterest in or displeasure over scribbles may get sidetracked doing neat coloring or premature realistic drawings and letters in an effort to please you. These activities require restricted hand and arm movements which inhibit normal development, and may be, in part, responsible for the many reading and penmanship problems children have later on.

> When adults have a consistently approving reaction to all work made, without overemphasizing appreciation of what they like best, the child functions best in art.*

Every child progresses through this scribbling "alphabet" (above) before moving on to the next stage. You will recognize

* Rhoda Kellogg, *Analyzing Children's Art* (Palo Alto, Calif.: Mayfield Publishing Co., 1970), p. 69.

easily that these twenty shapes can be put together to form the alphabets of every language in the world. Later on, that is exactly how and why your child will be able to read and write.

A note about materials: Very young children draw by making large movements from the shoulder, not by hand control. You will therefore need to buy paper that is as large as the child's arm is long. Anything smaller will logically result in drawings that continue off the paper onto the floor, wall, or tabletop. Paper wrapping on children's crayons serves no useful function and discourages use of the broad side of the crayon. The only explanation I have seen for it, in fact, is that it helps keep the hands clean, and clean hands are not a valid goal for the child experiencing an art activity. Buy large, blunt, unwrapped crayons that are easy to hold and will not break easily under pressure. Sharp points are for pencils, not crayons, and it's too early to offer pencils now. Too many children use their crayons sparingly to preserve the sharp points and I have seen children throw away crayons because the tips broke or because they broke in half. At Young at Art, we always started a new semester off with new crayons. The very first thing we did with them before embarking on our first project was to break them in half. Crayons are working tools, not prizes, and drawing with the broad side is just as useful as drawing with the point.

Offer one crayon at a time, since choosing colors and changing crayons in the middle of a picture is distracting from the main value of scribbling for toddlers.

> Is it essential—is it necessary that we provide the child with many colored crayons? No, it isn't necessary at all for scribbling. The child most definitely remains with one color in continuous scribbling. The experiments which we made when we gave children different colored crayons showed that most of them remained with one color. They just pick yellow or red or blue and remain with this color throughout their scribbling. Only those children change colors who lack confidence. They like to pick up one and then the other; through this they interrupt their scribbling, which is most welcome to them because they lack confidence. So, in the beginning, I would say that a black crayon

would be the best for scribbling.*

Children can still be expected to scribble after they have started school and the worst thing any adult can do is "teach" a child how to draw or give the child adult-drawn pictures to color-in. Children's art is a form of self-expression that precedes writing and storytelling, and, frequently, talking itself. Your reaction to his or her early works helps in establishing your child's self-image and, if you handle it correctly, adds immeasurably to his or her self-esteem. Scribbling is the first introduction to drawing and is most useful when it is self-taught through experimentation. Giving a child a coloring book or showing the child how to draw discourages problem-solving and obliterates the need for original thinking. It is like giving the child the answer in place of the math problem or a brief summary instead of the book. Coloring books tell the child that drawing, to be worthwhile, must be realistically rendered by an adult. The small, tight, back-and-forth hand movements required in neat coloring are completely different from those required to produce a scribble. These are the same as one of the earliest stages of scribbling. Coloring-in can arrest development at that point. It enforces a repetitious back-and-forth hand movement that ignores the child's need to experiment with the hand and eye movements that will later be used in drawing and writing. Coloring books, similar connect-the-dot books, paint-by-number sets, paint-with-water sets, molds, and "art" machines are exercises in creative mediocrity; they have absolutely no redeeming qualities. Machines that produce drawings with the turn of a dial also work against your child's development, and computers that are programmed to make drawings are totally inappropriate for children of all ages.

As I said in The Anti-Coloring Book®:

> We give them coloring books that consist of drawings by highly skilled professional artists: we ask them to abandon their own adventurous journey toward creativity and stay within the lines. By the time they have completed the first few pages of the average coloring book, the only thing they will

* John A. Michael and Viktor Lowenfeld, The Lowenfeld Lectures (University Park, Pa.: Pennsylvania State University Press, 1982), p. 145.

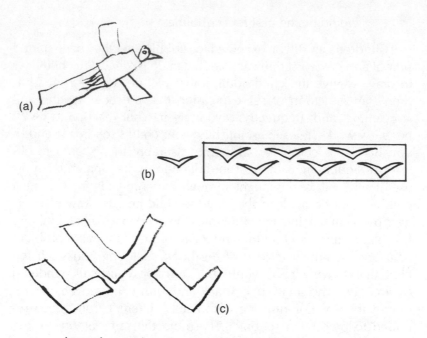

have learned is that adults draw better, by adult standards, than they do. At this point most children spurn their own refreshing and expressive drawings. Dr. Irene Russell's classic example is typical of the proof research has uncovered that the imitative procedures found in coloring books rob children of their abilities to think independently and to express their feelings through art. The first drawing (a) shows a child's depiction of a bird before the child was exposed to coloring books. Once asked to copy a coloring book illustration (b), the child lost originality in subsequent drawings of birds (c).*

Fortunately, children instinctively know this, and will probably ignore the lines and scribble over coloring book drawings anyway!

In addition to giving children predrawn outlines to color-in, we also have a tendency to try teaching them how to write far too early. Demonstrating for a child how to draw or write will encour-

---

* Susan Striker and Edward Kimmel, *The Anti-Coloring Book*® (New York: Holt, Rinehart and Winston, 1978), p. ii.

age that child to turn away from scribbling in an effort to live up to your expectations. The child who is "taught" how to draw a circle is not having the same valuable experience as the same child who, when allowed to develop normally, "discovers" the circle, as every child does, about midway through the scribbling stage. The toddler who has free, positive, joyful experiences scribbling will progress very naturally, and painlessly, into writing.

All children are born with the impulse to scribble, and their development in this area follows a predictable pattern.

> Any keen observer of the development of infants and young children cannot help but be aware of the fact that later development depends upon earlier accomplishments. The child cannot speak in sentences until he has mastered words. Must often he cannot walk until he has crept. He cannot become annoyed over his mother's departure until he has become attached to her.*

Our lack of understanding and support during this crucial scribbling stage produces generation after generation of people who are convinced that they "can't draw" and who must rely on patterns, paint-by-the-numbers, molds, and other crutches. If we would learn to leave our scribbling toddlers to their own devices, and be quicker to praise their efforts than we are to punish for drawing in inappropriate places, we would finally produce a new generation of people who were not so handicapped in this intellectual area. Even older siblings, proud of recent accomplishments, can discourage exploration when they try to "teach" a baby how to draw. I once observed a child happily scribbling until a four-year-old sat down next to him and drew a human being. His mother told me that the younger child didn't draw again for three days! Parents need the cooperation of their older children in this matter. Art classes in preschools, daycare centers, or elsewhere should take the child's level of development into consideration more than the child's chronological age.

Reading, writing, and arithmetic are commonly called the three basic skills. Perhaps even more basic is the elementary skill

---

* Frank Caplan, ed., The Parenting Advisor (Garden City, N.Y.: Doubleday/Anchor Press, 1978), p. 311.

.

that leads to the ability to do all of the above—scribbling. A creative, self-motivated art experience involves problem-solving (as in
math), thinking, and using symbols (as in reading and writing).

> . . . The public school's problems with non-learn-
> ers could be greatly reduced through reforms in art
> education. . . . *

Scribbling transcends historical styles and geographical boundaries. It is done by children in America, France, Alaska, Russia,
China, and the rest of the world. Michelangelo, Rembrandt, Van
Gogh, and Picasso all started as scribblers. The reason some of us
abandon art forever while others grow up to be talented artists is
largely environmental. With readily available materials and encouragement from significant adults, artistic endeavor can flourish.

* Rhoda Kellogg, *Analyzing Children's Art* (Palo Alto, Calif.: Mayfield Publishing Co.,
1970), p. 142.

SIX

Movement

*. . . There is a Japanese saying that "A superior
mind dwells in an active body."**

A newborn baby has no control over body movement, but by the
end of the first year he or she can usually walk unaided! So much
of how the baby feels about his or her body and what it can or
can't do will stay with him or her for life. You can help your baby
feel confident and good about his or her body by providing interest, support, encouragement, space, and time. Show interest in
even simple movements such as lying on the back and kicking,
which looks simply like fun but actually also provides readiness
and coordination for later crawling. Show support by offering
smiles, cheers, and encouragement to give your baby the stimulus
to continue. Support of the emotional kind—such as giving a
round of applause to a child who has just bravely gone down a
slide or a helping hand to one who wants to go, but not alone—
makes all the difference.

Give your child a chance to really feel what his or her body is
capable of doing without the intrusion of artificial devices such as
"walkers," which remind me of wheelchairs for healthy children.
I generally object to this type of unnatural interference in a child's
development. There are some toys and devices, however, that aid
rather than intrude on a child's normal physical development. For

* Masaru Ibuka, *Kindergarten Is Too Late!* (New York: Simon and Schuster, 1977), p.
150.

111

Lying on the back and kicking provides readiness and coordination for later crawling.

instance, wheeled push toys and sturdy wagons that the child can control, rather than be confined in, will serve the purpose of a potential walker admirably by offering incentive for learning and practice. The sense of independence that the child feels with this type of toy is most beneficial. Read *The Parenting Advisor* for more information on this issue.*

Children need ample opportunity to fall and scrape their knees without undue parental fear or concern interfering with the learning experience. Drop ''be careful'' from your vocabulary. It rarely

---

* Frank Caplan, ed., *The Parenting Advisor* (Garden City, N.Y.: Doubleday/Anchor Press, 1978).

prevents accidents but does cause fear. Space to stand up and to move around in without bumping into things and time to try doing things over and over and over are what is needed now.

Be generous with praise—not only for accomplishing feats, but for attempting them as well. When you notice that your child has set goals for him- or herself, use your tone of voice, words of encouragement, and incentive toys to help in attaining those goals. A new walker will take an extra step for a doll, a climber will reach higher to ring a bell.

There are gym classes for babies springing up all over the country. In a good babies' gym class the teacher will help you do activities with your baby that will encourage use of the whole body while encouraging social interaction. Many of these activities are reminiscent of games mothers have always played with their children—they just didn't always know how healthy they were! In the following illustrations, toddler fitness teacher Peg Nickerson demonstrates games you and your baby can play together that strengthen the baby's body and increase his or her spatial awareness:

In movement activities, your goal should be to help your child get in tune with his or her body. Hold the baby in your arms and dance in time to music. Do so in front of a mirror occasionally— as soon as the child is mobile he or she will be dancing! Make up dances as you go along—the sillier, the better. One of our favorites was the "pee-pee dance," which Jason invented shortly after learning to use the potty. He was in a real hurry to get to the bathroom but wouldn't go alone. He jumped from one foot to another and held his penis while yelling "pee-pee," to get our attention— hence the name. Children love to take off all of their clothes for a dance in the rain. Marches, particularly to appropriate music, may get your toddler where you want to go very efficiently. A song like "Tick-tock" will help make the child aware of rhythm in everyday objects. Clap slowly and quickly, quietly and loud—always verbalizing the activity to increase the child's understanding and to increase the child's vocabulary.

If one is available, visit a well-equipped playground every day from the time the baby can sit up in the sand and look around at the other children at play. Dress the baby appropriately and comfortably in long pants; girls don't need dresses at all at this stage. Knee guards give a crawler freedom to go anywhere. You can knit

1) Lean Forward and Back (helps develop thigh, back, and tummy)
2) How Big Is the Baby? So Big! (stretches muscles)
3) Upsy Daisy (for back and neck)
4) Bottoms Up (strengthens arms, pectorals, and back)
5) Over We Go (spatial awareness)

The games mothers have always played with their babies strengthen bodies and increase spatial awareness.

If your baby doesn't love the water, don't feel that swimming is something that "should" be done. If your baby does love the water, let him or her swim!

or crochet your own, or sew pads right into long pants, add pockets to the knees and put sanitary napkins or other padding in them, or buy well-padded knee guards in a sporting goods store.

For playground visits, always carry a bag filled with: diapers, extra pacifiers, wipes, tissues, a complete change of clothes, extra shoes or lightweight slippers, a snack, and a few small toys. The change of clothes will discourage you from saying "stay dry" when it's water your baby is fascinated with, or "stay clean" when he or she is conducting major experiments into the properties and characteristics of mud. I always had lightweight rubber-soled slippers at the bottom of the bag so that if Jason decided to jump into a puddle, our day's excursion didn't end with frozen toes. A light snack may be just what the child needs to be refreshed before continuing play and is also very useful for coaxing the baby back into the stroller for the ride home. The toys are not only to play with, but can be used for bartering with other children who have toys your baby wants to play with. Since there is no way for you to know in advance what exactly your baby will need when, the bag should always be ready. This may not seem like a very significant contribution to your baby's development, but knowing that Mom can always be relied on to provide bottle, pacifier, or other necessities adds to a child's feeling of security.

If your baby loves the water, let him or her swim! The swimming motions that are made in the womb continue for quite a while. There are many "water-babies" classes that will give you the expertise and opportunity necessary to swim with your infant. You need two adults, one to hold the baby and one for the baby to swim to. The latter should always be the primary caretaker, not a friend or the swimming teacher. Infants cannot keep their heads above water, but can swim perfectly under water. Don't ever push your baby forward under water for this forces water into the tender nasal passage and can be very painful. If your baby doesn't love the water, don't feel that swimming is something that "should" be done. You may want to wait to begin swimming with your baby until you feel sure that your baby likes it. When I took Jason at three months I felt unsure of his comfort. When I tried again at five months, he squealed, splashed, and giggled, making it very clear that he was ready for the activity. Your child, not you, can be the best judge of readiness.

SEVEN

Music

Although we are surrounded by music, even in elevators, attentive listening has diminished. You can help your infant develop the skill by setting aside a time each day when the two of you sit and exclusively listen to music. Or, if you prefer, make mealtime also music time. Keep in time by tapping a spoon on a cup, sing even if you feel you can't, and clap your hands. Your baby may be the only one in the world who loves the show—to him or her you are a star! When your child begins to make music it won't sound much like music, but reciprocating and treating the baby like a star help encourage further experimentation. Help your child to develop the habit of listening by stopping to hear the birds, a far-off fog horn, or church bells and sirens. Describe and name the sounds you hear, try to imitate them, and encourage the baby to do the same. Make sure that your child gets a chance regularly to hear truly musical music, not just those ghastly recordings of "children's favorite songs." In *Kindergarten Is Too Late!*, Masaru Ibuka tells of research which reveals that:

> The music about which the children were most enthusiastic proved to be Beethoven's Fifth Symphony! Popular songs such as are broadcast on television from morning till night were second in popularity, and the songs written for children were least popular.*

* Masaru Ibuka, *Kindergarten Is Too Late!* (New York: Simon and Schuster, 1977), p. 34.

Having a child is an elevating experience. You want the best for your child, and in providing it your life will be enriched. I knew my child would be constantly exposed to art because it was so much a part of my life. But I felt insecure about my musical background, and worried about how to do better for my son. My elementary school students always groaned or giggled when they heard classical music or opera because it was so alien to them. In school they sang only "children's songs," and at home their parents listened only to popular music. I knew nothing about classical music but, despite my ignorance, I vowed always to listen to classical music while nursing, and hoped that my baby would associate the pleasure of nursing with the sound of great music. Before I realized it, I was enjoying classical music myself and listening to it even when Jason was at the playground with a baby-sitter! As a parent, you expose your child to art, music, food, physical activity, dance, toys, and love for the very first time. Make it the best!

I think it is important not to "teach" music but to provide musical experiences which children can draw on later when they conceptualize. Take your child to hear a violin, piano, trumpet,

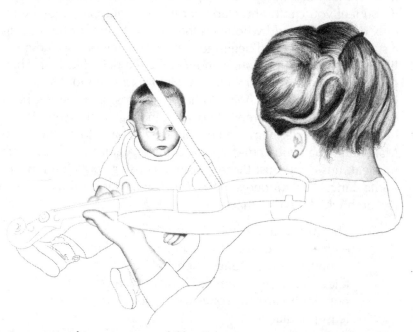

Just as you need to expose your child to great art, so too must you give a child the opportunity to hear the sounds fine musicians make with quality instruments.

Active exploration teaches the baby more about music than will months of lessons later on.

and flute well-played by a fine musician.

Just as you need to expose your child to great art, so too do you have to give a child the opportunity to hear the good sounds fine musicians make with quality instruments. Rehearsals, outdoor concerts, parades, and generous friends can provide invaluable experiences for your baby. For toddlers at Young at Art we stage concerts by a string trio. These classical musicians change their repertoire for us and have realistic expectations of the children's interest level and attention span. In the city, always stop to listen with your child to the street musicians who play for coins. It was a real exercise in discipline for me not to interfere when I saw a toddler twist his whole body around to observe such a street concert while his mother passed it without a glance or comment. How sad that when that baby reaches the age his mother is now, he too may have stopped noticing music. Seeing people make music is crucial to understanding and appreciating it.

Although babies need to hear professional musicians play music on real instruments, they will not be content to just sit and listen. "Please touch" should be your theme song now, as always. Plucking a violin or guitar string teaches a baby far more about violins and guitars than mere words ever could, and climbing into a piano to see how it makes music will teach more than months of lessons will later on. This active exploration is so very different from how we expect musical instruments to be treated that we tend to be uncomfortable with it.

Children need to hear the sounds that they can produce on fine musical instruments from the beginning. A real tom-tom, drum, and piano will sound a lot different from cheap, plastic toy imitations.

Rattles, like maracas, will probably be the child's first musical instrument. Bells will also be enjoyed. Percussion instruments such as drums, tom-toms, and cymbals are enjoyed enormously and help teach about rhythm. The least effective musical "instrument" is probably a music box. Most repeat part of a song over and over, out of context to the rest of the piece. Babies under eighteen months can't wind up most music boxes anyway, so these toys can make parents feel like slaves. By the time your child can activate a music box, these same manipulative skills could be put to better use on a participatory musical instrument.

It is essential for children to feel positive about and enjoy

music, and you can help by playing musical games with your child. See if you and your baby can bang quietly, then loud, fast, and slow, with the hand, foot, or nose. Most important is for your baby to realize from the outset that music is created, not just memorized. In addition to musicians, the world needs composers—the truly creative people who give music to the world.

The human voice is the greatest musical instrument of all. It's available wherever we may be—even on line in a supermarket or stuck in a traffic jam. Mothers have always sung to their babies because they know there is no sound a baby would rather hear than his or her mother's voice. Sing to your baby. It doesn't matter if you have an "awful" voice (I bet you don't, and no one else will hear you). Even if you're tone-deaf (I bet you're not—true tone deafness is very rare), sing made-up songs, well-known songs, baby songs, opera. Put common sentences to music. Your baby will love it. You can help your child realize that voices don't always have to sound pretty or good.

Voices and mouths can be used to make other kinds of sounds as well, such as clicking, buzzing, humming, etc. These sounds can be used by themselves or added to music to enhance it. Before traditional music skills are possible, children can make these sounds with their tongues and lips, as well as with their hands and feet, and they will so enjoy joining you in your game!

PART II

The Child: Age 1-2

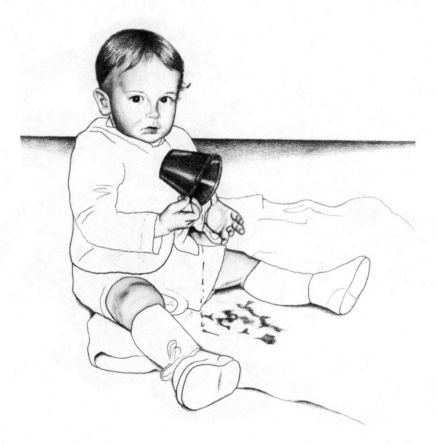

EIGHT

The
Second Year

This picture pretty well sums up the one-year-old's learning style. It can be maddening when you are trying to run a fairly civilized home, but a child can't learn about empty, full, pour, and spill without experiencing these things firsthand. Young children learn through active physical interaction with the environment, not by looking and listening. If the need to know comes during a parent-initiated water-play period, life goes smoothly. It's nobody's fault, however, if curiosity rears its head when you have just handed your child the last six ounces of milk within ten miles on the night of a major hurricane. Notice the old towel, which was placed under this child long before he even showed any interest in pouring. It can be hard to remember that the child isn't doing these things to bother you, but is driven by a force much larger than him- or herself. Children learn most from this self-motivated style of studying the world. Adult interference almost always does more harm than good. Living happily with your child for the next eighteen months means being prepared. Having a sense of humor helps.

You will find that as soon as your baby is mobile and can crawl or walk he or she will be into everything. He or she will climb up on the dinner table and into an open refrigerator. There is no need to say "no" to everything. The best way to help your child safely through this time of peak curiosity is to be there. Look at the food, the drawers and shelves with your child and explain things as you do. It is safer to look inside the refrigerator in your presence than it

This picture pretty well sums up the one-year-old's learning style.

is to do so after you have left the room. Persistence is another common quality now. If your intervention ignores the child's need to know, you only postpone the exploration. The one-year-old already knows that people don't belong in refrigerators, just as he or she knows that they sit on chairs, not tables. But he or she just needs to explore and, like Everest, the refrigerator and the table were there. You've been going to the refrigerator for the baby's whole life and bringing forth new and wonderful things. The baby has to see what it's all about. As soon as the refrigerator has been fully explored the one-year-old moves on to the cupboard, pot closet, and everything else in sight. Things aren't just explored, they are explored with a passion. Something may spill and others will surely be rearranged, but this is the price you pay for encouraging curiosity. If we could only preserve that passion for knowledge in all people through adulthood, the world would be a very different place. Preserving and nurturing it is what this book is about. Straightening our your shelves is a very small price to pay for encouraging the pursuit of knowledge.

You'll need the patience of a saint now. Every mother is sure that her baby will never live through the year. Babies whose parents say "no" all day are in the most danger, since they will try

The best way to help your child safely through this time of peak curiosity is to be there.

everything out when the parents' backs are turned. After enough recrimination, they will give up their quest—perhaps a few months before children whose parents encourage them do. That abandonment is permanent, and the recrimination switches from "Don't touch!" to "Why are you doing so badly in school?" Take heart— by age two and a half it's all over, and don't be surprised if you miss it so much that you start thinking of having another baby! By then, most of your home will have been thoroughly explored, and you and baby can relax more and talk about things together without taking them apart.

Nature provided your child with incessant curiosity for a very good reason. There are times when it is tempting to say "no" too much and try to control the child. Too often we feel that we have to "teach-teach-teach." The more we try to convince a toddler that parents know best, the more we suggest that danger lurks in every corner, the closer we bring our toddler to the point where his or her natural response to every new challenge is "I can't do it." That is the beginning of the end. The very curiosity and persistence that can be so maddening, and downright dangerous, in a toddler are the very same qualities that we find in successful and admired adults. The very things that children naturally do are the things that are best for them. Occasionally congratulate your toddler for being persistent. Jumping on beds is great fun and helps strengthen leg muscles; most parents forbid it. There is a danger of falling, but not if you have the patience to stand by and the foresight to put pillows in strategic places. Don't say "too high" when the child attempts to jump off the kitchen table; offer your hand or throw a soft pillow underneath to soften the fall. Don't say "Don't climb on the furniture" when "Let me help you take off your shoes before you walk on the sofa" is an option.

Now the child ricochets in his or her relationship with you. One minute you have a helpless baby, the next an independent child who resents your help. Don't be afraid to take your cues from the child's mood. There is no advantage to prodding maturity, it comes soon enough. Perhaps it is more fully developed when it grows in the security of your approval.

Children learn by doing more than by observing. Nevertheless, seeing you do things does contribute to their interest and attitude toward many things. Don't make the mistake of leaving your child with a baby-sitter when you go to get a haircut or visit a doctor. When I had a health problem, I took my son with me every week when I visited my doctor. The doctor let him squeeze the bulb when he checked my blood pressure and had him stand ready to kiss my arm after an injection. Shortly after these visits ended, I took Jason to visit his doctor. After being given an injection, he cheerfully offered me his arm to kiss. The doctor was astonished at the child's calm acceptance of procedure and cheerful cooperation. A first haircut can also be a terrifying experience, but not for a child who has seen you enjoy getting your own hair cut.

This is also the time to slowly ease your child into group play, always in your presence. Instead of sitting on a park bench and reading a book, be ready to step in and intervene in difficult social situations. By your example, you teach your child how to deal with others. If another child tries to grab your child's toy, you can step in and divert the grabbing child's attention with another toy. Soon, your child will get the idea and be able to handle these situations without help. You will be able to slowly ease back toward that tempting bench very soon, and can safely focus your attention on the book when you know your child can handle him- or herself well with others. As you walk home from the park, talk about how well your child handled certain situations. By verbalizing the tactics used and praising those which you want emphasized, you help your child learn how best to get along with others. These valuable lessons in social interaction will serve your child well and avoid what for many is the stark terror of nursery school later on.

NINE

Home Environment

By the child's first birthday, he or she is either a very mobile crawler or a new walker. Your entire house, yard, and garage must be completely child-proofed by now. I have lost count of the many homes I have visited where parents stubbornly cling to some mysterious tradition about keeping soaps and detergents under the kitchen sink. One mother told me her daughter "never touched" the detergents under the sink. Just a few weeks after our conversation, that same little eighteen-month-old girl drank a bottle of baby lotion, that could just as easily have been Lestoil, in the few minutes it took her mother, who had a doctorate in Early Childhood Development, to go to the bathroom. No matter which of the many books parents read on child care, they will find these standard safety precautions, yet too many parents still think their "well behaved" offspring are "different." The ideal child's environment will have *nothing* in reach that a child cannot touch or mouth.

If a child lives with you, or even visits, your entire home is that child's environment. It is unrealistic (and unfair) to expect a child to live and play only in a nursery. For the first three years of your baby's life, you should remove all valuable, dangerous, and fragile objects from your home. This is important, not only for your baby's safety and well-being, but also so that your baby can truly explore your whole home with the freedom and comfort that encourages future exploration. If you put toys, old books and magazines, pots, brushes, and old hats in all of the accessible drawers and closets in your home, your baby will feel secure and free to explore everywhere. I kept one plastic milk crate full of toys in every room in my house, which made clean-up simply a matter of picking up everything and throwing it into a box. Cooking toys were kept in the kitchen, water toys in the bathroom, art supplies in my office, etc. This helps provide a sense of organization to the toy collection, and places toys in the spots where they are most likely to be desired. It is also one way to keep your baby happily and safely with you no matter where you are.

Once the child can get around, he or she will resist being confined in any way. Playpens are unfit for human beings and are good only to protect recently decorated Christmas trees or freshly baked pies! It is crucial at this point not to stifle curiosity except if real danger exists. The child will open restraining gates quicker than you can. You need bars on every window and locks that are out of baby's reach on the doors. Your family's convenience or your busy schedule don't qualify here as reasons to restrain a toddler when the real physical and psychological need is to walk, touch, and explore.

We are all very well aware of the disadvantages of being poor. Many children suffer intellectually because their parents can't afford stimulating toys, books, and art materials. Yet I have observed another kind of deprivation in the offspring of wealthy parents— families whose homes are so beautiful and elegantly decorated that the children who live and play in them aren't allowed to do anything that might make them dirty. Many three- and four-year-olds enter nursery school without ever having painted, much less finger painted! Such children may be rich, but they certainly are not privileged. They are, in the truest sense of the word, deprived— deprived of essential learning activities and opportunities for development because these activities would interfere with the preservation of the home environment. No home, even if it is a palace, should become more valuable than the development of a child's mind.

Children learn through active, physical interaction with the environment. Adults may be able to learn through looking and listening; young children do not. They must touch, taste, and manipulate every new thing that they come in contact with before they can understand it. Children who are prevented from engaging in active participation and manipulation become frustrated at first, indifferent later on. Too many of us live in homes that make it

Your child's development, not your possessions, must be the highest priority.

impossible to permit our babies enough freedom in their quest for knowledge. Before they can learn to write, children scribble. They have very strong urges to do so, and often impulse strikes when the nearest thing is a wall or tabletop. Washable paints and furniture finishes allow you to clap and cheer your budding artist on while he or she draws on the furniture, then wait until it is forgotten and scrub it away. Your child's development, not your possessions, must be the highest priority. That does not mean that you have to live like a slob for the next three years, or that your home and furniture should be destroyed by an inconsiderate new family member while you pretend not to notice. It does mean that you have to accept your toddler's messy style of learning as normal and necessary, and provide for it in planning your home. Plastic laminate, glass, and enamel paint all wash easily; unfinished wood and wallpaper do not. A polyurethane finish on wood surfaces can do more to encourage creativity than all of the art supplies you can buy. It makes a lot more sense to adjust the environment to your children's needs than it does to try to ignore their needs in favor of your taste. If you refuse, you, your child, and the environment will all suffer. It is a lot easier to be understanding when damage can be easily repaired. My own home was planned very carefully to be maintenance-free. All its painted surfaces are high-quality, washable enamel, all furniture is plastic laminate, and all cushions are made with zipper openings for easy cleaning. Wipeable surfaces, washable upholstery, and a labeled place for every toy simplify life by providing for your child's participatory learning style while at the same time providing for your own need to live in a clean home. A quick wipe with a damp sponge will take care of just about anything—there is no longer any reason to spend a lot of time caring for your possessions when you can be caring for a human being.

There are alternatives to easy-care materials. In one home I've heard about, the first of six children drew on the kitchen wall. Instead of washing it, her mother began a family tradition that has already lasted for two generations. As subsequent children came along, they were encouraged to follow suit. Last I heard, that wall of sentimental masterpieces had not been painted over after twenty-six years, and the son of the originator of the idea had just contributed his first scribble. I asked the proud grandma if her children drew on walls all over her house and she assured me that it was never a problem. Blackboard paint, found in hardware or paint stores, will also transform a wall into a washable, more temporary version of this family's art gallery.

Modern platformed spaces are also very popular with children, who need a lot of time and place to practice going up and down safe steps. Children have always crept under furniture to find a safe, secret haven, but you may want to consider including such a niche in the design of your child-proof home. Of course, if you own a house full of fragile antiques, or don't care for contemporary design, many of my suggestions will be useless—they are intended for open-minded people who are considering how environment influences life with children.

TEN

Excursions

Education doesn't begin on the first day of school; that is merely when it is taken over by strangers. Your child will really learn more from you than from any teacher. From you the child picks up an attitude about life. Whether the world exists within your home or is a much larger place depends on how much you venture out together. During these precious years before school begins, you have the child with you during the peak of curiosity. "What dat?" and "How dat work?" are questions you will begin to hear soon after the baby begins talking. Your answers may not seem profound to you, but from them your child's attitude toward learning is shaped. In addition to making your home an enriching environment, you will also want to plan frequent excursions. Further enrich these trips by talking about the experience before and after, reading a book about a similar place, and presenting toys that encourage related play. Some excursion ideas are listed below. You will find others in *Tours and Visits Directory, A Behind-the-Scenes Guide to Factories, Mines, Business Firms, Government Agencies, Cultural and Educational Institutions, and Other Facilities Which Receive Visitors* (Gale Research Company, Book Tower, Detroit, MI 48226).

1. *Take bus, taxi, train, trolley, and, if possible, airplane rides.* A ride to the next stop and back can provide a child with the thrill of a lifetime.

2. *Visit an airport, train station, or bus depot.* You don't have to be planning a trip to go there.

3. Visiting *art museums,* which may seem like a very adult pastime, is, in reality, a very appropriate activity for toddlers. Children love looking at pictures. (Why shouldn't they look at the very greatest pictures in the world?) Exposure is the surest way to ensure a lifelong love and understanding of art. Point out objects that you think might interest the child, then comment about them on your child's level. Describe things in a personal way for your child, not as you think an art historian might. "Look at that doggie, he is the same color as Fido!" or "See the red flowers? We picked some red flowers this morning!" are simple comments that help sustain the child's interest. Running through this Alexander Calder sculpture was great entertainment for an afternoon museum visit, provided priceless contact with the world of art, and was a most effective

Running through a piece of great sculpture can provide the best lesson in art appreciation.

way for a child to learn about space. Stuffy museums with "don't touch" signs all over the place are inhibiting, but there is an increasing amount of exhibits that encourage participation by viewers.

Taking children to museums is difficult during this time, since their attention span is short and the need to be on the move constantly and touch everything in sight is great. Modern art often has a sense of fun and adventure that young children instinctively respond to. Comments they make about the art are frequently surprisingly insightful. This period of time is one of tremendous growth and I firmly believe that children are absorbing everything they see. It's well worth the work to spend some time in art museums. Your child doesn't have to see the whole collection for the trip to have been worthwhile. If the child really looks at and focuses his or her attention on just a few pictures, the trip should be counted as a huge success. And remember that in addition to art museums there are also science, nature, toy, history, and other types of specialized museums that are of interest as well.

4. *Children's museums* are wonderful places to spend an afternoon. Some are specifically directed toward preschool children; other are for older children, but may have a lot that will be interesting to an infant or toddler. During Jason's early years, we regularly drove from New York to the "Please Touch" museum in Philadelphia, because that was the museum that was closest to us whose activities were designed for very young children. He also spent a great deal of time, particularly on cold or rainy days, playing in the vast halls of New York's Museum of Natural History. Although this is not specifically a children's museum, many of its exhibits fascinate children. Most people think that a year-old child is too young for a museum visit, but knowledgeable New York City mothers speak of the Gem Room at the Museum of Natural History, with its many levels and low display cases, as if it were an elite club designed just for them and their crawlers, climbers, and new walkers. All you and your baby need for museum visits are eyes and an open mind. I wouldn't recommend visiting museum exhibits that force you to say to your child "don't touch" every two minutes, but a good children's museum or a participatory exhibit does just the opposite. This child is shown moving a car along a track on a map of the United States at the Capitol Children's Museum in Washington, D.C.

This child is shown moving a car along a track on a map of the United States at the Capitol Children's Museum.

Your child will have favorite spots in a museum you visit regularly. As he or she grows and develops, your child will approach the exhibits with fresh eyes, new interests, and increased skills. When we took our son to visit the "Please Touch" museum in Philadelphia for the first time in at least fourteen months, on the trip down he wondered aloud whether certain things he remembered from our previous visit were still there, and his recollections were accurate down to small details. (See Appendix I for a list of children's museums or museums with special children's exhibits throughout the United States.)

5. Stop into *the local fire station*. If you are lucky, you may find some firefighters with the time and interest to show a wide-eyed toddler around. If no one seems helpful, try another station. We were ignored at a few and treated like royalty at others. In one, my son was allowed to sit on a big red firetruck and ring the fire bell, and was given a gift of a child-sized fire hat which he treasured for ages.

6. Use a visit to *the local police station* as an excuse to have your child finger-printed. Save the prints at home as a memento

Contact with animals is the best lesson in zoology.

and as a safety precaution should your child ever be lost.

7. No child is too young to visit a *zoo*. Most modern zoos now understand how important contact with animals can be, and provide for it in their exhibits.

One zoo we visited allows children to climb into a turtle shell and be a turtle, a far cry from the days when zoos showed animals imprisoned in too-small cages. See Appendix VI for a list of zoos in the United States.

8. *Pet shops* delight animal lovers and are often closer to home than zoos.

9. Visiting a *friendly craftsperson, carpenter, shoemaker, or painter* and observing him or her at work can provide a child with a life-long interest that can lead to a vocation. So many children who are hospitalized decide to become doctors or nurses. The contact and exposure to real, live workers when the child is so impressionable can have a profound effect on a child's life even though the actual visit is forgotten.

10. *Parades,* complete with costumes, marching, and music, have delighted children down through the ages.

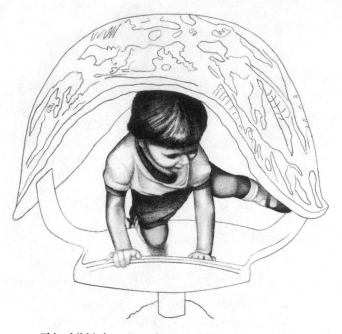

This child is learning what it feels like to be a turtle.

11. *High school band or chorus rehearsals* provide live music without added expense of concert tickets.

12. Visit *amusement parks with age-appropriate rides*. Children age eighteen months and over adore them; they provide wonderful opportunities for fantasy play.

Always stand and watch a ride, explaining to the child what is happening, before putting the child on it. Accompany the child on the first few rides and never let a frightened child continue to ride. Attendants should be there to stop the ride if requested to remove a frightened child. Frequent only parks that have rides specifically designed for this age group and steer clear of very fast or frightening rides. Recent additions to amusement parks involve active participation such as tunnels to crawl through and nets to climb; refer to "Funparks Directory" (Billboard Publications, Box 24970, Nashville, TN 37202, phone 615-748-8120), which costs $30.00 and is updated annually.

13. Go to *the circus*. Don't wait until the child is "old enough" to understand the show. Go every year, and with each subsequent visit the child will appreciate the experience on a different level.

Amusement parks provide opportunities for fantasy play.

For this year, you may want to plan to leave well before the end of the show, but the rich visual stimulation provided in only thirty or forty minutes is well worth the cost of a ticket. You can economize by bringing your own snack and flashlight to avoid having to buy them at the show.

14. *Picking pumpkins, strawberries, or apples at a farm* will give a child a feel for the land and farming as no picture book ever can.

15. Visit *an office* where typing on the typewriter, pushing the button on the copy machine, and stapling pages together (sloppily) are permitted.

16. *Regular attendance at a local playground* where your child can meet the same children with some regularity while exercising large muscles is an enjoyable exposure to socializing. Believe it or not, nursery school is just around the corner. Preparation for it helps ease the change from home to school.

ELEVEN

Toys, Playthings, and Playmates

Many people decry the alienation of youth, and wonder why all communication has broken down between children and their parents. Perhaps some of this problem starts during infancy when crying babies are given teddy bears with simulated heartbeats instead of physical closeness with their mothers, and are put in front of a television when it's company they crave. Most children spend far more time playing with battery-operated toys each day than with their own fathers. The most popular toys claim to encourage solitary play, but although playing alone is an important aspect of play, it needs to be supplemented by playing with other children and playing with an adult. Your involvement makes play time even more valuable to the child.

Even though children are now much more object-oriented than they were last year, and you are no longer the child's main source of entertainment, your child still needs your input and interest at play time. Each day, some of the child's play time should be devoted to playing with you. Not near you while you work, but really *with* you. Sit on the floor and observe your child. Instead of "showing" the child how to do new things, comment on what the child is doing. "I can see you are using the biggest blocks at the base of your building. That will make it strong." Really look at a drawing and describe it to help the child understand his or her new-found skills. "The red line crosses over the blue line," may seem obvious to you but is helpful information for a one- to two-year-old, and much more helpful than "teaching" your child how to draw can ever be.

Books and Storytelling

Set aside time every day to read books together. Among the current popular books we find "one-minute bedtime stories." You can't hope to instill a love of literature in a child who was raised on one-minute stories. You will need to read some stories over and over and over, until you both know them by heart, because children learn from repetition. The fact remains that it is at home, not in school, that a child will learn to love books. One of my friends, who is a writer and loves words, was very upset when her son was told by his high school teacher to read a classic comic instead of an assigned book. "How," she asked, "can a child learn to love words if all he reads is summaries?" Nevertheless, no matter what his teachers failed to teach him, this boy learned at his mother's knee to delight in the written word.

Now you will begin reading rhymes and stories to your child instead of just looking at pictures. But as Dr. Fitzhugh Dodson points out in *I wish I had a computer that makes waffles,* a real favorite of mine:

> . . . the environment of today's toddler is, of course, vastly different from those earlier days. In "Mother Goose" rhymes people only walk or ride horses. In today's environment we find cars and trucks, tractors and trains and airplanes and space capsules.*

As Doctor Dodson suggests, Mother Goose rhymes need to be looked at and thought about by conscientious parents before they are read. Don't just read them because they were read to you. In addition to simply being out of date, some are quite scary and full of violence.

> The King of Hearts
> Called for the tarts,
> And beat the knave full sore.

---

* Fitzhugh Dodson, *I wish I had a computer that makes waffles* (San Diego: Oak Tree Publishers, 1978), p. 10.

When I read rhymes or stories to children, I always eliminate these references to violence and antisocial behavior. A quick pencil slash and change of words assures that no one will be killed or beaten. For example:

> The maid was out in the garden,
> Hanging out the clothes,
> When down came a blackbird
> And snipped off her nose.

In our version of Mother Goose, when the blackbird came down to visit the maid who was hanging out her clothes, he "kissed her on the nose." In our Babar books, Babar's mother was hurt, not killed. Tiny Tim swallowed a bubble, he didn't drown. Kids have enough to worry about as it is. The possibility of a stranger coming along and shooting Mommy and the idea of a baby brother being drowned seem unnecessarily gruesome for a toddler, even one who has already been tempted to drown his or her own sibling.

Sex role stereotypes should have long since been put to rest. For example:

> What are little boys made of?
> What are little boys made of?
> Frogs and snails and puppy dogs' tails,
> That's what little boys are made of.
> That's what little boys are made of.
> What are little girls made of?
> What are little girls made of?
> Sugar and spice and everything nice,
> That's what little girls are made of.

Responsible publishers are publishing modern versions of good children's literature to replace these old standbys.

Pop-up books are more like toys than books, and battery-operated toys at that! They are fun to play with but are so clever themselves that there's not much left for the child to be clever about. Active children of this age love to be involved with everything and enjoy pulling the tabs and opening the doors, but this activity should not be confused with reading. Pulling tabs and turning levers is not literature. My son loved the poem "The Night Before Christmas" by Clement C. Moore, so when I came across a pop-up book of the poem I bought it for him. Although he usually loved to hear the poem read, he got so busy playing with the gimmicks in the pop-up book that he wouldn't let me read it to him. The plain sixty-nine-cent version of the book was far more valuable for him than the expensive pop-up version was. Never buy a pop-up book instead of a regular book.

In addition to enjoying books with your child, you also should make up stories and encourage your child to do the same. You can start by asking the child to make up a new ending for a familiar book. As soon as the child has made up a story, write it down and read it with as much respect as you would read Dr. Seuss. After all, people don't only read books—they write them too! The most obvious way to teach children to write is by having them make up stories now before they can write. You'd be surprised at how unusual this idea is in most schools.

The Best Toys

Some toys are terribly clever and some are not, just like children. The difference is that it seems as if the dull children are the ones who are always given the clever toys. Toys that walk, talk, wet,

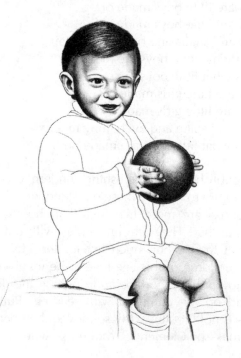

eat, shoot, and generally wear themselves out with battery-operated activity need no mental or physical input from a child. Children are learning every waking minute; the toys we give them often determine what it is they are learning.

What is an educational toy? Adults have an image of a boring toy that teaches a child all of the capitals of the states, the dates of all of the wars, and the names of all of the presidents of the United States, but a simple rubber ball is an example of the best kind of educational toy your child can own. With a rubber ball and an interested adult, a young child can learn about near and far, over and under, fast and slow, in and out, and high and low, in addition to something about the effects of gravity, density, and weight. Balls can be thrown, rolled, passed from person to person, held between the feet while lying on your back, and used in many ways that encourage active body movement.

Of course, you can have lots of fun with them too! A child can also play alone with a rubber ball, but will miss out on the descriptive words you provide for what is happening.

You should be encouraged, not discouraged, by the fact that your child tires of some toys so quickly. Good toys are learning tools that grow and change with the growing child. Boring toys are the ones that are so clever that they don't even need a child to control them; they work all by themselves. Whatever the cost, the criterion for judging a toy, after checking it out for safety, should be whether it, or the child, does all the playing. The more "clever" the toy is, the lazier and duller your child will become. You will see a wide array of battery-operated and remote-control cars in the toy stores, but watching children push their own cars around should convince a parent that battery control is really toy company

control versus child control. Child control provides exercise, problem solving, and coordination, while battery-operated cars are still working after a child has gone to sleep.

Toys that invite participation and involvement are ultimately the most fun. If the battery is the only thing at work, your child is losing out. We made a blanket rule in our house regarding toys: No battery toys of any kind. When friends who didn't know the rule gave Jason battery toys, they were either returned or played with minus the battery.

During this year, your child will probably need more toys than at any other time. If your funds are limited, don't be discouraged; help your child to discover that an imagination can work miracles. Keep in mind that an excursion on the subway can become a trip to the moon. You can also save money by packing a few old toys

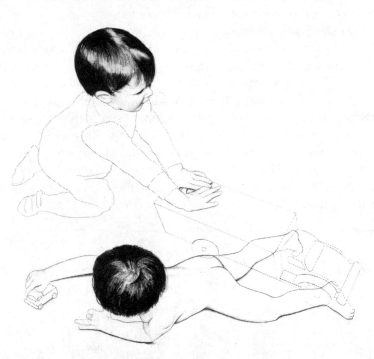

Toys the child can control and operate him- or herself provide exercise, problem solving, and coordination benefits, while battery-operated cars provide none of these and are still working after the child has gone to sleep.

up and trading with another child. When you trade back a month later, the "old" toys seem new again, and the maturing child can use them in new ways. Check out local thrift shops and church and school bazaars. We bought a whole set of hardcover books for 25 cents each from a local ten-year-old boy who had spread his old toys out on the sidewalk in hopes of raising money to buy new toys. The tighter your budget, the more expensive and loosely "labeled" your toy purchases should be. As soon as you buy a cheap painted firetruck, you will find that you need to buy cheap painted police car, tow truck, ambulance, farm truck, etc., etc., whereas a solid color, sturdy wooden vehicle can change roles and be all of the above and more.

Each year, new timely toys come on the market and then disappear only to be replaced by new ones after a season or so.

Classic toys are loved generation after generation. They grow and change with the child, and their visual, conceptual, tactile, or emotional qualities bring children back to play with them again and again. Traditional favorites, such as blocks, books, drums, dollhouses, child-propelled vehicles, crayons and paper dolls that don't even walk or talk, much less wet, rubber balls, hoops, and red wagons, give children freedom to fantasize and create. Except for the crayons and paper, they all last practically forever and transcend the time in which the child lives. Children devote most of their play time to these basic toys, become most attached to them, and remember them the longest. Some are even saved for future generations. Use most of your toy budget for these kinds of basic toys and buy the highest quality available.

Sometimes the best toys aren't toys at all, but things you use at home. Everything is so new to a child this age. Encountering an ear of corn for the first time will provide more excitement than an adult can imagine. "Don't play with food" or "No, that's for dinner" is not the kind of response that will help your toddler develop and maintain his or her natural curiosity.

Children are beginning to pretend or fantasize the first time they hug or "feed" a doll or hide to play "peek-a-boo." Substituting a book for a truck is something most children understand by their first birthday. The more open-ended the toys, the better. The toys that are available to them and the feedback they receive from you help to encourage or stifle this creative dimension. Offer a bucket for a hat or a pretend banana to eat. Once, while on a short

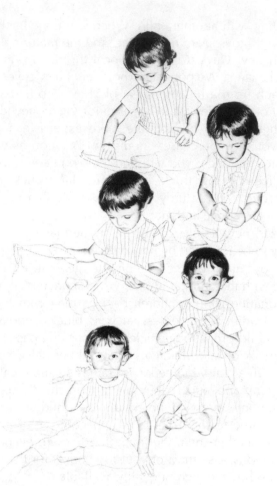

Sometimes the best toys aren't toys at all.

trip where my son saw many boats, we stopped at a restaurant. Although I had brought along our usual bag of toys and books for him to entertain himself with during the meal, I had failed to include in it any toy boats. As he clamored for a boat, threatening to ruin our dinner, I reached into the roll tray and scooped out the dough from half of a long, thin roll, saying, "Here's a boat." He laughed, played with the boat for quite a while, then said, "Eat the boat," and did so. Of utmost importance always is your example. When you value creative play and engage in it yourself, your child will too.

Using a pot as a hat is an example of early fantasy play.

Your child learns not only through playing with you but by observing you at "play." If you never read a book or draw a picture, neither will your child. If you drive a car, that's what your child wants to do; sew and soon your child will be imitating you. You may find that a toy telephone is no substitute for the real thing. The same is true of cameras, typewriters, calculators, etc. Children want and need to learn about the real world and do so more effectively with adult "toys" than they do with imitations. The child will be more interested in the objects you use than in purchased toys. If you type a lot, it's the typewriter your child will be fascinated with. The red plastic toy version won't do, you will find. Real typewriters, telephones, vacuums, hammers, steering wheels, etc., are what the child needs now—not a toy designer's poor idea of an imitation.

> . . . real tools allow for real work; children's tools often inhibit it.*

---

* Susan D. Shilcock and Peter A. Bergson, *Open Connections: The Other Basics* (Bryn Mawr, Pa.: Open Connections, 1980), p. 80.

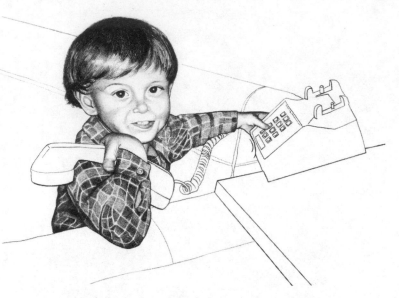

Toy imitations cannot substitute for the real thing.

Try a toy version only if offering a real tool is impossible. Don't expect a fourteen-month-old to do the same thing with a toy typewriter as the six-year-old for whom it was intended will, and put it out of sight at the first sign of frustration.

> In fact, it is important not to forget, when buying a toy, that a child may get a great deal of pleasure from a toy which she cannot yet use "properly," either by playing with it at a lower level or by persuading adults to contribute the difficult bits. For instance, a baby who is only beginning to shunt around on her bottom and is still at a push-and-swipe stage may well enjoy a wheeled musical toy designed for a toddler, even though she can only push it to and fro from a sitting position. Or a child who has no idea of building up graded pile-ups will be delighted to have an adult do the piling up while she does the knocking down.*

* John and Elizabeth Newson, *Toys & Playthings* (New York: Pantheon Books, 1979), p. 52.

Given the opportunity, an 18-month-old can even take photographs.

Of course you will have to examine everything that interests him or her. You can remove real safety hazards by using quick thinking yourself, to locate a more interesting item when possible.

When your child sees you using a grown-up "toy," he or she will want to try it and probably won't be satisfied with toy imitations. I used a very high-quality camera to take the photographs for the illustrations in this book. I almost always had it with me and my son became fascinated with it. In keeping with my philosophy, if reluctantly, I let him take pictures with it when he asked to. At first, I gave it to him without any film in it. I showed him how to use it and he very proudly "took pictures" all over the place. Occasionally, he'd ask to use it when it was already loaded with film and he actually took some very fine photographs! He also took a few pictures of feet and ceilings, but so did I! When I found a 35 mm camera that looked very much like mine on sale for about the cost of an expensive toy, I bought it for him.

Imaginative play begins very early and it is important to encourage it at every turn. Allowing the child to experiment with a toy rather than always "teaching" how to play with it is one way to encourage it. Puzzles, shape sorters, and other toys that have a "correct answer" and only one right way to be played with should play a very small part in your child's life at this stage. Don't eliminate them completely, since they do teach some skills, but limit your child's exposure to these kinds of activities if confidence and creativity are your goals for your child. Most puzzles have only one correct answer. They can be frustrating for the child working to master them, and boring for the child who has. There are some more acceptable ways to present puzzles. A parquet puzzle, which is correct no matter how it is put together, is always different and more likely to stimulate creative thinking than the more usual picture puzzle. However, this quality is destroyed by toy companies that insist on packaging it with patterns to follow! Throw out the patterns as soon as you unwrap the package.

Making Puzzles

You can create variations of parquetry puzzles by cutting out different color cardboard or wood square or diamond shapes. The artist Paul Cezanne gave his paintings to his young son to cut up and use as picture puzzles. Unless you are one of the world's master painters, consider using prints of famous paintings in this manner. It is a wonderful way for children to be exposed to art. If improved self-image is of more concern to you than exposure to art, mount a large photograph of your child on cardboard, cut it out in simple puzzle shapes, and let the child put him- or herself back together again. "COMPOZ-A-PUZZLE" and "Whitehall" make blank white cardboard puzzles in assorted sizes. Let your child draw or paint on one to create a meaningful puzzle experience. All of the above are alternatives to the simplistic commercial art available on most children's puzzles.

Toys should be chosen to stimulate flexible thinking and because they are appropriate to the level of development and interest of the child. Toddlers need a wagon or other push toy when they begin to show interest in walking. This toy gave the new walker a sense of independence and freedom by allowing him to pull himself up on it and walk unaided by an adult before he could actually walk alone. It also was used later as a ride-on toy, adding value to the investment. Pull toys that make some sound reassure the toddler that the toy is still behind him or her. At eighteen months the child is physically developed enough to use a ride-on motorcycle. Because so many are too tall or too close to the ground, and several

Toddlers need push toys when they begin to show interest in walking.

can cause serious accidents, it seems appropriate to mention here that the Marx motorcycle is the safest and most comfortable that I've found for this age group. The leg muscles and coordination it helps develop are essential for both boys and girls.

Sometimes children seem to want to play with only one kind of toy, such as cars or dolls. It is tempting then to offer the kinds of toys they clearly want. Responding to a child's interest by providing the right toy at the right time is a way of helping your child develop. However, that type of toy should be made available along with others to help your child's interest expand and grow. Avoid buying only "boy" toys for boys and "girl" toys for girls. Girls who adore dolls will still learn through playing with cars, and boys who seem obsessed with vehicles still need some cuddly dolls. When my son ignored his stuffed animals and dolls and played exclusively with his cars, I made him a stuffed car to cuddle.

Responding to your child's interest by providing the right toy at the right time is a way of helping your child develop.

Block Play

Creating and cuddling are strong instincts in children. Blocks help foster and encourage the creating instinct, and so soft cloth blocks, which can also be hugged and chewed on, are a good introduction to block play. When your child is between one year and eighteen months, it is a good idea to invest in hardwood unit blocks. You can expect this toy to be among the most important your child will play with for many years to come. It is one toy which presents a child with endless possibilities and provides excellent opportunities for stimulating the imagination. Block play encourages language development, teaches science concepts, stimulates creativity and imaginative thinking, increases awareness of architecture and the world in which we live, encourages learning about space and form, provides impetus for dramatic play, helps foster self-awareness, and provides opportunities for social development.

For variety and to boost interest in block play, it is nice to also have other different kinds of blocks. "Bristle" and snap blocks, such as Legos or "Imagine It Construction Sets," have the added

Children don't need blocks to build.

advantage of staying where they are placed. At Young at Art we use soft wooden blocks and polymer glue as a sculpture project. Alphabet blocks promote familiarity with letters, and multicolored blocks add the excitement of color to block play. All of the above are worth buying, if your budget permits, as additional toys, but are not a substitute for the basic unit block set. Buy the highest quality hardwood set you can afford to provide maximum durability and stability. Plan to add new pieces to it over the years. After making these financial sacrifices for your child's education, don't be surprised to find your child happily piling up the old soda cans you thought were safely thrown away and ignoring the blocks!

The Art of Block Building by Harriet Johnson (Bank Street College of Education, New York) tells of the seven stages of block play that children pass through, no matter at what age they are introduced to blocks.

Read the following books to your child to stimulate interest and reinforce learning through block play:

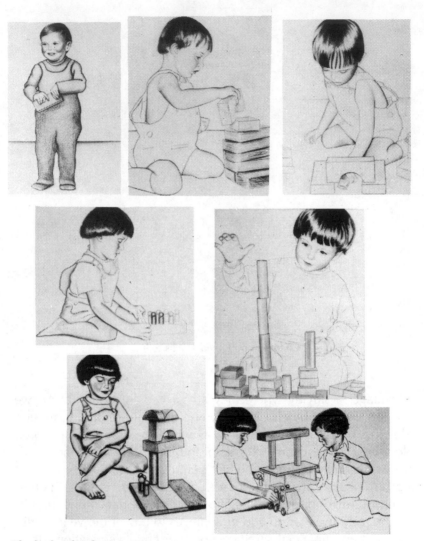

Block-play development

Stage 1: Blocks are carried around rather than built with.
Stage 2: Child begins making horizontal or vertical rows.
Stage 3: Child connects two blocks with a third.
Stage 4: Child encloses space with blocks.
Stage 5: Buildings are decorative and symmetrical.
Stage 6: Structures are named and dramatic play begins.
Stage 7: Dramatic play increases and buildings imitate familiar architecture.

Harriet Johnson, "Stages in Blockbuilding." National Association for the Education of Young Children, *The Block Book,* Washington, D.C.: Elisabeth S. Hirsch, ed. 1974.

Changes, Changes, Pat Hutchins
I Can Build a House! Shigeo Watanabe
My Hands Can, Jean Holzenthaler

See Appendix II for my reviews of these books.

Bathtub Play

Last year the baby learned through direct contact with water. This year your child will benefit from experimenting with it with plastic funnels, pitchers, slotted spoons, assorted-sized containers, sprinkling cans, squirting toys, and soap crayons. The most versatile bath toy we owned was a toy boat by Fisher-Price. It had in it a sailor, a duck, and three nesting containers with varying sized holes in the bottom, and was complete with a barge to tow. Of course, nothing beats having a friend (or relative) for bath play! An investment in a vinyl tablecloth from the five-and-ten goes a long way toward preventing simple spills from becoming bothersome or dangerous.

New soap-base crayons bring scribbling into the bathtub in a way that is easy to clean up after. Since, as we have seen, the more

Nothing beats having a friend for bath play.

Changing materials and settings can be all it takes to revive a waning interest in scribbling.

free scribbling the child does, the easier learning to read and write will be, you want to encourage an interest in it. Changing materials and settings can be all it takes to revive a waning interest in scribbling. Drawing on the walls is approved by all when the wall is the tile of the bathroom and the crayons are soap-base. Soap-base crayons are also great for makeup and body decorating. Soap-base finger paint is also available, or you can make your own by adding a little water to some Ivory Snow and mixing until you achieve a pasty consistency. Let your child sprinkle in a few drops of food coloring, mix, and paint. Soap-base finger paints will sting if they get in the eyes, so caution is advised.

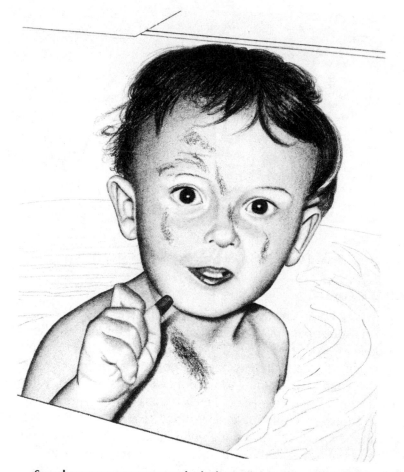

Soap-base crayons encourage body decoration and are easy to rinse away.

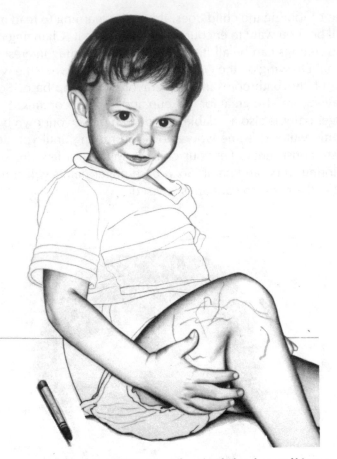

How you respond to your child's art exploration helps shape self-image.

Nature's Toys

As always, children know best. The most valuable toys are based on materials found in the environment. It is helpful to know how children learn from these toys and nice if you can afford to buy them, but if you can't that is not a problem. If you don't have blocks, your child will pile up old boxes or cans and learn the same concepts. Long before the creation of blocks, children were piling up stones and fulfilling their instincts to create. Can't afford clay? Sand, earth, and bread dough will have the same effect and even the poorest of children will have some very rich experiences making mud pies! If you don't buy your child crayons, a stick in the dirt or finger in the dust provides enough scribbling experience to form a sound foundation for later writing and drawing. Good toys can be good teachers, but even with no toys at all, children will play in the same ways. Children know what they need to do, and what kinds of toys they need to play with. Observing them at play and meeting their needs at the right time is the best way to make their play provide maximum benefits.

Play Dates

Regularly scheduled, supervised play dates with one or two other children of the same age provide important readiness for school. When supervising play dates, there are many lessons conscientious parents can learn from the way preschools deal with young children. Three or four interesting activities are set up for the children before they come in. Quiet activities are alternated with physically active exercises. Duplicates of most toys are provided to avoid arguments. Children are never left by themselves—an adult is always present, though not interfering with the children's freedom. Attend a toddler gym, art, or music class which is under the supervision of a trained instructor with your child regularly.

Initial play date experiences should not be lessons in sharing. Your child was not born with the instinct to share his or her toys—it's up to you to teach the concept. Before being able to share, the child must feel very secure about ownership of his or her things. You will have to set a good example; your child will notice it when you offer to give away a bite of your apple or lend your lawn mower to a neighbor. Don't expect your child to be a better human being than you are! The visiting child should always bring one or two toys of his or her own, understanding in advance that they are brought for the host child to play with. Favorite toys that the child can't easily part with should be put away with the coat upon arrival. At the same time, the child who is being visited should be told that if there are any special toys that he or she does not want to share, they can be put away for safekeeping. After all, how would you feel if a visiting adult made a beeline for your bedroom and started raiding your drawers and closets to use your favorite possessions?

The play date should be held in the presence of the two adult caretakers. A carton, laundry basket, or low table should hold several *identical* pairs of toys. When there are two of each toy, sharing is not an issue, and the children can relax and enjoy each other's company. These pairs of toys provide an important lesson in friendship for your child. Soon after getting to know each other, without the risk of losing their precious possessions, they will be ready to start to share. For children this age, consider obtaining:

- 2 xylophones
- 2 small cars (same model and color)
- 2 identical dolls
- 2 crayons and 2 sheets of large paper
- 1 container play dough
- 2 identical stuffed animals

Both caretakers should stay for the whole play date, which can last for ninety minutes (with breaks in between to cuddle on Mom's lap and have a snack). Since the children will want to be in the same room with the caretakers, you may want to close the door to the child's bedroom and set up the sharing box of toys with you both in the living room. A nice way to end the play date is with the host mother holding both children on her lap to look at a picture book together. Often the visitor does not want to leave. A snack can be taken home to soothe the leave-taking and make the trip home more pleasant. Remember what toys were used and what activities you presented. Be consistent and have some of the same available for the next visit so the visitor will feel "at home." Repetition and routine help create a feeling of security.

After children have gotten to know each other and had several play dates that involved no sharing, you can make more toys available. The visitor should still bring one or two toys, understanding in advance that they are for the host child to play with during the visit and will be returned. Both children should be told in advance to put away special toys that they don't wish to share. Keep a timer handy and when both children reach for the same toy and prepare to do battle, step in and say firmly: "Nicky can play with the car now and when the bell rings he has to give it to Elizabeth." Set the timer for two minutes, and when the bell rings be sure that the second child gets the toy. If necessary, set the timer again so that the toy is passed back to the first child. By then, though, he or she will probably have lost interest and moved on to something else.

For most children, waiting for "your turn" always involves sacrifice. I first taught my child the concept in a swimming pool where he was enthusiastically jumping in. A friend and I "took turns" catching him and as he clambered up the stairs we said: "Mommy's turn," or "Pat's turn." Either way, Jason came out ahead. You might try a kissing game where baby is kissed first by Mommy, then by Daddy. Mommy's turn is next and soon the baby catches on and learns the concept of sharing or taking turns with pleasant associations.

Some play date activities, alternated with free play, that children this age have enjoyed in my home include:

- Painting at a two-sided easel.
- Making collages out of prepasted stars or circles.
- Helping prepare mix, from premeasured containers, for baking cookies.
- Printing with alphabet stamps.
- Experimenting with play dough or clay.
- Pasting empty boxes together to form a sculpture.
- Sandbox play.
- Taking a bath together with bubbles, containers, and soap-base finger paint. (You must be present throughout.)
- A make-up session. You will need an area that can get dirty, face paint or make-up crayons,* cold cream for removal, and a large or double-sided mirror.
- Block play.

Midway through the play date, offer the children a snack. Eating together at the table (not nibbling while they play) counts as one of the planned activities.

When things get too lively or seem out of control, instead of scolding, try holding both children on your lap and reading to them or looking at a picture book together. It is much more effective than scolding.

For several weeks, both caretakers should stay for the entire play date. One reason that some children feel threatened by play dates is that they know that their parents use the time to be away from them. After the children are well acquainted with each other, the environment, and the other child's mother, one mother can, after staying about half an hour, leave for a very brief time. When the child is settled in and having fun, mention that you are going

---

* Fantasy Face Paint Kit #404, Toys to Grow On, 2695 East Dominquez Street, P.O. Box 17, Long Beach, CA 90801.
Theatrical Make-up Crayons #9006, Polymark, Waltham, MA 02254.

"to the store to buy a snack" and will be back in ten or fifteen minutes. When you return to share a treat with the children, you are establishing trust. You kept your promise and returned after a very short time, and with an enjoyable snack. Next time you leave, your child will not feel threatened. If he or she does get upset, don't go.

Clearly explain and frequently repeat the meaning of the words *borrow* and *lend*. If your child is playing with another child's toy and the other child wants to use something belonging to your child, make it clear that your child must allow it. We were at the beach and a little boy spent half an hour playing with my son's boat while my son played in the water. Then Jason asked if he could use the other child's pail and shovel. The child said "no." His mother shrugged and said, "Sharing is so hard for a two-year-old." I would have handled it quite differently. "Since you were playing with his boat, you must let him use your pail and shovel." Sharing then is not a sacrifice, but more like bartering. Adults use money in exchange for goods and services, and children learn this concept through sharing before they can understand true charity. As long as you are fair and consistent, your child will be able to accept the rules.

A child who hits or performs other antisocial acts should be quickly removed from the room and gently reminded that we "never hit (bite, snatch toys from . . .) people." When setting the rules of behavior for your child, I think you need to be very firm about how other human beings are to be treated, and very flexible about what can be explored. Spilling and taking things apart can be taken with good humor, but hitting, biting, or grabbing things from another child should be strictly forbidden. Visiting children need to know that you will defend their right to have a toy or protect them from being hurt just as much as you do for your own child.

If the visiting parent does not agree to abide by the same rules, do not invite them back and let your child know that you don't approve of the way a certain situation was handled.

If you don't hit your child, your child won't hit other children. I've lost count of the number of times I have seen parents smack a child—to convince the child not to hit another child! Once you resort to hitting for simple discipline, what do you do when your child does something really bad (which even good children occa-

sionally do)? Hit harder? Longer? With an object? All of these examples of extreme cruelty teach your child to be cruel; they
provide no understanding of unacceptable behavior.

Jason had weekly play dates with his friend Jeffrey from the
time they were about eight months old. I got to be very good
friends with Jeffrey's mother Anna, and these weekly social encounters were most enjoyable for all of us. When Jeffrey was about
fourteen months old, he started hitting and pushing Jason quite
often. When it started to look as if a pattern was emerging, Anna
and I reluctantly suspended the play dates. We waited two months
and scheduled a thirty-minute trial date. The children were thrilled
to see each other again. We told them that the date would end the
very instant that either child hit. We kept the date short so that the
children wouldn't get tired. During the hiatus, Jeffrey had become
very verbal. He could now express with words what he used to say
with a shove. With only one exception, which we handled as we
had promised, the problem was solved and Jason and Jeffrey related to each other as equals thereafter. They both proved to be
very gentle, sweet-natured children with several common interests,
and played beautifully together.

When they were three, Anna and I began taking turns, with
one of us caring for both boys on alternate weeks. It was the one
enduring relationship from this period, I think, because Jeffrey's
mother made it immediately clear to Jason that she was as concerned for him as she was for her own child. Jeffrey loved and
trusted me as well. Both boys learned from the experience that
hitting is not acceptable social behavior, and that it can be counterproductive.

TWELVE

Art Experiences

Scribbling

The need for a child to scribble is very strong and universal. When the impulse strikes, your toddler must draw on whatever is at hand. Providing appropriate drawing utensils, large paper, and a place to work is the best way to help your child in this endeavor. But even if you banish art materials from your home and forbid scribbling, your child will almost certainly find a way to do his or her scribbling work. Observe any child; spilled milk becomes paint and a straw becomes a paint brush, foggy windows are a wonderful

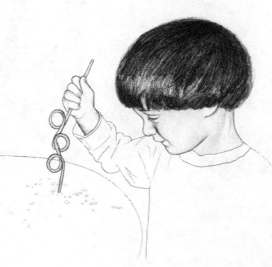

background for drawing with the finger as is dust on a tabletop, sand at the beach, and leftovers on a dinner plate. All provide stimulation for the instinct to scribble. So can the walls, your freshly washed mirror, your important papers, or whatever else is handy. Keeping crayons and paper handy and in sight but out of the child's reach can prevent mishap. Your child can ask for them, a signal to you to be on the alert if your priority is to protect your walls. Your interest and encouragement play a large part in the child's progress in self-taught art, but even without it, all children do find a way to draw.

Every art teacher will tell you that parental response to a child's work may be one of the important elements in the child's feeling for his or her work. Therefore, please never say things like, "What is it?" and "That looks like a car" (when the child had no intention of drawing a car). Children do not attempt to render real objects until they are about four. Pushing them can be as inappropriate as

Children scribble even when they have no access to art materials.

suggesting that a one-month-old walk. Better say, "I see you've done something round (or red or exciting)." By asking "what" a child's picture is, you suggest that it isn't good enough for you to tell what it is by looking at it. Even the very first scribbles should be recognized as a child's first use of a tool of communication and, therefore, noteworthy. The end product remains significantly of less interest to a child than does the process of working. Contact with adults who criticize or undervalue the work changes this. Paying vague compliments like "very pretty" becomes hollow after a while. After all, what makes one picture pretty and one ugly? It is most helpful for the child if your comments describe what the child is doing and what the picture looks like. Be a mirror for the child's efforts; reflect verbally what the child is doing. The most helpful comment provides vocabularly, describes what the child is doing, and includes praise. Positive feedback from parents is an essential ingredient for children who will keep up their artistic endeavors and continue to learn through art.

It is inevitable that your child will draw on a place that you will find "inappropriate" one day. Since you can be sure of that in advance, plan ahead on how you will handle it because how you handle it is crucial. It is important to realize that your response to this instinct will determine your child's attitude toward art, much more than it will shape his or her attitude about cleanliness and tidy housekeeping.

One friend, whose child was in my art class, called to say that her son had drawn on the walls and she had punished him by scolding him and taking his crayons away from him. I could only answer that it was she who had been naughty, not the child. She had forgotten to put his crayons on their high shelf and had left the child playing unsupervised in his room while she cooked dinner in the kitchen. The one-and-a-half-year-old boy was really "doing what comes naturally." Punishment is more likely to communicate the parent's own lack of respect for child-made art than the desired respect for property. Be honest with yourself. If Picasso, Renoir, or Michelangelo walked into your living room and drew a mural on the walls, would you be upset about your ruined paint job? If you painted your child's room before birth, why not count on redoing it when the child is three, and enjoying the child's decorations up until then? The fact is that when Picasso was a scribbling toddler, his father, a professional artist, always encouraged him to draw and paint. When he did a bird, his father declared the child's bird better than his own and gave him the job of painting all of the birds in his own art. Picasso probably started out with the same potential your child has. What his father gave him was an overwhelming confidence in his art.

I never admonished my son on the few rare occasions when he drew on walls, and he seems to have outgrown that stage much faster than did all of his friends, who had quickly learned from their angry parents that it was an ideal form of rebellion. An easel stood in Jason's room with paper clipped to it and materials nearby. When the urge to draw or paint struck, it could be instantly, and constructively, satisfied.

> One might wonder why a sensible mature mother would permit what many would consider a mess. And I must confess that I not only permitted it, I held a basket of crayons while it was being created. We encouraged the creation of "mess" and a lot of others, because we are raising our sons to be artists, fathers, astronomers and all of the myriad roles in life that are enhanced by creative thinking and expression.*

My own child, bored on a four-hour car trip, picked his crayon up off his picture and decorated the ceiling of our car. I was pleased to see it, but my husband wasn't. Paper, as always, was close at hand. Daddy explained that he would have to wash the car, while if the drawing had been done on paper, we could have saved and enjoyed it forever.

I don't want to sound as if you should encourage your child to draw on walls, but merely that, since you can count on its happening no matter what, it is best to be prepared to handle it in a way that doesn't turn children away from art. If you use the new crayons that are intended for wipe-off books but are great for walls as well, these episodes will be easily remedied.†

Parents of young children should enjoy living with the art

* Loretta S. Marshall and U. E. Marshall, *CTW Newsletter,* vol. 2, no. 4, p. 4.

† Dixon-Ticonderoga Co., 756 Beachland Boulevard, P.O. Box 3504, Vero Beach, FL 32964.

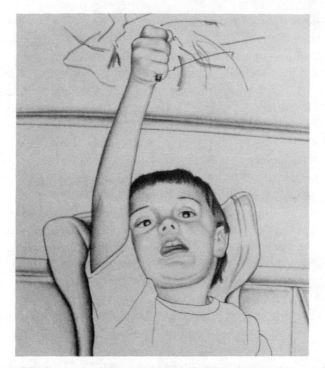

It is inevitable that your child will draw on inappropriate surfaces, so plan an appropriate reaction in advance.

expressions their youngsters make. If you introduce acceptable art materials early enough, your child will associate paper and crayons with drawing, and stay away from your walls as long as these materials are available. Greg's mom was becoming concerned with his penchant for drawing on the walls. Here, his paper is much too small and invited moving out onto a large surface. I advised Greg's mother to get 16" x 20" paper instead of the small pad he'd been using and to stop saying "no" each time he drew on unacceptable surfaces. So, for the next few days, whenever Greg took a crayon to her walls she handed him paper and even though she was crying on the inside, said, in her most cheerful voice, something like: "Oh, good, I see you want to draw. Here's your pad." Greg quickly learned to associate paper with crayons and broke his association with rebelling through drawing on the walls. This gave both Greg and his parents a more positive attitude toward Greg's art; so much so, in fact, that when his parents commissioned a professional artist to do Greg's portrait, they asked the artist to use one of the child's scribbles as a background. Soon after his parents changed their attitude, Greg stopped trying to get their attention by drawing on the walls.

It is important to keep in mind that whether you act as I suggest, pleased to see your child's art work anywhere, including your walls, or if you discipline your child for drawing on the walls—it makes no difference in one significant way. In either case your child will not still be drawing on the walls when he or she is four. The difference will occur only in the way the child perceives him- or herself and his or her art. The children whose parents understand their offspring's overwhelming need to draw and encourage freedom in the pursuit of art activity will have far more confidence in their own work and will be much more likely to solve new problems on their own.

Wise parents recognize the importance of scribbling and material manipulation and their significance for later learning. They provide materials and space to work in, thereby diminishing the child's need to draw on walls and furniture, but accept the fact that without constant vigilance some destruction is inevitable.

Another problem that parents often face with children this age is what they view as destructiveness. Important papers left out momentarily may be crumpled or torn. In reality, children need to crumple and tear paper in order to learn about paper's qualities

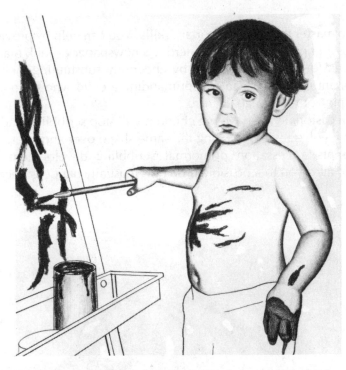

Providing adequate materials and a suitable place to work will prevent your child from drawing on the walls.

and to master these two important skills. You can help by providing disposable papers, such as yesterday's newspaper or junk mail, to be used for this purpose, and by cheerfully substituting them for important papers instead of reprimanding a child who is about to crumple your marriage license.

Occasionally, very young children will stop scribbling and become involved with repeating the same shape over and over. This represents a cessation of normal scribbling development and should alert you to a possible problem. It usually happens because

there has been too much direction of the child's art. An adult who "entertains" the child by drawing pictures, one who prematurely "teaches" the child how to form letters, an older sibling who mocks scribbles, all contribute to tearing down the child's self-confidence. Occasionally a child will accidently draw some lines which resemble something realistic. If an adult singles this picture out for praise, while ignoring other work, the child quickly picks up an idea of what it is that the adult prefers, and may try to repeat it in order to win approval. At this point all development stops. The child needs to go back to being a child. He or she will learn much more effectively by discovering these simple shapes for him- or herself in two or three years than as a result of adult imposition now. The lines and shapes the child makes now actually are put together to form letters later. He or she must familiarize him- or herself with the shapes before the letters themselves can be understood. Early childhood supervision that emphasizes pictures and letters at the expense of scribbling can cause more reading problems than it cures.

Beginning at age one, children should be given an opportunity to scribble every day. Some days they won't be interested, and that's fine. Other days it will seem as if they are drawing all day. One way to spark interest is to offer new drawing utensils. Crayons (unwrapped) are the obvious. These can be followed by water-soluble markers (permanent ones really are permanent and shouldn't be mouthed either). Other drawing materials may include "Playpen" markers, felt-tip pens, pencils, colored pencils, erasers, chalk, pointed sticks, or ballpoint pens, which may be used on a multitude of surfaces, including paper, walls, mirrors, windows, floors, bodies, bags, bathtubs, and boxes. Be on the lookout for other new materials in art and stationery-supply stores. An occasional silver marker can stimulate a veritable frenzy of art activity.

Computers are now being programmed to scribble, create graphics, and mix colors for children. Encouraging your child to be a wizard with computers is fine, but don't sacrifice art development to do so. A computer cannot substitute for the learning process that goes on during drawing and painting activities, or provide the magic of mixing two colors to create a third. No machine can give your child an experience more valuable than he or she has during free, open-ended scribbling.

Art games, machines, and computers can never provide art experiences.

Painting with a Brush

The child who is beginning to show an expertise in using such tools as a spoon or shovel, and who already has had exposure to other art materials such as crayons and finger paint, will now be ready to begin painting with a brush. If you've been doing some of the activities that I recommend, such as scribbling and food and finger painting, your child will be ready to paint with a brush at the age of eighteen months. In our home, the event was met with all of the excitement we could muster and we videotaped it clapping and cheering. Jason surely knew that we found his efforts of value.

You don't need to buy an easel, but if you do, make sure that the paint you use is not too watery. If it is, keep the paper on a flat

The two-sided easel permits socializing and communication while discouraging copying.

surface. I find Childcraft's Primart Tempera a good quality for easel painting. I favor the double-sided easel—painting can be a lovely social activity. The single, wall-hung easel saves floor space but necessitates "waiting your turn." Papers hung side by side on a wall or placed on a tabletop subliminally invite comparison and copying. The two-sided easel permits socializing and communication while discouraging copying.

If you decide to invest in an easel, get the sturdiest, best quality model you can afford. One that has adjustable height that changes with the rapidly growing child is essential. If you can't spend the money, remember that cork board works well, as does a cardboard box cut in half on the diagonal to sit on a tabletop like a pyramid-shaped table easel. Be sure to clip or tape the paper to the easel or tabletop. You will also need 11" x 14", 16" x 20", or 18" x 24" paper. I would never offer anything smaller than this to a child of this age. Invest in fairly decent quality paper. Cheap newsprint rips so easily that I recommend it only if your budget is so tight that the alternative would be not buying paper. Painting on printed news-

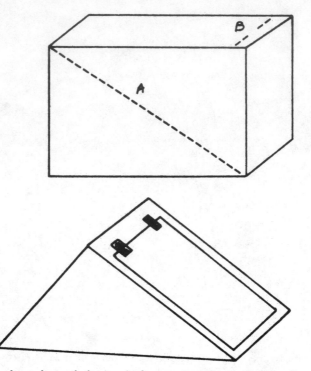

Two easels can be made from a single carton cut diagonally along line A. Cut two slits in the long side at B to use in fastening paper with spring-type clothespins.
(From *Creative Art for Learning* by Merle B. Karnes, page 11. Copyright 1979 by The Council for Exceptional Children. Reprinted with permission.)

paper presents the problem of the child's work getting confused with the printed page. This causes too much confusion to be worthwhile.

Hang a large towel on a hook right on the easel, and keep a bucket full of soapy water within reach to facilitate hand washing. A trip across the house to wash one's painty hands can create quite a mess.

Start with a ¾-inch bristle brush and a quart jar of nontoxic tempera paint. Whatever you do, don't put out the whole quart jar at once. For this first painting experience, pour only an inch or so into a separate container. This will prevent the frustration of dipping the brush all the way into a full paint container and having the paint drip all over the hand. You can add more paint when necessary. After much searching, I discovered that the large size plastic Vaseline jar fits perfectly in the popular Childcraft easel that I purchased. It closes tightly and its mouth is wide enough for a

Hang a large towel on a hook right on the easel and keep a bucket full of soapy water within reach to facilitate hand washing.

beginning painter to fit a brush inside. Childcraft also makes spill-proof jars that experienced nursery school teachers always buy. For a flat surface such as the floor or table, coasters, ashtrays, pet food dishes, and jar tops are ideal paint containers. Paper cups and juice cans tip over too easily.

One color of paint is all the child needs. Use the very same color in several subsequent paint experiences before switching to another. A logical sequence for presenting new colors and materials can be found in my book *Young at Art, The First Anti-Coloring Book for Preschoolers.* In fact, you will find that a toddler will be very satisfied with only one color for quite some time to come. Unless it's very cold in your home, I strongly recommend painting in the nude (or in a disposable diaper) right before bath time. The artist Jackson Pollock has been credited with the discovery of the significance of really "getting into" a painting—toddlers have always known it!

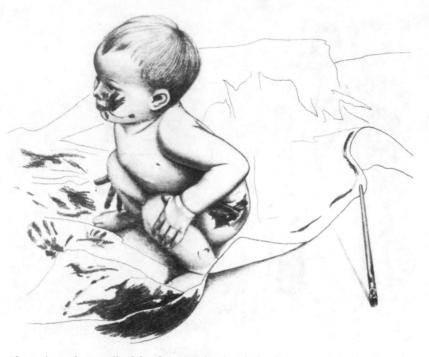

The artist Jackson Pollock has been credited with the discovery of the significance of really "getting into" a painting. Toddlers have always known it!

Your proud painter will almost certainly want a hug as soon as the work is finished, so dress accordingly yourself as well. Place oil cloth or vinyl over your floor and clip five or six papers on the easel at once. Tell your child that you are making all these preparations for a very important event, and generate a feeling of excitement because he or she is going to *paint!* Place the brush in the jar of paint and make two or three marks on the top paper with a brush. As a child shows interest in the brush, remove your paper from the easel. It is an imposition to draw or paint on your child's work.

Your child can then do a painting, with your encouragement. Remember that each stroke is important. Your child is doing a painting, not a picture of a house, dog, car, or dragon. Never point out accidental similarities to realistic objects. Doing so interferes with a natural development through experimentation. When the painting is finished, remove the top sheet so that the child can do another new painting without delay. One good habit I got into

One of the first painting experiences inevitably becomes an exercise in body painting.

while teaching art was always to write the child's name and age on the back of the paper in pencil before painting commenced. This gives you a record for posterity. Children grow up so fast; like photographs, artwork is a wonderful way to record their growth. Your child's first painting should be viewed as just as important a step in development as the first time he or she walked. The main difference is that you, not the child, will choose the time and place. Painting time is over when your child loses interest. If you are well organized, the transition from painting to water play in the bath will be a happy one. If you try painting too early and your child does not seem interested, put everything away for a few weeks and try again.

One of the first painting experiences inevitably becomes an exercise in body painting. I have never encountered a youngster who didn't need to do this as part of an early introduction to painting. If you expect this and plan for it, it can be a lot of fun as well as a valuable learning experience for your child. Once the child has gotten past this stage without reprimands and tears, he or she will show great growth in art. If body painting has been thoroughly done, it won't be repeated. The child who is not allowed to do this misses out on an important experience. My child did it at eighteen months. Most other children don't have painting experiences that early. They do it at age two, three, four, or five, or whenever they first encounter paint. I always planned a body painting class early in the term for my toddler art classes at Young at Art. We provided mirrors and photographed the occasion. It was always everyone's favorite class, including the mothers who had started out thinking I was a madwoman! You can well imagine that that most daycare center or nursery school teachers, with perhaps

Body decorating is a significant learning experience and should not be discouraged.

twenty students, can't possibly allow this kind of behavior, which would quickly produce bedlam in a group situation. Therefore, it is important that you, as a parent, offer art experiences in a setting that assures the freedom your child needs. Do it now and your child will completely outgrow the need by age two-and-a-half.

Freud referred to the phenomenon of playing with messy textures, but called it the anal-erotic age and felt that it was their own feces that children liked to play with. Art educator Viktor Lowenfeld sternly, and I believe wrongly, cautioned teachers not to offer fingerpaints and the like, lest children be "led . . . again to the enjoyment of playing with dirt." Frequently the child engrossed in painting will need to put down the brush and use his or her hands. This should not be viewed as regression. Thwarting these natural, observable needs in children can serve no useful purpose. Whatever the deep psychological reason, children clearly need to play with "dirt" and also to decorate themselves with it, as part of their growth and development. A good art experience can help them do this.

Play Dough and Clay

Play dough and clay provide very significant three-dimensional art experiences for a child. Play dough, along with appropriate cooking utensil toys, provides an early manipulative experience combined with pretend baking. It provides readiness for working with clay, which is harder to manipulate. Clay, which is actually mud or earth, plays a very large part in the development of the young child.

My Play Dough

I play with my Play dough;
See what I make!
I play with my Play dough;
I make a cake.

I play with my Play dough;
I shape it and mold it.
I play with my Play dough;
I bend it and fold it.

I poke it and punch it;
I roll it and scrunch it.

With a squeeze and a pat,
I squash it down flat!*

I like the above poem because it gives vocabulary to what the child is doing without imposing adult standards. Children do bend, fold, poke, punch, roll, and scrunch clay or play dough—they don't make realistic boats or cars. Making recognizable objects for your child is a no-no, so is using molds or cookie cutters. Their use causes dependence on adult ideas and emphasizes a preference for realistic subject matter. I am against using them in every situation. Children enjoy using rolling pins, plastic knives, and other safe kitchen tools with play dough, but you can encourage manipulation of the material by demonstrating on your own piece and offering encouragement as your child experiments on his or hers. Children learn most through direct physical contact with the material. Simple observations of what you see provide valuable feedback and add to the child's vocabulary. It is by learning the words that describe the activities that the child is best able to retain information and repeat desired actions.

Children who never have an opportunity to work with clay duplicate the experience every day all over the world with mud. Children begin by squishing, pulling, poking the clay. By observing the changes made while the clay was handled, the child learns to control the material. Pounding and banging on clay also provides for a healthy release of energy and tension as well as a lesson in how to flatten the substance itself. Children seem to name and assign roles to their clay creations somewhat earlier than they are ready to do so with their drawings. Working in three dimensions may help the child make the connection between the art produced and reality. I wouldn't be surprised if a clay coil quickly named a "snake" isn't the very first creation to have a name applied to it by most children. Fantasy play develops around clay experiments far earlier than we see it in most other areas of the child's play.

I advise having a work table set up in the child's play area with a manipulative material such as play dough or clay on it every day. Do not use molds, cookie cutters, or play dough "machines." They

---

* Fitzhugh Dodson, *I wish I had a computer that makes waffles* (San Diego: Oak Tree Publishers, 1978), p. 46.

Both play dough and clay provide important manipulative experiences for children.

provide the same imposition of adult art that we see in coloring books, and should have no place in your child's development. Instead provide encouragement and approval of the child's experimental work.

THIRTEEN

Movement

In the first year the child began as a helpless creature with little body control. Now he or she can walk and is beginning to talk. Within this short, miraculous time, the child learns with your help, as well as on his or her own, what the body is capable of doing. If every effort meets with concern on your part, your child becomes fearful and doesn't get a chance to fulfill his or her potential. If every time the child attempts something new you say "Be careful," your child's self-confidence is undermined. By moving in at the very first sign of apprehension, parents reward fear. On the other hand, saying "You can!" gives your child's self-confidence a boost. You need to strike a balance between not coaxing a reluctant child and not inhibiting a daredevil. Children must develop according to their own instincts.

The new walker is both exhilarated and frightened by his or her new-found independence. The aquisition of this new physical skill involves differentiation on two levels; physically, the distinction is made between gross motor activity and increasing specialization in the body; emotionally, it involves no longer thinking of the mother as a part of oneself and recognizing that one exists separately from the mother. The new walker will leave you, but needs to know that upon returning you will be there waiting. Sometimes the child will run from you, and find the chase reassuring (it's good exercise too!). The child is motivated now by two conflicting urges: curiosity and the lust to explore are very strong while the emotional need for one caretaker is simultaneously of prime importance. The child moves away on the one hand and becomes clingy on the other.

You can learn a lot about your child by observing how he or she reacts to physical challenges. The child who stops short of success may be doing the same in other areas as well. Some children try certain feats only if they have an audience, others only in private. Does your child see a challenge as an opportunity or as a threat? What is more important to him, the physical enjoyment or Mom's approval? All of these cues help you to better know and work with your child. Frequently you will be alerted to the fact that a child is about to master an important new skill by that child's irritability. If you can recognize the clues, you can help your child obtain the goal he or she has set rather than confusing the issue with a counterattack. Applause, hugs, incentive toys, and approval are all ways to help the child work toward goal attainment, and are much more meaningful than focusing on the child's expression of frustration. Some props can be used as aids. Children will run, crawl, and climb after tempting toys. When my son was eight months old, he spent weeks trying to figure out how to crawl and spent most of that time rocking and whining. We tried to help him and even demonstrated how to crawl, with no success. Then I took him to visit an office, put him down on the floor, and watched stupefied as he crawled, with perfect coordination, to a great big dog who was sleeping under someone's desk. The idea of reaching the dog was tempting enough to stimulate mastery of a new skill. When helping an aspiring climber you may want to try holding a triangle or bell at the top of a ladder on a slide and let the child climb toward it. Hand the child a stick when he or she reaches the goal to ring the bell with.

Be sure that your child is having wide and varied experiences that encourage skill attainment and coordination. I've noticed play sets in stores and many in backyards with tempting characters, bright colors, and high prices. Five or six different ways to swing are often all they offer. A good piece of equipment will offer climbing, balancing, chinning, *and* swinging. If you plan to purchase equipment, invest in something that is sturdy and offers a variety of activities.

Children do fall occasionally and sometimes even hurt themselves. This experience is a necessary evil and helps them learn about their bodies and their own capabilities. Children also choke on food occasionally, but we don't tell our children not to eat. My son was very active and frequently attempted feats of physical skill that surprised and frightened me. Once we were in a new playground and I spotted Jason ready to jump off a very high tree house. I screamed "Don't jump!", but he didn't hear me from across the park and jumped anyway. He landed in the sand and promptly climbed back up to repeat the trick. I was so glad that he hadn't heard that public declaration of my temporary lack of confidence in him. The only serious injury he suffered during his first three years happened in his own living room when he was simply walking, slipped on a scrap of wood a careless carpenter had left behind, and needed three stitches in his forehead. He always seemed to know what he was capable of far better than I did. Since children somehow know what they are ready to do safely, negative messages from doting parents serve only to confuse this self-knowledge and produce short circuits in the mental wiring that knows "I can" but says "I can't."

Children learn with body movement. When we restrict this movement through excessive fear of injury, we curtail learning. The unhealthy effects of underusing our bodies are much more dangerous to our overall health and well-being than the cuts, scrapes, and even broken bones of an active childhood. You can be more helpful pointing out the difference between the "safe" and the "dangerous" way to do something than "right" versus "wrong." The best supervision involves protecting, not controlling. Instead of backing off and yelling "no," stay close and assist the child in accomplishing his or her own goal. At the same time, goading a child to do something he or she isn't ready to do can be very frightening. There is a very fine line between what is helpful and what is inhibiting. We need to find a whole new way to talk to children: "Find a place to put your hand." "Hold the bar with two hands and you won't fall." "You got all the way up by yourself. That was great! Do you want to come down, or shall I hold you?"

Visiting safe, well-designed playgrounds is another way to protect your child. Cement floors in playgrounds should be extinct by now; sand is the safest cushion for falls. Here in New York City, often reputed to be an unfriendly city, a group of parents got together one fine spring day to clean and sift acres of sand in the local playground. All agreed that the adults had even more fun that day than the children did! That playground was donated to the city by a wealthy couple who wanted a nicer, safer playground for their young child than the existing old-fashioned cement one that had only swings, monkey bars, a small sand box, and a slide. Lacking a wealthy donor, you may find that many families together can accomplish a lot. Many suburban communities have pitched in to build modern, safe playgrounds for their children. Under the direction of an architect who is an expert on playgrounds, the parents built the entire thing themselves. (For information, contact: Robert S. Leather, 919 Bostick Road., Ithaca, NY 14850; 607-277-1650.)

Allowing a child to set his or her own goals seems to be the hardest thing for adults to do. I watched a toddler standing at the top of the stairs that led down to the subway. She was fascinated with them and curious about where they led. Her impatient baby-sitter kept saying, "Come on, we'll be late for gym class." I couldn't help feeling that at that moment the child would have benefited much more, both physically and intellectually, from climbing down those stairs to see the train and then climbing back up again, if that's what she wanted to do, than she would have in most teacher-directed gym classes for toddlers. Adults can either prevent or provide opportunities for growing and learning, so you must be flexible enough to recognize it when an opportunity just seems to present itself.

Occasionally a child will climb to the top of something and then be too nervous to climb back down. It is terribly important here to focus more attention on the accomplishment (climbing) than on the fear. Focusing on the fear produces a feeling of failure, when actually getting to the top is the accomplishment that should be applauded. Simply ignore the latter and praise the former. Learning about what the body can do is the most important aspect of movement for the child now. You need to try to encourage creative, rather than mechanical, self-conscious movement.

Repetition of sequence helps a child to learn. You need patience and must allow time, not only for the child to complete the process, but also for him or her to "recover" and absorb. Watching a child climb up and down stairs endlessly or move chairs all around the room and back again is quite the same as reading a favorite bedtime story over and over and over.

Help children see the endless possibilities of various props or equipment. Children this age love tunnels. They can crawl through

them, chase balls (and mothers) through them, and hide in them. Build one by rearranging furniture, make one from an old carton, or buy one. In addition to being banged upon, drums can be used to walk around, sit on, stand on, jump off. They can be played fast and slow, soft and loud; hit with nose, one hand, two hands, feet, and behind. They can also set the rhythm for an activity. They can be scratched with fingernails or brushed with hair. Simple rubber balls are as popular as ever because they can be used in an infinite number of ways. Stretch your child's creative thinking abilities, while stretching his or her muscles, by encouraging him or her to think up new things to do with balls. You can catch them, pass them from one person to another, sit on them, bounce them, roll them and roll on them, crawl after them, squeeze them, and play hide and seek with them. The child who doesn't catch the ball should not hear "too bad!" but should hear instead "That was terrific! You really ran fast after that ball." It is far more important for the child to learn what he or she *can* do than what he or she can't do.

FOURTEEN

Music

There is a huge difference between learning a song and making one up! You'll want to encourage both activities, of course. It's hard to make music if you don't know how to listen to it first, but if we only teach our children songs other people have written, who will be left to write new songs? Singing songs together is a very worthwhile activity, but making up songs is a truly creative endeavor. Just as all children make their own drawings and paintings, so can they improvise their own songs, rhythms, and dances. Children naturally sing, hum, repeat sounds, and move rhythmically. It is important for us to recognize these natural abilities and try to strengthen them. If music is always presented as complete songs to learn and be sung in only one correct way, creative musical activity is inhibited. Teaching children songs doesn't teach them how to make music.

One way to encourage this activity is by doing it yourself. When I played "This Little Piggy" with my son, I rarely used the same words twice. Variation always included friends, family, new foods, and things my child enjoyed:

> This little piggy went to Cantina
> This little piggy stayed home
> This little piggy ate tacos and nachos
> This little piggy ate none
> And this little piggy cried "olé!" all the way
>   home!

On the next night it might become:

> This little piggy went to Aunt Gail's house
> This little piggy stayed home
> This little piggy ate tomatoes and chicken
> This little piggy ate none
> And this little piggy said "Oy vey" all the way
>   home!

Of course, the tickle came at the same point in the rhyme each time and the effect of the finger game was the same as if the words had never changed. By stretching my imagination I was giving my child an understanding of improvising and helping him understand that there can be many "correct" solutions to problems. As soon as his vocabulary permitted, I would hesitate at a line, pretending I couldn't think of a phrase, and see if he could make it up for himself. Efforts were enthusiastically praised, never corrected. You and your child can make up songs about everything you do: work, trips, meals, etc.

The act of creation, whether it be in art or music, always involves an element of risk. You can provide a feeling of security for the child by providing activities which are nonthreatening at first and assure success. Adults can demonstrate acceptance of risk-taking. Singing songs that the child can finish by adding a rhyme is one way. Once the pattern of success is set and the child has gained confidence, he or she will be freed to create music. "The Bus Song," with accompanying hand gestures, encourages children to make up new words for it, and also stresses listening to sounds and rhythm. In addition to the "wheels on the bus go 'round and 'round," verses can include something about the passengers going bumpity bump, the driver saying move on back, babies crying, wipers swishing, etc.

It is a mistake for children always to experience music in group situations such as camps or classes. It's very hard to elicit individual music-making in large groups because they tend to be inhibiting. Group music experiences therefore often involve only the parroting of old songs as demonstrated by the leader. Children learn from these experiences, but their music education should in no way be limited to them. Some children won't seem to participate at all in groups, but take it all in and try it on their own in private or with Mom or Dad. These children need accepting, encouraging parents. Parents can provide a nurturing environment where music exploration is encouraged and rattles, bells, and other age-appropriate instruments are found. Your enthusiastic praise should not be saved for the music creation you like best, but offered for the bravery of trying something new.

Rhythm is the first aspect your child will understand about music. There are many ways to help heighten your child's awareness of sounds and rhythm. Singing and dancing with your baby are one delightful way. In addition to the rhythm created by body movement and in music, nature provides rhythmic sounds for us to observe. Rain or snow falling, the wind, ocean surf, dogs barking, bees buzzing, all provide distinctive sounds and contain natural rhythms we can help our children hear. People create many sounds in addition to music; sirens, typewriters, door bells, telephones, motors are all heard by children although we adults may tune them out. Rhythm is everywhere.

Go outside with your child, perhaps to a park, and listen to the rhythms around you. You can hear them in a bird's song, the flapping of its wings, balls bouncing, phones ringing, the wind through the trees, and the honking of horns. Even the very act of walking in the park is done in a basic rhythm: left, right, left, right —walk, walk, walk, walk. Chant with your child "left, right, left, right—walk, walk, walk, walk," etc. Your child may start to walk faster and faster. Go along with his or her natural rhythm. Start to say "run, run, run, run." See if the child can discover any other way to walk. You may ask, "Besides fast, how else can we walk? Of course, we can walk slowly." Say: "Slow-ly, slow-ly, slow-ly, slow-ly—left, right, left, right." Even slower, say: "Oh so slow-ly, oh so slow-ly, oh so slow-ly, oh so slow-ly—left, right, left, right."

You don't need to leave your house to listen to sounds. Of course the radio and record player provide music, but so do the rain on the roof, the vacuum cleaner, doors and drawers sliding and slamming, and an endless number of other things. Even crayons on paper make a sound. My noisiest classes always took place on the day when one child would bang the crayon on his or her paper to make dots and soon the whole class was following suit in a kind of rhythmic symphony. So many teachers put a stop to this kind of activity, but it is a valuable rhythm exercise. Listening to the swish of brushes on paper can make the resulting picture quite different than it would have otherwise been. Try painting to music.

MACHINE SOUNDS AROUND THE HOUSE

Even the moving of a paint brush can be rhythmical. See what kind of picture your child will create with the "walk" rhythm, the "running" rhythm, an uneven rhythm, or a "slow" rhythm.

Helping children to listen, discriminate between sounds, and imitate some are all ways to heighten sensitivity to sounds. Machine-made rhythms in our environment, such as ticking clocks, metronomes, and windshield wipers, all have their own sound and rhythm. The song "Machine Sounds Around the House" can help increase your child's awareness of sound and rhythm.

There are several books you can read with your toddler to increase an awareness of sounds around us. See Appendix I.

Children can create the basic rhythms—fast, slow, even, and uneven—with other parts of their bodies, too—not just their feet. They can use their hands, fingers, whole body, and even their mouths. Music should be experienced by as many of the senses as possible. Certain songs lend themselves to certain body movements—swaying, clapping, slapping your knees, whole body movement, stamping feet. Children can decide what movement would be appropriate by listening and getting the feeling of the

Songs from *A Pre-School Music Book,* Angela Diller and Kate Sterns Page (1936).

CLAP CLAP

MARYANNE CRAVEN

Clap - clap   clap your hands   clap your hands to - geth - er,

clap - clap   clap your hands   clap your hands to - geth - er.

song. Here is a song you might want to sing with your child. Let the child perform the action words as you sing together. He or she may change the words to "stomp your feet," "nod your head," "slap your leg," or anything he or she wants—even "paint, paint, paint today."

Babies instinctively understand rocking and respond to being rocked. Rocking, or swaying, has a calming effect, as does the "swaying" music below. This music, like the movement it represents, can be most effectively explained through its contrast with something faster like running. Children in this age group tend to sway in a steady, well-ordered rhythm in contrast to the more erratic rhythm they utilize when running. Just as you need to learn to walk before running, so you need to understand the slower, simpler, swaying movement before dancing.

Children use their whole bodies when they move and their tendency with running to music is to move all body parts quickly.

SWAYING

STEPPING SOFTLY

AMARYLLIS   GHYS
Andante con moto

RUNNING

Presto   FLEMISH FOLK-TUNE

Don't be surprised if the movement seems uncontrolled, since children will want to move their hands, head, and hips, etc., as well as their feet.

Since rhythm encourages whole-body participation, in tiptoeing children tend to scrunch up their bodies to be small like the sound and feeling of the music. They understand the music instinctively, and by pointing this out to them you can reinforce learning.

Help expand your child's musical experiences through rhythm games. Clap to music, clap in substitution for an anticipated word, clap simple rhythms. Play the "echo game" with clapping or with voices, responding to your child's cues and vice versa. Play a game of rhythmic polyphony, beginning with an upbeat chant and, as your child expects a similar finish, coming in with a surprise downbeat ending ("Let the piper call the tune/Mad as a hatter/Is it time to get up?/No way"). You can also use speech in many different ways that stimulate careful listening. Use varying levels of pitch in different registers. Hum, whisper, speak in falsetto, and growl. Play games that increase the child's awareness of loud and soft, fast and slow, and high and low. Many musical instruments aren't really musical instruments at all. A wooden spoon banged on a plastic-covered coffee can, two pot tops clapped together, a stick run along a fence, or the gong of a wooden spoon on a pizza tray are all sounds children discover on their own and, with your encouragement, enjoy making. Ask your child to close his or her eyes and try to guess how you are making different sounds. Try:

- clinking two glasses together
- running your fingers along the teeth of a comb
- banging on pots
- jingling keys

The next step in this game is to close your own eyes and let your child try to outwit you!

Many simple musical instruments can be made at little or no cost by you. Remember that the smaller the child, the bigger the instrument should be! A pitch pipe makes a great horn.

1. Using either glue or nails, cover two 2" x 4" x 1" blocks of wood with sandpaper and add a knob to the back of each. Rub the blocks together to produce a marvelous swishing sound.

2. Sew bells on a band of elastic that your child can wear on wrist or ankle. With each movement of the arm or leg, the bells ring.

3. Attach bells to the edges of a paper plate with the wire twist ties that come with garbage bags to make a tambourine.

4. Fill empty film cannisters with different types, sizes, and amounts of dried beans. Glue the tops securely closed with Elmer's glue. Each cannister will produce a different sound when shaken.

5. Two wooden dowels approximately 10" long can be banged together as rhythm sticks.

6 Another variation of the rhythm stick is to use one smooth stick and one fluted stick. The smooth stick is rubbed over the ridges of the fluted stick.

7. If you cannot provide a real stringed instrument like a violin or guitar, stretch some large rubber bands over an empty Kleenex box for a substitute.

8. All one-year-olds love to bang. They'll hammer on everything in sight, and most indulgent parents buy some sort of workbench and a drum for this activity. Real skin-covered tom-toms make the best drums, but if you don't have one, an empty cardboard Quaker Oats container is a better substitute than most toy plastic drums are. A lump of clay stuck on the end of a pencil can become a mallet.

A toddler who joyously bangs two pot tops together is discovering a musical instrument of his or her own invention.

9. Make your own dooley sticks by hammering flat metal bottle caps or coins. Nail two loosely to a wooden stick, with the metal sides facing each other.

10. Make your own triangle out of a 17¾" length of aluminum wire and a large nail. Bend the wire into a triangle at two 6" intervals, leaving an opening at one end. Hang it on a string, and use the nail as a striker.

Music toys and other sound-producing objects give your child a background in making and listening to sounds that forms the basis for later music appreciation. Experimentation at this age lays the foundation for creativity in music making. Too often, such experimentation is met with resistance from adults. Young children play with sounds but often hear "stop that racket!" Working against our kids is an adult perception of what music should sound like. In a *Life* magazine article (July 1982), popular electronic music composer Vangelis (Evengelos Papathanassiou) is quoted as saying:

> Actually, my first electronic instrument was the radio. I played the radio. I liked the sounds it made when I moved it from station to station late at night when I was a little boy. Ever since then, I like to play with sounds.

We cover our ears when a toddler joyously bangs two pot tops together when what we should do is congratulate the child for creating his or her very own musical instrument. We can be helpful by offering other similar pot and jar tops to allow the child to see which ones make the loudest, deepest, and highest sounds. Well-timed questions can add to the child's experience. It can be helpful when adults ask appropriate questions, such as, "How soft (loud, fast, slow) can you play the drum?" and "Which is louder, the foghorn or the fire truck's siren?" These questions encourage your child to listen to and discriminate between differing sounds.

Praise is more appropriate than correction. Instead of "You're giving me a headache," the child should hear "You must be so smart. You discovered cymbals without anyone showing you. This warrants a call to Grandma (or Daddy or Santa)!" If necessary, consider buying earplugs, because like early art experiences, "pretty" is not the goal, "experiment" and "observe" are.

> Leopold Stokowski advised parents to encourage their children to improvise and experiment with sounds on the piano before they were given formal lessons. He taught adult attitudes towards a child's "playing" with sounds had an important influence on musicality.*

---

* Miriam B. Stecher and Dr. Alice S. Kandell, *Max, the Music Maker* (New York: Lothrop, Lee & Shepard Books, 1980).

PART III

The Child: Age 2-3

FIFTEEN

The Third Year (The Terrific Twos)

I think it's a mistake to call the twos terrible. Whether they are terrible or terrific is entirely shaped by your perception of your child's natural development. During this year, your child will be asserting independence and at a peak of curiosity. When your child says "no" or "me do it," you shouldn't be discouraged. You can view each "no" as another step on the road to independence and be delighted to know your baby is developing normally. The child who stamps his or her foot and says *"No!"* is not a brat, but an individual well on the way to having a mind of his or her own. Now is the crucial time for you to encourage, not discourage, the skill of thinking for oneself. Independence is one of the primary concerns of the two-year-old. There is a very fine line, however, between encouraging it and forcing it. You can't force it, but you can foster it. The need must come from the child, as it surely will eventually. When it does, be ready.

Curiosity may have killed the cat, but it is your child's best motivation to learn. There is rarely a good enough reason to squelch it. The child below surprised the two mothers sitting nearby with a casual, "Catherine, may I please see your vagina?" Before anyone had time to react, he looked and moved on to something more interesting. There was nothing in the least bit sexual in the curiosity, despite the fact that it involved sex organs. Children want to see and know about everything, and if Catherine's nose had always been covered, he would have wanted to see her nose. An adult who looks shocked or expresses anger when

A child's curiosity in sexual matters is no different from the curiosity shown in all other areas.

curiosity rears its head is doing more negative than positive teaching. Children need to learn the facts of life as they become curious about them. Not all facts of life are sexual. Death, divorce, poverty, insanity, and sickness are all issues that should be discussed openly and must be dealt with. I know of one father who, when asked by his child where his own father was, responded: "He went away." His own problems about dealing with his father's death were thus handed down to the next generation. As parents, we must offer guidance and a good example on difficult problems, so they won't become problems for our children.

You can also help your child grow by allowing him or her to make as many decisions as possible. "Would you prefer an apple or a banana?" simplifies decision-making and is preferable at this age to the open-ended "What would you like to eat?" "Would you rather go to the playground or the toy store? Read or watch TV?

Paint or work with clay?" are all simple, limited decisions that can help prepare your child to make more complicated decisions later on. The best way to encourage your child to be creative and independent later is to foster self-confidence and a sense of security now. The child who is permitted (not pushed) to be independent now will carry the habit with him or her for life. The child who is taught total obedience learns to rely on others to make decisions.

> Highly dependent children don't suddenly blossom into mature, confident adults.*

On the other hand, the child who is forced to be independent before he or she is ready will resist and feel insecure. Of course you are bigger and stronger than your child, and you both know it. But believe it or not, you are not always smarter than your toddler, who knows best what his or her needs are and what he or she is most ready to do. At this point, you can easily win each "fight" with your baby, either by punishment or bribery—but if you always win now, over the long run you will be the loser.

When your child starts to say "no" to everything, it is important to respect his or her need to do so. Lord knows there are enough times when the child has to respect our need to say "no." Listen to your child and your child will listen to you. In her book *Your Child's Self-Esteem*, Dorothy Corkille Briggs, teacher, family counselor, and child psychologist, states:

> When autonomy is respected, the two does not carry this unfinished task into later stages of growth. In adolescence, the youngster will again concentrate on independence, but he won't have to blast the roof off the second time around if it is already well established.†

If your child says "no" to a bath or a meal, take it seriously and treat it with respect. Say "Okay," wait until later, and try a new approach. The feeling of control this gives the child makes life more pleasant for everybody. And the child eventually gets washed and fed, though without a threat to his or her self-esteem. There are some ways to lighten the pressure of negativism. Jason insisted

---

* Dorothy Corkille Briggs, *Your Child's Self-Esteem* (Garden City, N.Y.: Doubleday & Co., 1975), p. 51.
† Ibid.

on calling a banana an apple, although he knew the difference quite well. He adored seeing me pretend to be very upset by that, smack my head in mock astonishment, and scream, "No! Banana!" If he could talk for laughing so hard, he'd yell, "No! Apple!" and this game could go on forever. Once, while Jason and I were cuddling, I said, "Jason, do you love me?" and he looked at me with a devilish glint in his eye and said, "No." We had lots of fun with that and encouraged him to use "no" in a joking manner in other ways, as well, always showing approval for his imaginative ideas and ignoring whatever we didn't like about it. These games are simple, early forms of pretending that stress the innovative aspects of a child's ideas rather than the need to always conform. It's important to encourage your child to occasionally say and do ridiculous things, and to occasionally make up imaginative white lies, without fear of correction or ridicule. During this stage, I'd worry if my child was too acquiescent. Children who are always obedient may be afraid to be bad. A touch of rebellion or brattiness is a desirable characteristic in young children.

I watched a family on the street; the man had an ice cream cone and the child was screaming for one too. The father was arguing: "But you'd never be able to finish your own ice cream cone. You can have as much as you want of mine." The child absolutely refused to even taste the man's ice cream cone and became hysterical as it became clear that the father would not buy him one of his own. The decision to buy the child ice cream in a case like this should not be based on whether or not the child can consume it all. The need to have "my own" is as important as the financial logic. No one likes to waste money, and to most people an unfinished ice cream is wasted money. The man could have had it his way, while respecting the child's need for independence, by simply buying the child his own cone and eating the unfinished portion himself or asking occasionally for a bit of the *child's* cone. This would have preserved both the family budget and the child's integrity. My guess is that the man could have afforded to buy a cone for a child who would be able to finish it. In that case, given the importance of the independence issue, he should feel he can "afford" to buy a cone that will be partially "wasted," since the uneaten ice cream isn't really wasted at all—it is providing a sense of pride and independence for a youngster.

Children are exerting their wills now because instinct tells them they must learn to do for themselves. Don't take these actions personally or view them as being directed against you as a parent. They are not rebellious acts, but work toward a goal set by an inner clock, not a parental timetable.

I visited a home where the conscientious mother had a chart hanging in her child's room. It was headed: "Goals for Eliza."* A two-page list of goals followed, such as "By the end of the month, Eliza will eat unaided with a fork" and "By November, Eliza will use the potty." Each goal listed was scheduled for the average child's readiness time according to the experts. One key ingredient was missing: Eliza's control over her own life's goals. Learning is far more effectively done when it comes from the child's own initiative.

Encouraging your child to make decisions means keeping quiet when you don't approve of the choice your child has made. Someone who once visited brought my child a package of lollipops which sat unopened in the kitchen for a long time. One morning Jason refused to eat breakfast and indicated that he wanted a lollipop instead. Despite the fact that I am very well aware of the evils of sugar and the importance of good nutrition for young children, I gave it to him without comment. As the day progressed, he continued to refuse food and requested lollipops, and I gave in to his request each time. By late afternoon, he had consumed only lollipops and bottles, and I must admit that I was beginning to doubt my own philosophy and worry that perhaps I had made a mistake. Then I realized that he had a fever and was coming down with a cold. He had probably awakened with a sore throat, in which case a lollipop was the ideal thing to soothe it. He was too young to tell me that he had a sore throat, but nevertheless knew exactly what was best for him—more than I could have. After his recovery he resumed normal eating habits and never again requested lollipops for breakfast. A lecture and a lesson in nutrition—along with an all-powerful mother withholding lollipops—would have given sweets an unnecessary importance that could have lasted for years. By eating a nutritious breakfast yourself each morning, you probably teach far more about good nutrition than you do with rules and lectures.

Children's need to establish their independence is very strong. This instinct allows them to survive on their own later on and your

* Not the child's real name.

most significant role as a parent is to prepare your child to survive in the world as a self-reliant adult. Parents must expect children this age to be somewhat rebellious, and should allow children to make some decisions. Chaos will not reign in your home if your child occasionally chooses the family's dinner menu or changes the schedule for visiting the park. At the same time, you and the other members of the family have needs too. It would be very frightening if you always let your toddler run the show. You therefore must expect an occasional tantrum, and can be certain that it will come at an embarrassing, inconvenient time. Your toddler knows very well that tantrums don't work ten minutes after you've all had a restful nap and are in the privacy of your own home. Tantrums begin not only when the child is tired, but when you are too. It also helps to be sick or expecting important guests momentarily! Tantrums are an expression of frustration. They happen occasionally to every two-year-old and therefore should not embarrass you if they occur in public. Squelching every tantrum means that your child will need to relearn assertiveness as an adult. It is helpful for the child to know that the parents accept his or her individuality and can be flexible about some issues while still being very firm about others. When you do set down a firm rule, you must let your child know that you mean it. Knowing what the rules are helps a child feel secure. If tantrums occur very frequently, you may have too many rules or your child may need to learn how to channel energy into physical activities. Growing up is hard work and deserves your understanding and support. We all fear that "wild" children are the result of parents who relinquish control and give in to every little thing, but that doesn't mean that you can never be flexible. There is nothing wrong with recognizing that your screaming child is genuinely miserable, and occasionally changing your mind. The key is to be absolutely inflexible about some essential rules, but not to make too many rules.

What about presenting a "united front" with your spouse? This may be considered heresy, but still I think there are times when a disagreement between the two of you can be advantageous to the observing child. When my husband proudly displayed his new camera for us, Jason asked if he could take a picture with it. When my husband said "absolutely not," I spoke right up. "Jason is very smart and he knows how to be extra careful with a camera because he uses mine. I think you should let him try it." Jason listened nervously, nodding his head in agreement at the words "smart" and "careful." As his father was convinced, Jason excitedly approached the camera with near reverence, and treated it with special care. Hearing my vote of confidence in him, even if I had not won that argument, would have added to his self-confidence. Married couples have to differ on some aspects of child care and it does no harm for children to learn this lesson early—provided they come away from the experience with bolstered self-esteem.

Everyone expects some bedtime and night disturbance with a new baby, but by the time a child is two, parents tend to pull that old "You are too old for this nonsense" lecture. They expect to "put" a child into bed to fall asleep instantly and not awaken until morning. This is unrealistic. The two-year-old probably needs more comfort at bedtime than the two-month-old. The transition between being awake and aware and giving up and going to sleep is often a difficult one for this active age group. They want so much to be a part of everything and seem to need special reassurance that they are. Bedtime for many families is a battle. The child wants to stay up, kiss Mommy again, or have a glass of water long after exhaustion has set in. Mom and Dad know it's time for bed and take the adversary position. Of course it's not water the child needs, but company at bedtime. What's wrong with lying down with your child till sleep comes? It makes monsters and ghosts disappear and fosters a feeling of warmth and security. I believe that the expectation that children must sleep alone in rooms of their own, perhaps fueled by Dr. Spock's stern advice "Better not let the child in your bed,"* has perpetrated more misery in more homes than any other child-rearing myth. Relaxed parents of happy, well-adjusted secure children know that children fall asleep the quickest when being held and have no nightmares when they sleep with their parents. Most nightmares at this age are caused by fears of parent abandonment, a hard feeling to have when you're sound asleep in Mommy and Daddy's bed!

> Bad dreams and other night disturbances in sleep
> are frequently related to the child's fear of being
> deserted by his parents. †

* Benjamin Spock, M.D., *Baby and Child Care* (New York: Simon and Schuster, 1976), p. 201.

† Ashley Montagu , *Touching* (New York: Columbia University Press, 1971), p. 159.

Parents who have ignored advice about putting infants in their own rooms to let them cry themselves to sleep tell of nightmare-free offspring sleeping contentedly in their parents' bed without any Freudian ill effects. Of course, some children are happy sleeping alone in their own rooms and that is fine. But children who desire physical closeness at bedtime are the rule, not the exception.

Children may be upset or afraid while alone, but even if nothing in particular is bothering a child, it is quite normal and natural to want to sleep cuddled up to Mom, just as every other animal sleeps pressed up against its mother. Both calories and kisses contribute equally to a child's growth and development. Many people banish their children to rooms or beds of their own, firmly discouraging bedtime chatter or cuddling—only to proceed to bed themselves, cuddle up to their spouses, and wind down with quiet, intimate talk. We must change the phrase "going to bed" from being a euphemism for sexual intercourse before we can mentally free ourselves to provide for our children's basic need for intimacy. Not so many years ago you couldn't even hint in a television show that married couples shared the same bed. The notion of a whole family sharing a bed would have been a scandal. Beds should be a source of comfort and the ultimate place to relax.

Children soon outgrow this need, quite on their own. Whether it is at six months or six years varies with every child. My child decided, at three and a half, to leave our bed for a sleeping bag on our bedroom floor, and at four and a half he announced that he wanted to sleep in his own bed after falling asleep in ours. I somehow always knew that I would not have to worry about making room in my bed for his wife!

Some children can sleep alone at most times but need the comfort of their parents' bed during times of crisis. Children have nightmares because something is frightening or bothering them. "Crying it out" doesn't cure the problem, it compounds it. From it the child learns that "Mom and Dad don't care that I'm in need." They stop crying eventually, but so do most abused children. Just because they are not crying doesn't mean that they are not miserable. My son, who was still sleeping in my bed, did not have a nightmare until he was three. I had enrolled him, at his own request, in a summer day camp. After the first day, which he said he had enjoyed, he woke up screaming twice in the night. Both times his dreams had been about camp. I spent the next day in camp with him, as the counselor spent most of her time yelling at the children. Jason was told, in no uncertain terms, that he would not be sent back and that he would never have to be in a situation with such a bad-tempered leader. His nightmares ceased, and he didn't have another until a year later, when he witnessed my husband and I screaming at each other like two raving maniacs.

Routine can be so important at bedtime. Some families establish routines without even realizing it. We once were staying at a motel near an amusement park. We could hear every word spoken in the room adjoining ours and night after night we heard exactly the same thing. First, the mother put her daughter in her crib and told her to go to sleep. The little girl talked, sang, jumped on the mattress, tapped on the walls, and called to her. Each time the child called to her the mother gruffly said, "Go to sleep." After about fifteen minutes of this she spanked her soundly. The child then cried and fell asleep. I couldn't help wondering if the mother ever realized how predictable each evening ritual had become.

Contrasted with the nightly routine in our room, theirs seemed so unnecessary. We gave Jason a bath, one of us read to him, and then we turned out the lights and all three of us got into bed. We talked about the day and what we'd be doing tomorrow. "Pleasant dreams" and "I love you" were repeated at least three times as part of the nighttime ritual. Jason was always asleep within fifteen or twenty minutes and then my husband and I both got up and were free for the rest of the evening. We spent the same amount of time putting our son to bed as that other mother did putting her daughter to bed. The difference was that she viewed the child's need for her attention at bedtime as naughty; we did not.

As children are breaking away and becoming independent in some areas, they tend to rely even more on some of the crutches they used as babies. These security devices make being on one's

own a little less frightening. Parents who decide to take away a child's security device now delay development. You move the focus of attention from the issue at hand to the issue of having or not having the security device. Anxiety is displaced. Relax and let your child grow at his or her own rate.

> Because establishing independence is a monumental task, outside pressures become formidable roadblocks to the twos. Yet, around this age parents often decide to take away the bedtime bottle, get the thumb out of the mouth, or remove the security blanket or pacifier. These demands are like asking a confirmed smoker to kick the habit at the very time he takes on a stressful new job.*

Children are born with the capacity to grow and develop. If left alone about the issues of giving up all of infancy's paraphernalia, they will do so quite on their own. Your child will gladly abandon the bottle, pacifier, or whatever has been used to help him or her through bad times, at the appropriate time. What is appropriate for one child is too soon for another. Let your child decide when the time is right. I have never seen an eighteen-year-old still drinking milk from a bottle, but I've seen many who smoked, bit their nails, and overate—all signs of anxiety and frustration. Parents should see themselves as being on the child's side. Life is difficult and frustrating for a toddler. It helps if the child feels secure in the knowledge that Mom and Dad are for, not against, him or her. Taking away a child's emotional crutch is cruel and causes problems to surface later on. It's far better to let the child grow at his or her own pace.

My own child's security device was to drink his bottle and hold my ear. I always let him know that I was a staunch supporter of this need. When others made comments to him like, "Big boys don't drink from bottles," I always was the first one to respond with, "Jason is a very big boy. He knows how to share and he can put on his own clothes, but he likes bottles." There was never any question about whose side I was on. One friend of mine took her child's bottle away quite early. She insisted that he ate much better

* Dorothy Corkille Briggs, *Your Child's Self-Esteem* (Garden City, N.Y.: Doubleday & Co., 1975), p. 128.

Dolls and stuffed animals can provide friendship and comfort to a child in need.

because of it, which I'm sure was true. He visited once and was playing with my son in his room when Jason screamed for me that the child had taken his bottle from him. When I entered the bedroom, the child was nowhere to be found. I had quite a scare and began searching for him. I found him in my bedroom hiding behind the long dresses in my closet and sucking guiltily on Jason's bottle. No two-year-old should have to feel guilty for fulfilling normal instincts. Children may eat more if deprived of a bottle, but obesity is much more common in this country than are children who starve themselves.

> When sucking needs are unfulfilled, they do not disappear. They come out in thinly or thickly disguised ways. A baby may continue sucking his thumb, a child his eraser, and an adult his cigarettes and cigars. Babies may bite all objects, children may bite their nails, and adults may make biting remarks.*

* Haim G. Ginott, M.D., *Between Parent and Child* (New York: Avon Books, 1965), p. 179.

Parents whose children become attached to special teddy bears or blankets also need to be supportive of their children's needs. The most loved bear will be dropped and forgotten when a child is distracted by interesting things. It is then Mom or Dad who has to trudge through airports, stores, beaches, or parks clutching a teddy bear for a child who will need it later. It's Mom or Dad who has to remember to pack Teddy or Kitty when the child is excited about an impending trip and may forget. But that child may be sleeping in an unfamiliar bed that night and will surely look for his or her special friend.

Self-Determination

Somewhere around eighteen months or so, the terrific twos rebel against being put into their strollers. I chased Jason through the streets of New York until he was about two and a half, when he suddenly settled down and enjoyed the ride. If you ignore the protest against strollers now, you'll have quite a different fight in

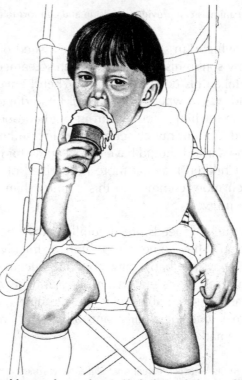

Food should never be used as a gift, bribe, or behavioral incentive.

two years, when your child refuses to walk. I met one woman walking down Broadway with her three-and-a-half-year-old daughter wrapped around her leg and whining. The mother looked up at me apologetically and said, "I'm trying to teach her to walk by herself instead of always riding in her stroller." As I ran ahead with my own empty stroller to catch up with two-year-old Jason, I said, "I bet you bribed her to stay in it two years ago," and she admitted that she had often bribed her with food and that it had been a big mistake. Ice cream is fine as an occasional supplement to meals, but not as a bribe.

It is important for parents to remember that spending two hours walking to the corner grocery store is as much a part of properly raising a child as is changing diapers if you want your child to thrill at the prospect of discovering new things and feeling self-reliant and independent. Stopping to look at trees, flowers, fire hydrants, and even trash provides an education. Now your child will learn about the true meaning of learning as it can never be taught in school.

Curiosity can be nurtured in every activity your youngster participates in. There is never only one right way to cook a dish, or to solve any problem for that matter. From getting dressed in the morning to going to bed at night, the day is filled with hundreds of questions and choices. The more questions your child answers for him- or herself and the more decisions made by the child, the better off we all will be. When my son decided to "prepare dinner" one day, I provided him with each ingredient he requested. He mixed together (measurements are approximate):

> 1 cup frozen yogurt
> 1 cup Tab
> 1 cup peas
> a lot of salt
> 1 cup croutons
> 3 broken cookies
> pepper
> 3 pretzels
> a few more croutons
> 1 crumbled potato chip
> ½ cup coffee
> 6 ounces apple juice

Children can be very creative in the kitchen.

He proudly mixed it all up and didn't taste it until he was all finished preparing it. After one taste he informed me that he wasn't hungry anymore and moved on to another activity! If he did this every night it would have been very wasteful, but the cost of the above ingredients provided him with a long afternoon's self-directed play and the feeling of being a grown-up cook. It was a very cost-efficient activity. If you were raised as a member of the "clean plate club" and can't bear to permit the wasted food, your child can also do "pretend" cooking, with the child thinking up ingredients to add to such things as a wicked witch's brew, a magician's magic potion, a doctor's medicine, or a poison.

Children are seeing the world with fresh eyes. They don't know how to accomplish goals that they set for themselves. Figuring the answers out for themselves is what they need to do. I'd never let a child struggle with something if that child wanted my help, but at the same time, I'd never offer help to one who wanted to find the answers for him- or herself. Let your child put his or her shoes on and you can tie the laces; let your child pour milk, even if it means a few spills. (The experienced child will have fewer spills than one

You can encourage independence by permitting the child to handle some grown-up tasks.

who's never poured liquid before.) You can facilitate pouring by transferring liquids to plastic containers before putting them on the table and by not filling them too full. Keep a sponge handy. The child will enjoy mopping spills as much as he or she enjoys pouring, and learns to take responsibility for action, rather than waiting to do as told.

"Be careful" is all you have to say to scare a child. It's much more useful to give specific directions if you feel the need to offer guidance every time your child attempts something new. "Hold on with both hands," "Hold the flat side not the pointy side," "Put the scissors down if you want to run" is helpful, specific information your child can use. One day as I nonchalantly left my apartment building, two-year, nine-month-old Jason struggled along behind me dragging his motorcycle down the stairs. A neighbor stopped to help him. Jason began by saying, "I'll do it!" and ended up by stamping his feet and screaming, but still the man proceeded to "help" him. Finally I intervened, assuring the man that while we appreciated his concern, Jason was better off and happier struggling down the stairs without help. "Sorry," he said, "I can't get used to it. My children are the complete opposite. They say, 'He'll do it' instead of 'I'll do it.' " It didn't seem necessary to suggest that he had helped make them the way they are today.

Toilet Training

What, you may rightfully ask, does toilet training have to do with creativity? Parents frequently align themselves against their children in this matter and cause tension and loss of self-confidence by pushing it too early. They take away an important area of self-determination from the children. The child who is ready for bladder or bowel control can make the switch from diaper to potty literally overnight. This may happen early in the second year or well into the third year. Children vary greatly in this matter and it is most helpful to take a *vive la différence* attitude. You give your child more benefits by allowing him or her, like a flower, to grow at the built-in rate of growth. The child who is not ready should not be made to feel ashamed; shame in no way contributes to readiness, but can severely undermine self-confidence. *Training* is a poor word for what is occurring; normal development cannot be taught.

> Every child has an inner timetable for growth—a
> pattern unique to him. And his particular way must
> be respected.*

Toilet "training" is a waste of time and an unnecessary cause of tension in the lives of too many toddlers. Easiest for all is to make a small potty seat available, let your child know what it is for, and let the matter drop. Once the child has independently decided to use a potty, the issue solves itself and the child gains self-confidence and a feeling of control over his or her own life. As with bottles and pacifiers, toilet training is a normal part of development that parents make an issue over by pushing. Some children sleep dry as early as eighteen months of age, others still wet the bed at six. Development in many areas is uneven at this stage, but everyone catches up by the end of childhood. I even know one boy who could read at age three-and-a-half, but still wore diapers at night (and drank from a bottle) until he was five. His mother

---

* Dorothy Corkille Briggs, *Your Child's Self Esteem* (Garden City, N.Y.: Doubleday & Co., 1975), p. 113.

knew that he was ahead of other children in some areas and behind in others, and accepted that as being as it should be. To gain perspective on the matter of toilet training, stop, relax, and ask yourself: "What am I really worried about?" Do you seriously think your child will grow up and still wear diapers? I always said that if my own child did that, why worry? Let his wife worry about it! Of course, that is not what you are worried about. You know your child will eventually use a toilet like everyone else. It really is a matter of months. When you see two ten-year-olds walking down the street, it's impossible to tell which one was toilet trained or gave up the bottle first!

Shortly before their third birthdays, one of Jason's friends visited and proudly showed us his underpants, which had cars on them. Jason said he wanted a pair, so I bought some. Each time I dressed him I asked him if he wanted diapers or underpants. He always said "pants." Despite the fact that he soiled them more often than not, I let him wear them. Within three weeks he had completely "trained" himself. The important thing was that the motivation came from him, not me. When he was finally successful, we offered to buy him any gift he chose. He requested a "toilet train," which I believe was his first pun. That "toilet train" was also his first and only battery toy, but when you ask a child to choose anything he likes, you have to be prepared to accept the fact that he may choose something you object to! Another friend of mine had her two-year-old sit on the potty every day after lunch, for up to an hour, until he moved his bowels. He was "trained" at exactly the same age Jason was, so what was gained by making everyone crazy?

> Many of us fear that temporary regression halts forward growth. We feel youngsters will never "make it" if they aren't forever going forward. Oddly enough, we have faith in a plant's capacity to grow. We put the seed in a nurturing climate and trust the potential that allows it to develop in its own time, in its own way. Growth plateaus or a few brown leaves don't unnerve us. If things seem amiss, we attend to the nurturing conditions around the plant. But we don't push on it or try stretching its leaves. We sometimes have less faith

in our children's sprouting capacities than we do in our plants'. By pushing and urging and forbidding, we try to force growth. When progress bogs down, we focus on them, rather than on the climate around them. We forget that, like the seed, the push toward growth lies within each child.*

I feel that every little bit of help you can give your child to feel independent is important. We gave away all of Jason's stylish overalls as soon as he showed interest in bladder and bowel control and bought him only elasticized jogging-style pants or shorts. He, therefore, needed no adult help to use the bathroom. Velcro closings and drawings of arrows that point at each other on shoes will inspire a child to try putting them on him- or herself as well.

* Ibid.

SIXTEEN

Home Environment

Since independence is the primary concern of the two-year-old, you can make some changes in your home that will help make your child feel grown-up and independent. There is a very fine line between forcing independence and encouraging it. Adjusting your environment to the needs of a small person who possesses minimum coordination skills goes a long way in encouraging independent behavior. Once the habit of doing for oneself is established, it will carry over into other areas. Put a step stool near the sink, a window, or an interesting shelf. Buy child-sized furniture and keep a child-sized potty chair next to the toilet. Keep juice in a small plastic pitcher on the bottom shelf of the refrigerator so that a thirsty child can help him- or herself with minimum mishaps. Hang hooks and closet poles low enough to allow a child to take out and put away his or her own things. (You can also purchase an inexpensive closet expander that hangs from the existing bar in your closet and eliminates the need for a permanent alteration.*) Label toy boxes with pictures of what is in them. This prereading activity also encourages a child to find and put away toys without adult help. Set aside a corner of your home where incomplete art projects, block structures under construction, and unfinished puzzles can be left out without inconveniencing other family members. This will lend a sense of importance to the child's activities that is lost when "clean-up" rather than completion becomes your primary concern.

* Holst, Inc., Dept. MN0384, 1118 W. Lake, Box 370, Tawas City, MI 48763.

Encourage independence by adjusting the environment to suit your child's needs and size.

If you and your family have settled down in the home of your dreams, this chapter is not for you. If, however, you live in the city and are planning to move to the suburbs "for the children's sake," read on! Trees and wide-open spaces have appeal, but so do museums, playgrounds, and nearby gym, swimming, art, and story-time classes. The notion that rural areas are "safer" than urban areas can lull parents into a false sense of security. The need for constant supervision of young children exists wherever you live. You may find more opportunities for stimulating experiences in an urban environment. A ten-year-old student of mine who had recently moved from the city to the suburban community where I taught took to visiting my classroom every day after school. When I suggested that he try to get more involved with his new classmates he whined, "But there's nothing to do here." When I asked what he had done after school every day in his old neighborhood he responded, "We hung out at the Brooklyn Museum every day." The opportunities for absorbing information about the arts by "hanging out" in a museum daily cannot be equaled through books or classes.

Nevertheless, this child's parents moved to the suburbs because of the myth that it is a "better" place for children. His dad had a much longer commute to work, and he and his mother were uprooted because of this myth. Many conscientious couples move to the suburbs when they are raising children and back to the city after their children are grown. The fact remains that environments are what you make of them. The city can be a rich, interesting place for a child to grow up in, or it can be overwhelming and frightening. The suburbs can provide country air, a sense of community, and clean living, or they can be a boring wasteland. You and your husband should live where you are happiest—suburbs or city. After you have made your choice, live life there to the fullest, but expose your child to the alternative.

SEVENTEEN

Excursions

Multiple sensory experiences stimulate intellectual achievement. Children will be imprisoned within classroom walls, and busy doing homework all too soon. This preschool time is the most concentrated time you have together. I'm always saddened to see groups of thirty or so students, supervised by a harried teacher, running wildly through a museum. Children need to discuss what they see and have things explained to them. They need personal guidance and the interested attention of an adult who has the time to point out things and generate interest in new things. If you don't do that for your child, no one else can.

Museums

Museum visits are terribly important now, and your toddler is probably much more willing to sit in a stroller than he or she was last year and can concentrate for longer periods of time. Children of this age have some art experience behind them now and will be interested in the techniques artists use as well as in recognizing subject matter. Where last year you made only simple, personalized comments about the pictures like "Would you like to ride in a boat like that one?" this year, in addition to such comments, you can add information about the art. "The background looks like it was painted but the boat seems to be three-dimensional, almost like sculpture." Two-year-olds understand words like *sculpture, collage,* and *painting.* Use the correct terminology whenever possible to describe things. These trips can stimulate new art activities at home.

As you look at art work together, talk about how the artist made something, and how the techniques can be applied to your child's art work. Elevate your child's art to the level of a professional by comparing it favorably to what you are seeing in the museum. "I bet the artist who painted this picture was trying to make the same kind of wavy lines that you did on the picture we hung in the living room. You used more colors in yours than this artist did." If found objects were used in a collage, for example, suggest that your child find things on the way home to use in a collage too. Don't suggest copying, but do introduce new techniques in this way. Whatever your own tastes are, it's important to expose your child to abstract art now—it is the style most similar to child art (Picasso often said he wished he could draw like a child). Children can relate to good abstract art on an intuitive level. Its respected presence in a museum helps the child recognize the significance of his or her own work. There are books about art and artists that can reinforce this kind of learning: see Appendix I under Art, Artists, Beauty, Ugliness, Children Drawing, Children Painting, Looking, and Museums. See Appendix II for my reviews of these books.

Children can relate to good abstract art on an intuitive level.

Shows

A longer attention span also means that you can take your child to movies, the circus, puppet shows, and concerts without having to leave before intermission. A story line can be followed and understood. The more familiar a scenario is to a child, the more interesting it will be. If you are going to a show, try to read an illustrated version of the story beforehand. Prepare your child in advance for anything that might be frightening.

If you attend an exciting show, toys and books obtained there will stimulate fantasy play for a long while. A puppet show will inspire many home imitations that a new toy puppet, stuffed animal, or doll can add to. Most performances that are intended for children sell tempting souvenirs that can add quickly to the cost of the tickets. If you are on a tight budget, bring your own snack and drink, and spend your money instead on something that will help the child remember the performance. Since dolls, puppets, flashlights, and other souvenirs are usually overpriced, you may want to buy a reasonably priced substitute before coming to the show. Have it ready to give to your child when he or she sees other

A puppet show will inspire many home imitations that a toy puppet, stuffed animal, or doll can enrich.

children getting goodies. If you know that you can't buy anything during the performance, discuss this with your child before you arrive so that temptation and desire do not ruin the show. Help your child create original shows by providing appropriate props and being willing to play "audience." For a stage, cover a card table with a blanket or sheet, turn a large carton on its side, or have the performers work on the ground floor at an open window, while the audience remains indoors.

Educational Experiences

Plan exciting excursions with your child frequently. You don't have to go to Egypt to ride on a camel. These lucky children experienced an exotic trip at the Bronx Zoo in New York City. You can see so much of the world without going far from home. Circuses travel all over the country, bringing the alluring close to home. Aquariums allow a close-up view of sea life that few sailors ever had! Wondrous sights that fascinate and stimulate toddlers are within reach no matter where you live. Worthwhile trips don't have to scream "educational" at you. Visits to places that are new to the child can't help but be educational. A visit to a furrier, factory, garage, bookstore, and office can be as educational and stimulating to a toddler as a trip to a museum, zoo, or aquarium. A ride on a jet plane is not a better experience for a child than a ride on the subway; it's just different. Ideally, the child will experience both. Often children from wealthy families may have flown to Europe and been on luxury cruises but have never been on a train. It is not unusual for these children, who may be the apple of their parents' eyes, to spend all of their time at home with caretakers to whom they represent nothing more than $3.00 an hour. The truly rich child has exciting experiences to stimulate the mind and unconditional parental love to bolster a sense of confidence.

The most interesting and educational experiences a child can have often occur while accompanying Mom and Dad as they go about their daily lives. It is more difficult and time-consuming to tend to errands with a two-year-old in tow, so it can be tempting to save some jobs for when your toddler is busy elsewhere. However, these seemingly mundane errands can be turned into real adventures with just a little planning. If your trip will be to the post office, let your child buy fifteen or so one-cent stamps to use in a collage at home, or buy a postcard to use for "writing" a letter.

Any grandparent would enjoy receiving a colorful scribble in the mail. All you have to do is address it and let your child lick the stamp and place the postcard in the mailbox. While your child is occupied drawing, you can tend to your business. A visit to the grocery store can be turned into a treasure hunt, with your toddler tracking down something "orange" to serve for dinner. Giving a "job" to a child increases his or her sense of importance and infuses the activity with meaning. That job can simply be giving the ticket to the dry cleaner or money to the grocer. Encourage your child to ask storekeepers for receipts or other souvenirs. This lesson in poise and good manners will serve your child well in life. When you praise the child for a job well done, and then talk about the experience later at home, you help your child understand how society operates. If you carry a Polaroid camera with you, you can photograph highlights of the day and "write" a book about it. "Tommy's Trip to the Dry Cleaner" will probably not win next year's Pulitzer Prize for literature, but it will add to the value of daily excursions and enrich your child's life. Paste the pictures in a sketch book, let your child paste whatever papers were collected during the day in a collage, while together you write a few lines about the day's excursion. It is too early to suggest that your child draw a picture about his or her experience, since the concept of subject-motivated art won't be an issue for another two years.

There are some experiences you cannot provide that others can. I for one could never even stand on ice skates, but I didn't want my son to inherit my faults, so a baby-sitter who was a skilled skater was given the job of taking him on ice-skating expeditions. I am also a terrible cook, so a friend and I agreed to share skills. She invited Jason for the cookie-baking and bread-making experiences he lacked at home, and I took over her son's early art education.

School Visits

This is an important year to visit a school. It will be the second most important place in your child's life for many, many years. A gradual, pleasant introduction to school, before attendance must begin, is helpful. Try to infuse the visit with some excitement, and if possible add a sense of purpose to the visit by having the child bring some important papers to "the teacher." Perhaps an older sibling or neighbor can invite the child to meet her or him at school and provide a brief tour of sandbox, blocks, and other good things. Many parents told me that my hour-long toddler art classes at Young at Art were a good introduction to school. They provided a snack, some friends, and good fun, but primary caretakers never left the room. Thus, the classes presented no threat to the child. Perhaps you can find this kind of a class for your toddler.

Art Classes

If you are looking for an art class for your child, check first to see whether the program is, like most programs, sending all of the children home with "pretty holiday art" where one child's is indistinguishable from another's. If so, don't even consider sending your child there. Look instead for a place that provides art materials to be experimented with under adult supervision and encouragement.

My three-year-old son once returned from an art program sponsored by a museum with a pre-cut, adult-made felt Christmas tree he had decorated. I'd felt assured that at a museum he would be offered only sound art experiences, but even that was no guarantee. Shortly thereafter we visited still another museum where he was given a shockingly poor, black and white coloring-book-style rendering of one of the greatest paintings in the museum's collection with instructions to color it in! Some museums' education programs demonstrate little knowledge of child development and a great deal about the artists in their collections. The goals of these programs are frequently to disseminate information about the museum's collection, not to produce future artists to someday contribute to the collection. The Metropolitan Museum of Art, in New York City, produced a book of art projects for children with directions for imitating art objects in its collections. When I suggested to the buyer of the shop that they sell my Anti-Coloring Books® to encourage original art work as well as copy work, she informed me that the children's drawings stimulated by my books were not "real art" and hence the books would not be sold in the shop.

I once taught in an art program for two-year-olds that was housed in an elegant building. The building and its maintenance took precedence over the learning that took place there. No chalk projects were permitted since they tended to mess up the art room. Teachers knew they would be reprimanded if any clay, paint, or marker showed up on walls or floors, so their art lessons were planned accordingly. This prevented children from getting a well-rounded art experience. As soon as children deviated from the project as explained by the teacher, they were quickly corrected. Little room was left for creative variation.

As a school administrator, I observed many art classes over the years. One art teacher of young children did only pasting projects with them, week after week. She offered no variety of experience, only different materials. When I asked why she never did other projects with the children she said, "Pasting is easy and not too messy!"

One excellent art program for children this age had a huge vinyl tarpaulin covering the entire floor installed in the manner of wall-to-wall carpeting. The art materials were laid out on the floor and ready to use so the children could begin experimenting with them the minute they arrived. The teachers never told them what to make with the materials; the children were free to make what they wished. Adventuresome use of them was encouraged. If a painting child decided to include the tarpaulin-covered floor in his or her design, that was permissible. Once in a while, a child got involved in body painting. Additional materials were available for a child who finished early. Midway through the two-hour class, the children and teacher met as a group to discuss their work and have a restful snack. The teacher played guitar and the children sang. They were encouraged to make up songs and to teach the

songs to the rest of the group. Movement activities, often related to
art concepts learned during work time, then followed. In a program
like this, with so much personal freedom allowed, the children
were extremely well behaved and the class very orderly. Teachers
were always available to answer questions and provide encouragement and help.

In my own toddler art classes at Young at Art I always focus
my attention on one concept when planning for a class. For example, on "Red Day" we have an all-red snack, such as strawberries and cranberry juice, listen to songs about red, and read books
about the color. We draw and paint in red (or, with older children,
in various tints and shades of red) and we cut and paste red paper
of differing textures. This leaves the children completely free to
make their own creative discoveries while working within the confines of a structure. Freedom without this type of structural framework quickly becomes chaos.

These teaching techniques contrast enormously with some of
the highly structured art classes I have observed over the years.
When every child was required to make the same picture and use
the materials in the same way as every other child, learning was
totally controlled by an adult and behavior was affected adversely.
More learning was prevented or interrupted than was initiated.
Invariably, all hell would break loose at the first chance. A simple
break in routine, such as hand-washing, could provoke bedlam,
and passing out paint brushes invariably involved pushing, stealing, and tears. In "laissez faire" classes, on the other hand, where
children are free to work but without interest from the teachers and
without the structure of a routine, discipline also breaks down. In
classes where teachers provide a solid framework within which
total freedom is permitted, children have less reason to overstep
the boundaries of that framework. Teachers' expectations are very
important, and should never dictate the specifics of how a work of
art must look.

If your child does go to an art class, try to find one that parents
stay for. If you don't stay for the class, do find out what the teacher
did and plan some follow-up activities at home. When you pick
your child up after class, be sure to offer a warm greeting. I once
taught an hour-long class where mothers were not permitted to
stay, and noticed that some mothers returned after the class without even making eye contact with their children, while others

kissed them and paid special attention to the art the child was carrying. An hour away from your child seems hardly a long enough time to catch your breath, but is a very long time to the child.

Parental Excursions

Parents have to go on excursions as well as children do. As I said in Part I, I don't believe in second honeymoons for parents of very young children, since babies feel abandoned when excluded from the family circle. There does come a time, however, when you will want to leave your child overnight or for a few days and will feel that the child is ready to be left without suffering. Who the child is left with and how ready the child is to be on his or her own should affect the decision. I know one family who hired a baby-sitter that the child didn't know when they went away for two weeks. One day she found him on the floor of his mother's closet holding her robe to his face.

I felt my son was becoming increasingly independent and he seemed ready to be left behind when he was three, so I attended a professional conference for two days. Jason stayed at home with his father, not a stranger. This special time for them enriched the experience by cementing their relationship. Jason saw me off at the airport and picked me up on arrival, which, I think, helps a young child understand "where Mommy is." I planned busy days for him while his Dad was at work, setting up play dates with his favorite friends and dinner dates with his grandmother and favorite aunt. His dad worked shorter hours than usual. I called three times a day —first thing in the morning and at lunch and dinner time. With each call I revealed the location of another gift I had hidden around the house and he ran off to find it as soon as we hung up. Carefully chosen gifts can reassure a child that feeling lonely sometimes is okay. Nicki Weiss's book *Waiting* and Margaret Wise Brown's *The Runaway Bunny* both deal with being away from Mom. Stuffed mother and baby animal sets to be played with and cuddled can be nice and can be purchased or made out of old socks. A toy telephone allows the child to "talk" to Mom between real phone calls. Gifts do not have to be extravagant to remind the child of Mother's love; I made a crown out of (used) shiny wrapping paper for Jason that he loved. Other gifts he enjoyed that cost nothing include a picture of Superman I cut out of an ad in a magazine and pasted on a colored paper "card," a cape I fashioned out of an old baby blanket, and the Aquaman shirt I made by painting this su-perhero on an old, badly stained shirt with fabric paint (to hide the stains). Kiss and hug your child's pillow before leaving, and tell him or her that when he or she wants a hug and kiss to magically get one from the pillow.

EIGHTEEN

Toys, Playthings, and Playmates

Timing is very important with toys at this age, and that fact can be used to your advantage. If you are going to fly in a plane, for example, it can be tremendously exciting and will stimulate very meaningful play. After you have been settled in on the airplane for a while, present the child with a gaily wrapped, small toy airplane.

A toy airplane will surely be appreciated by the child who is taking an airplane trip.

This appropriate gift will hold your child's attention at this time for longer than a different toy would, will make everyone's flight happier, and will help the child digest a lot of information he or she is absorbing through imitative and fantasy play.

A new baby doll when you visit a family with a new baby, a doctor's bag before or after a visit to the doctor, a book about animals in conjunction with a zoo visit, a paint brush and a jar of paint after a visit to a museum, a "hard hat" after viewing construction and a car just like "our car" before a long drive are just a few ideas of ways to reinforce learning and enhance new experiences for your child. These well-timed gifts are so much more meaningful than a room full of toys on Christmas morning.

Two-to-three-year-olds, while they still want to do the things you do, are becoming increasingly fascinated with toys. You'll want to budget more money for store-bought toys during this year than any other. Listening to and observing your child are the most effective ways to know what toys would be of interest. One time I stood in line at the cash register at a five-and-ten with my son waiting to pay for an inexpensive plastic car he had chosen. A family stood on line behind us, with a child about the same age. He saw the car and asked his mother for one. She said, "No, I picked out a horn for you." He cried and cried, insisting with his limited vocabulary that he didn't want the horn, he wanted a car. I think that mother just didn't understand the value of listening to her child's expressed needs. She would have gotten far more value for her money if she had given the child the toy he was ready to play with. Decision-making is a difficult skill to master, and it should play a part in every child's life from the very beginning. Choosing between a horn and a car now paves the way for choosing between more significant options later on!

Protection versus Overprotection

Children need adult supervision twenty-four hours a day, but that supervision should *not* be in the form of preventing exploration. Good supervision involves offering guidance and assistance when it is appropriate. Children learn from their exploration, and occasional cuts and scrapes should be treated as medals of learning, not catastrophes. Once when we were visiting friends, my child found a razor in the sink and touched the blade to "see if it was sharp." He cut himself. He learned an important lesson about

Offer useful information instead of dire warnings to a child who shows interest in a sharp instrument.

razor blades and got only a kiss on his "boo-boo" and a bandage from me—no lectures. I knew that it was I who deserved the lecture, for allowing a two-year-old to explore a new house unsupervised.

How does a knife cut an apple? Long before a child can safely use this type of utensil, he or she will want to try. When a child reaches for a sharp knife, as every child surely does, don't say "No, don't touch." Saying "Never touch a knife, you might cut yourself" is the traditional way to handle this situation. Try instead, "Hold the brown handle, not the shiny blade. The blade is very sharp." Help the child hold it properly and describe how it works by guiding the child's hand while together you cut the apple. Giving the child a blunt knife and demonstrating its proper use while staying close by for protection will not only improve the child's skill with tools but, more importantly, will teach that child to be self-confident in approaching new and unfamiliar tasks.

> The watchful parent who guides and directs at every turn conveys the idea that the world is full of dangers that the child cannot handle. Overprotection says, "You are not competent," rather than, "You are lovable." It undermines self-respect.*

At one time my child reached for a hatchet, and even then I didn't scream "no," much as I would have liked to. I said instead, "The blade is very sharp, and if you drop the hatchet you would be very badly hurt, so hold it with both hands and hold it over the wood, not over your body." He did so, without mishap, but two other mothers in the room were so upset seeing him holding this potentially dangerous tool that they left the room. If I had said "no," I would have simplified life for myself at that moment, but I would have either stifled curiosity or postponed it to a more dangerous time—when my back was turned.

One friend whom I admire enormously has a son who is a

* Dorothy Corkille Briggs, *Your Child's Self-Esteem* (Garden City, N.Y.: Doubleday & Co., 1975), p. 62.

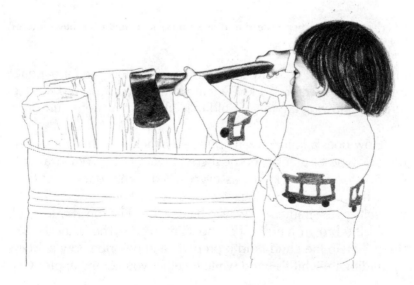

hemophiliac. In his case, a cut can be a cause for concern, but when he was at the age of peak exploration she bought him padded knee guards and was always prepared. Her son had as many cuts and scrapes as any healthy child, and probably as many as he would have gotten if she'd made him a nervous wreck screaming, "No, no," all day long.

Once a visiting friend bought a child a small cactus plant as a gift. The following day her mother noticed it in her room and said, "Oh look, a prickly cactus plant, let's see what it feels like." The child burst into tears and would have nothing to do with it. The well-meaning friend who gave it to her did so with a strong warning never to touch it. But a child never understands things merely by looking; touching is essential. She found this warning frightening and the cactus plant so ominous that it had to be thrown away.

My son was permitted to use scissors, knives, and even that hatchet long before other children were. But he never went out, even within our building or on our terrace, alone. You can't really say "Don't talk to strangers" to a child, who hears you being friendly and cordial to strangers every day. Also, the admonition not to talk to strangers is a direct order from you, an adult, not always helpful in every dangerous situation. You don't want your child to grow up suspicious of everyone, but no child should have to fend for him- or herself against neighborhood bullies, unsavory adults, drunks, etc. It is safest to teach your child to think for him- or herself, and stay close until he or she is old enough to do so.

Gifts

I am a big believer in "presents" to communicate love. I found that when I had to leave my child with a baby-sitter and he didn't want me to leave, an assurance that I would be back right "after lunch" and would bring a present diminished his anxiety. Gifts can be anything that shows the child you thought about him or her while you were away. They should be little toys or other objects rather than candy or cookies. Using sweets as rewards sets an unhealthy precedent. A lollipop may be slightly less expensive than a book or toy now, but over the long run costs much more, if only in dentist and doctor bills. I never made a big deal about sweets, one way or another. My son never liked them. I found that he was just as pleased when I excitedly handed him "the very first autumn leaf of the season" as he was when I returned with the top of the Fisher-

Price line. Fruit, picture postcards, art supplies, books, and toys were all ways to say: "I love you and I missed you when I was out." I kept a stock of five or six inexpensive wrapped gifts in case I didn't have a chance to find a gift when I was out. By the time Jason was two and a half, he was bringing home presents to me when he went out. I must say that even a handful of half-dead weeds made me feel very loved indeed!

Once when I was about three, my mother returned from a day-long shopping trip and when I asked her if she had brought me a present, she reminded me that I had been naughty in the morning —therefore no present. I still remember the feeling of painful rejection. Six or eight hours after the fact is no time to punish a toddler. I stamped my foot and replied, "When I grow up and have a baby, even if she be's bad I'll buy her a present." Everyone was terribly amused by my ungrammatical outburst at the time, but I've been true to my word. If I leave my son, he knows he can count on my always returning with a small gift. I bring it because I think gifts are one way to show him that I love him, even when he's naughty. It is a simple expression that a child can understand better than he or she can understand other sacrifices or more sophisticated, subtle loving expressions. Although my son did occasionally say, "What did you bring me?" before he said, "hello," I never doubted that he was glad to see me. Whether you call it bribery or behavior modification doesn't change the fact that gifts can work wonders.

Once I had been gone only a little while and hadn't thought to bring a gift. As I explained to Jason why I hadn't gotten anything for him, he listened glumly. I unpacked some groceries I had picked up on the way home and suddenly he brightened. "You didn't forget, Mommy. Look! You bought my favorite toothpaste." He was glad to accept the tube of toothpaste as his gift that day because children want and need to believe in their parents. I never let my secret stash of little gifts get so low again.

Children are not spoiled by having a lot of toys and can never be too loved. The "spoiled" human beings of our society are the ones who, as children, didn't get enough love and attention. For an object-oriented child, a gift of a toy does add to his or her sense of worth. As for his being "spoiled" by these frequent gifts as expressions of love, I can only say that when my son was three, he found a dozen or so gaily wrapped presents from Santa under the tree on Christmas and said: "But Mommy! What if there won't be anything left for all of the other children!" You can't give too much to your child. If you are generous and giving, your child will grow up to be also. Those who are stingy and covet what others have usually feel deprived. Those who receive objects *in place of* time and love, instead of as an expression of love, are really deprived. It can be how and why a child receives gifts that prevents "spoiling." I never found that frequent gifts made my son jaded. The right toy at the right time could send him into a frenzy of excitement, even though he did receive toys frequently. I always told him that if a stranger ever offered to buy or give him anything, he should say "no, thank you," come home and tell me what he'd been offered, and I would immediately get it for him! I wanted him to believe that.

Of course, children often ask for far more objects than we can possibly give them. They need to know that you *want* to give it to them much more than they care about the actual object. It is a good idea to communicate love by giving the child what he or she asks for as much as possible, and for no better reason than the fact that it was requested. When your budget won't permit, you don't have to give the child a lesson in finances. A lesson in love is far more necessary. So instead of "No, we can't afford it!" say something like, "Oh, I would love to be able to buy that for you," or, if the child's birthday is a safe distance away you can say, "Maybe I'll be able to save enough money to buy that for your birthday." "Maybe we should add that to our list for Santa," "Let's get it next time we're in a toy store," or "Why not?" were some of my favorite euphemisms for *"no!"* They work only when you have said "yes" enough times to convince your child that you really care about his or her desires.

Organizing Toys

As a toy collection grows, it is easy for it to get chaotic. A sense of security is fostered through organization of play space and materials. It is helpful to separate the toys into categories. This facilitates clean-up and also lets you see when you have too much of one type of toy and not enough of another. Some categories:

Puzzles	Art supplies
Books	Dress-up clothes
Records	Blocks

Tools

Vocational toys
    (doctor bag, typewriter, etc.)

Vehicles

Trains

Ride-on toys

Airplanes, rocket ships

Dolls

Animals

Sand toys

Water toys

Housekeeping toys

Push-pull toys

Draw or paste a simple picture of a car on the outside of the closet or box where cars are kept, a bear on the stuffed-animal shelf, an airplane on the airplane shelf, etc. Buy an inexpensive children's dictionary or save toy catalogs that come in the mail to obtain the pictures you need. Cover the picture completely with clear Con-Tact paper to prevent it from peeling off. This picture-reading is an introduction to reading. When Jason was five and drawing realistic pictures he drew new labels for all of his storage bins during a long, rainy afternoon. It is just a matter of time before

Use picture labels. Picture decoding is a pre-reading activity.

the child begins putting things in the proper place for him- or herself. In addition to separating and labeling all toys, keep them near the spot where they will be most likely to be used. Keep all water toys accessible to the sink and bathtub, art supplies near the easel, etc. A child who wants to play with a car and always knows exactly where to find one gains an important control over his or her own play, a feeling of independence, and a sense of security. Don't keep toys on high shelves as this creates an unnecessary dependence on adult assistance.

Toys in Nature

Despite a love affair with toys and objects, and except for other human beings, the natural world is still the thing that most fascinates children and is their best teacher. Sunlight, sand, and water are the three best toys in the world. The sun tells us all about shadows and time, water play gives us an opportunity to deal with the properties of liquids, and sand demonstrates gravity and encourages building.

Your reactions to your child's play and the play experiences you provide have a profound influence on your child's life. One sunny, warm afternoon after a heavy rain, I took Jason to the playground, which had a huge puddle right in the middle of it. Naturally, he made a beeline for it. My only comment was "That looks like fun!" After a few minutes I realized that all of the other mothers were glaring at me, and I heard things like, "Tommy, don't you dare go in that puddle," and "Just because that boy is allowed to go in the puddle, don't think that you can." For the remainder of the afternoon, I remained one of only two mothers who permitted our children to get their feet wet. Jason had a great time and played in the puddle for a full hour and a half, proving that attention span is directly related to interest level. Unless it is frigid outside, why not let your child play in a puddle if he or she expresses interest in doing so? Wet feet aren't really a disaster on a warm day, and I'm sure that the puddle was at least as educational as any piece of equipment in the playground. Being a good parent really is providing these open-ended opportunities and being willing to offer the support your child needs to grow. Sometimes being a good parent can be as simple as being willing to always carry along an extra set of dry clothes and extra shoes, or being willing to mop the floor. It makes all the difference to your child. On the next rainy day,

Rain puddles are educational and fun.

remember that a rainy afternoon is entertainment in itself. Instead of hiding indoors, go outside with your child and take a walk, wash your hair in the rain, or take your shoes off and do a rain dance.

Use your imagination to plan other water-play variations that will stimulate the child's interest as well. For instance:

1. Have a "car wash" with sponges, rags, and soapy water, a hose if possible, and, of course, all of the toy cars you can find.

2. Add a drop of food coloring to the bath or to a sinkful of water. Have two cups of different colored water so the children can experiment with color mixing.

3. Fill a sink, a giant plastic bowl, or other large container with water and a small amount of liquid soap. Show your child how to make bubbles with an egg beater.

4. Provide funnels, sprayers, and various sized containers to provide experimentation with volume and measurement.

5. Provide doll babies to bathe, boats to sail, etc.

6. Invite a friend; a rainy afternoon can seem to go by in an instant with a friend and a bathtub full of bubbles.

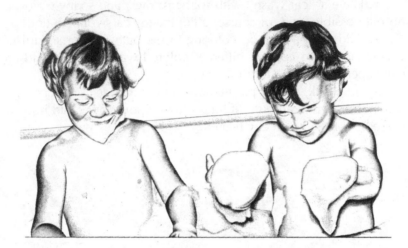

Since your supervision is required for water play, you need to be creative about using your time well. I've paid my bills, written books, and read newspapers sitting on the floor of the bathroom while my son played in the tub. I've cut up many salads at the bathroom sink instead of the kitchen sink, and if I ever have another baby I'll be sure to have a telephone installed in the bathroom too. If you feel that you can't supervise your child in the bath or at the sink all afternoon, fill a bucket with water and water toys and place it on the floor near you, which you can cover with a vinyl tablecloth.

Books for young children about water are listed in Appendix II. My reviews of these books can be found in Appendix III.

The best play always has to do with expanding one's understanding of the environment. How does the world look through rose-colored glasses? Or blue?

What will paper scraps look like reflected in two mirrors at the same time? All of these, and many more, are very important questions to be pondered, given the time and, hopefully, the interest of adults. The real world is what your child is preparing him- or herself for, and play time reflects this. Your child will frequently be

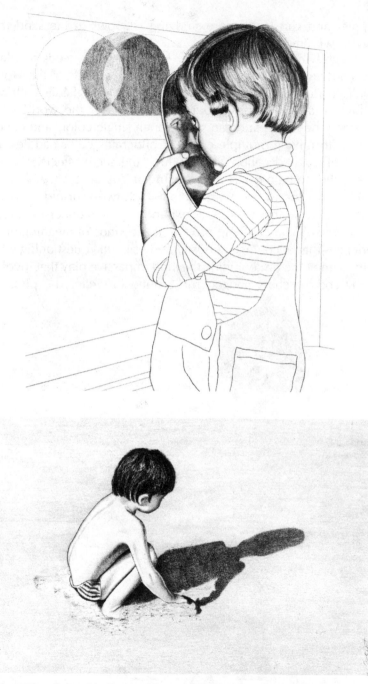

The best play always has to do with expanding one's understanding of the environment.

happier and can learn more studying shadows in the sand than playing with most toys.

Magnifying glasses, magnets, kaleidoscopes, seeds to plant, and aquariums all help your child see new aspects of the world. Small World Toys make "color glass play"—eyeglasses with red, yellow, and blue lenses. Your child can view the world while adjusting the lenses and can see through single colors and experiment with mixing multiple colors. Childcraft's color paddles and scraps of colored cellophane produce the same effects. We use these props to help teach color mixing at Young at Art. A kaleidoscope and a periscope will fascinate the two-year-old. Shovels, funnels, sifters, and buckets all expand a child's understanding of the universe. You can help provide these kinds of meaningful experiences that encourage curiosity and scientific questioning while at the same time discouraging the kind of passive play that involves sitting and watching gadgets run around in circles, beeping and

Toys, like children, should start life with infinite options and possibilities for action.

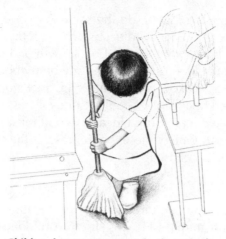

Children learn grown-up jobs through play.

flashing lights. Toys should, like children, start life with an endless amount of options and possibilities for action.

There are some books that stimulate thinking about sand, shadows, and environment that your child will enjoy: see Appendix II under Shadow and Clay.

Vocational Toys

Some toys and experience experimenting with adult "toys" help a child understand adult work. My son was fascinated with my copy machine, so at age two he was appointed "copy man" of the office, and was very proud of the title. He knew that I was writing

a book, so I suggested that he do the same. We bought a book of bound, blank pages, and he did so. The scribbles he did in it regularly are an important record of his growth and development, and surely as valuable to our family as any of my books have ever been. Fisher-Price makes every child's favorite vocational toys, which have interchangeable people: sturdy garages with ramps and hand-activated crank-up elevators, dollhouses, firehouses, cars and trucks, etc. One of these that represents the child's special interest should be purchased.

Weapon Play

I let my son know that we didn't like guns because they are used to hurt people and animals. He was strictly forbidden from the very beginning to ever hit, kick, or bite another person, so why would I let him shoot anyone? Although he, no doubt, played with guns at his friends' houses, I felt this was an important way to help him understand our family's philosophy regarding how other human beings should be treated. Fantasy play is a rehearsal for adult life. Guns and swords provide opportunities to act out frightening, aggressive, and violent solutions to life's problems. Since these are not the solutions we want our children to find for life's difficulties, weapon play is dangerous. I know that playing with guns does not mean that a child will grow up to be a killer, but, since a child learns at every play experience, why encourage the child to learn that killing is fun? We may not always be able to prevent weapon play, but why encourage it? When someone bought a battery-operated space gun for Jason's birthday, we took it back to the toy store and told Jason to choose anything else he wanted in exchange for the gun. Although he cooperated very reluctantly, the gun cost $12.00 and Jason was delighted to discover that he could choose four $3.00 toys in exchange for it.

New York police officer Michael Cafarella says, "Children use guns to point at people. Many of the accidents we have to deal with involve people who pick up real guns and use them as they did toy guns. Police officers and soldiers often have problems learning how to handle a real weapon because the way they used toy guns comes so naturally to them. Using a real gun actually requires a lot of skill." Officer Cafarella, who carries a gun daily in the course of his work, said he would never buy one for a child of his own.

NINETEEN

Art
Experiences

Two-and-one-half-to-three-year-olds come to a point in their scribbling where they recognize that, quite by accident, shapes they have drawn resemble realistic objects. They will therefore give names to their pictures after having drawn them. The next time they view the very same drawing, they might see the similarity in the shapes to a completely different object and choose a new name for the picture. The adult can best help by pointing out what it is that the lines have in common with the objects. For example, "That certainly is round, just like a wheel." The following day can become, "I can see that shape is as round as the sun." Both statements are equally accurate and help the child see how all round shapes are related. The roundness of the shapes remains, but the title and description of the picture changes. Sometimes parents and teachers accept the first name as the "true" meaning of the picture and write the child's description on the paper. They do the child a disservice and stifle flexible, fluid thinking. By writing the child's original comments on the child's picture they offer that all-powerful adult sanction to the idea, often eliminating the possibility for the child to see the appropriateness of a new title for the picture later on. Amanda's cheery mandala drawing might very well have become the sun, a flower, and a multitude of other things, but her teacher's acceptance of the first title removed those later possibilities.

Treat your child's art as you would professional art in your home. Display it in frames rather than on the refrigerator. Try not

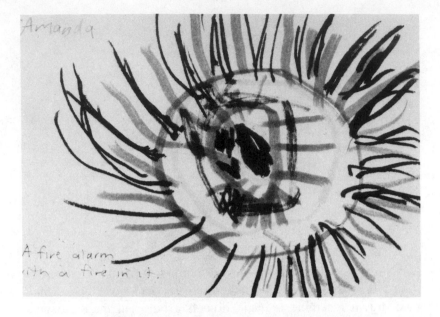

to choose the pictures you like best but rather the ones the child seems to have shown the most interest in doing. It is difficult not to impose adult standards of what is "pretty" on children's art. Children very quickly pick up on what their parents like and don't like and can sacrifice development in exchange for approval. Don't be surprised if your child doesn't remember if he or she actually did a certain picture, or if the child throws it away. The process is what is important to the child, not the product. Nevertheless, you should never be the one to throw away your child's art. Invest in a 24" x 36" folder to store the pictures in. We use about two a year, which should give us forty folders by the time our son is grown up. I think he'll enjoy having them to show his children, and if not, there is plenty of time to throw them out!

Children are not fooled by parents who hang framed realistic art in their living room and tape scribbles and early drawings to the refrigerator. It is never too early to think of giving your child's art an important place in your home. You can invest a very small amount of money in a simple, standard-sized frame from the five-and-ten. Buy the same-sized pads of inexpensive drawing paper, and when your child proudly shows you a work of art, you'll be ready to display it as professionally as in a museum. Sticking it in a standard size 11" x 14" frame is as simple as is taping it to the

THE FAMILY CIRCUS®   By Bil Keane

"Mommy hung my plaster handprint in the LIVIN' ROOM, not the recreation room!"

refrigerator, but it looks so much nicer. Your child will know the difference. Giving it a prominent place in your home signifies that it is important and valuable to you.

If you want your child to be confident in the area of art, it's important to reinforce the idea that you appreciate and value his or her work. Your interest, and the fact that you proudly display it, is never lost on the child. If others criticize, laugh at, or don't appear to appreciate it, it undermines your efforts. An older sibling, in another stage of art development, can have a devastating effect on a child. Part of your job as a parent is to "protect" the child from the older child's comments, which may wound, and whose example may confuse and cause feelings of inadequacy.

As an art teacher, I frequently spent several weeks working with children as they painstakingly and lovingly made gifts for their parents. "What is it?" is the first thing many well-meaning parents asked. If Mom doesn't even know what it is, it couldn't be very good, could it? Or, if it was a present for Mom, Dad frequently also took the child on a shopping trip for another gift—thereby communicating to the child that his or her efforts were not really good enough to give to Mother and that "store-bought is better."

Maintaining Interest in Scribbling

When your child appears disinterested in scribbling, it may mean he or she is concentrating on other areas of development. Drawing with a new utensil, on a different shape paper, or on an interesting texture such as sandpaper, corrugated cardboard, parchment, or fabric will offer a stimulating change and new challenges, and may stimulate a renewed interest in scribbling.

Fingerpainting

If your child is just beginning to fingerpaint now, you should offer only one color at a time and allow for free manipulation of the material. However, if the child is an experienced finger painter, provide red and yellow to magically create orange, blue and yellow to make green, or red and blue to become purple.

Challenge your child by offering new materials.

Painting

Between the ages of two and three, painting with a brush is still a kinesthetic experience for a child, so offering a lot of colors can detract from the experience. You can provide variety by offering black paint on white paper one day and white paint on black the next. Children love Day-Glo paint, which is particularly effective on black paper. Variety can be achieved through simple additions to the basic project, such as occasionally trying to paint on corrugated cardboard or sandpaper. By all means, let your child indicate color choice and suggest new and exciting backgrounds, but keep in mind that basic materials are the most important. Pablo Picasso painted every day of his life using the same simple materials. Artists

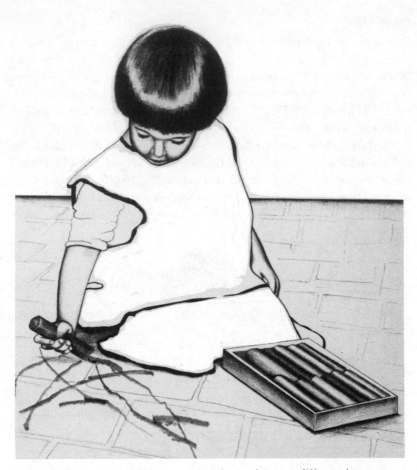

Chalk, which can be blended, smeared, and erased, is very different from crayons and pencils.

do their most creative work with materials with which they are most familiar.

Chalk and a chalkboard are wonderful materials for this age. The contrast of white chalk on a blackboard (which is more fun than the green version, though harder to find) provides a vivid negative image of the usual black lines on white background. It's easy to wipe off and blend with the fingers. Children also love to erase and/or wash it! Chalkboards may be wonderful, but so is the sidewalk if you don't have a chalkboard. The next rain will wash away the chalk after the child has lost interest in it and won't be saddened to see it disappear.

Pre-pasting Activities

Self-stick labels from the stationery store provide a wonderful pre-pasting activity. Brightly colored circles on contrasting paper reinforce learning about the meaning of round without requiring an advanced skill like pasting. As with colors, geometric shapes should be offered one type at a time. Today you can work with circles and then point out some in the environment through the next few days. Play circle games, and read books and sing songs about circles. Save squares for next week. Nothing is to be gained by demonstrating that circles can become pictures, wheels, or lollipops, etc. The child has not yet made the mental connection between making lines and shapes on paper and making realistic objects, despite the fact that he or she can clearly understand (i.e., "read") pictures in a book. Avery and other companies make many different sticker shapes in assorted colors that provide an ideal introduction to pasting. Recently, Avery marketed an "art" kit, but it includes those deadly patterns of trite drawings for the child to fill-in and is overpriced as well. Don't offer your child the new stickers that come in the shape of rainbows, pigs, etc. Those already completed shapes quickly become substitutes for art activity, rather than stimuli for it. Stars are about the most realistic shape I would offer. Pieces of plain and colored masking tape are another way to provide an introduction to pasting that does not require real pasting skill and coordination. You will need to provide the bits and pieces of tape for your child to use. It is important to allow the child to freely arrange the shapes as he or she wishes. As with every new art material the child is introduced to, stickers will also be incorporated into body decorating.

Pasting

If your child has been painting with a brush and has had pre-pasting activities as described above, by age two or two and a half

Self-stick labels from the stationery store provide a wonderful pre-pasting activity.

Different kinds and colors of tape introduce pasting without requiring real pasting skill and coordination.

Stickers will also be incorporated into body decorating just like every new art material offered to the child.

he or she should be able to master pasting. Mix some water with Elmer's or Sobo glue and offer your child a small amount in a low, spill-proof container. The addition of food coloring to the glue makes the smeared paste that is inevitable in early pictures an attractive addition to the art. Do keep in mind, however, that "attractive" is not the goal; learning, stretching one's mind, and growing are! Most children apply paste all over the background paper as they would on a painting. Try not to say "no" or "That's not the way to do it." Remember, how the picture turns out is not as important as is material manipulation and bolstering your child's confidence.

Give your child scraps of one type of free form or geometric shape cut from construction paper. Demonstrate how to apply paste to the small scrap, put the brush back in the container, and place the scrap on the background. Don't impose your own expectations on the child. Learning about paste involves stickiness, so don't worry if there is glue all over the paper.

Body Decorating

Face and body decorating is a universally practiced art which can become feminine or masculine depending on the society in question. Being of a society that considers it a feminine activity doesn't automatically negate the urge in little boys. It's better to let them get it out of their systems now—it will not affect their masculinity later on. Here, two-and-a-half-year-old Jason and Jeffrey, in an outdoor setting that posed no threat to the pristine interior, were stripped and told they could do whatever they wanted as long as they stayed in their seats. The boys had a glorious time, looked marvelous, and had as much fun cleaning themselves off as they did doing the body decorating.

You can make your own easy-to-remove makeup by putting two teaspoons of cold cream into a paper cup or cupcake tin, adding a few drops of food coloring, and mixing. The child can apply it with the fingers. It won't stay on for a long time, but it is fun and ideal for play that will be followed up by a very simple clean-up. What a valuable Halloween experience this would be for a child, in contrast to the more usual one of wearing a store-bought replica of a famous cartoon character, and one frequently chosen by an adult too! A little cold cream followed by soap and

Having an adult put makeup on the child "correctly" is missing the point. Adults should never do for children what they prefer to do themselves.

Experimenting—not looking beautiful—is the fun of it.

water renders the child as good as new, though greatly enriched by the experience.

Pipe Cleaners

Pipe cleaners are also fun. Your child can bend, twist, and curl them into endless shapes. No need to frustrate the child by introducing stick figures. The fun comes from the manipulation of the material. Free experimentation is the best way for the child to learn new skills.

Clay and Play Dough

Clay and play dough are favorite materials of this age group. Buy it or prepare your own by mixing

> 4 cups sifted flour
> 1 cup salt
> 1½ cups water or more (mix slowly to desired consistency)
> 1 tablespoon cooking oil
> a few drops of food coloring.

If you use a little less than the required amount of flour and put the remaining flour in the shaker, your child will enjoy shaking it over the play dough. Add the food coloring to the water before mixing to achieve even color. Modeling clay, mud, and firing clay offer interesting variations of texture and potential.

Molds that produce adult-made shapes are of no value and should not be offered either with clay, play dough, or sand. They don't encourage manipulation of the material, which is the way children learn from this kind of play.

Spontaneous Art

The avant-garde notion of conceptual art is understood by all young children, though their notions are frequently at odds with what most adults think art should look like. When my son very purposefully climbed up on our kitchen counter and proceeded to stick pieces of paper he had drawn on all over our toaster, I praised him for inventing an original art object. Instead of pointing out the inherent problems (like the hazard of fire), I unplugged the toaster and told him that we wouldn't compromise the art by making toast for a while.

Even the kitchen toaster can stimulate conceptual art.

Fostering Creativity

It is essential for adults to recognize and encourage their children's creative actions. It can be difficult for adults who do not experience inventiveness in their own lives, and who never work with art materials themselves, to recognize creativity in children. Too often they view a deviation from the norm as "wrong" or "naughty." We are all born with curious minds and the capacity for creativity. For most, the ability atrophies early on. It is discouraged at every turn and quickly abandoned along with bottles and diapers. Creative actions are hard to recognize when we are accustomed to calling pretty flower pictures "creative," even though they may have been done according to numbered directions.

Frequently people say they offer preschoolers art activities from my Anti-Coloring Books®. When I reply that the books were intended for much older children, the answer I frequently receive is, "But my child is very bright." High intelligence doesn't mean that your child can skip over the need to do age-appropriate art now. Presenting the infant with a task that is too difficult will only frustrate him or her and elicit dependency responses. If the child shows signs of readiness, present appropriate, reasonable challenges that encourage development. Just because a three-year-old is smart doesn't mean he or she should draw realistic objects. I have seen some children of this age draw realistic people or objects and that ability did not indicate either high intelligence or art talent. It is much more indicative of a type of upbringing. Parents who undervalue scribbles and offer "instruction in drawing" will occasionally influence their children to abandon scribbling and draw to please adults. The developmental sequence is thus interrupted and advances will probably never be fully regained. The loss is evident later on when art is abandoned and when writing becomes difficult.

> Creativity is a way of thinking. It is not synonymous with a high IQ.*

The creative individual approaches problems with fresh solutions and is not afraid to come up with new ideas. You don't always have to get out the paints, paste, or clay to stimulate your child's creative thought processes. You can do so while driving the car or waiting your turn in a doctor's office. Make up a silly song and then encourage your child to do the same. Ask questions that have many correct answers: "What if . . .?" "How could we . . .?" "What else could we use a . . . for?" "What would it feel like to

---

* Barbara Kuczen, Ph.D., *Childhood Stress* (New York: Delacorte Press, 1982), p. 188.

Encourage the child to find new uses for tools.

be a . . . ?" "How else could you do that?" Respond positively to your child's new ideas, rather than pointing out difficulties in them.

Finding new uses for tools can be creative. Turning a rolling pin, traditionally used to roll out clay, on its side to poke holes in the clay shows an open-ended thinking process that should be praised and encouraged. Intervention to show the "correct" way to use a rolling pin prevents further experimentation and learning. This action, far more than how "pretty" the resulting sculpture may (or may not) be, is what should be focused on. Emphasizing the process, not the product, is the key rule here.

One reason art has been sadly neglected in early childhood development may be that art is not a widely respected profession in our society. Many artists are thought of as "wild," and financially very few artists do well. Parents, therefore, having no desire for their children to grow up to be artists, neglect art education. Art is, however, "a way of learning, not something to be learned."*

Plato described a whole system of teaching children through

---

* Viktor Lowenfeld and W. Lambert Brittain, *Creative and Mental Growth,* 6th edition (New York: Macmillan, 1970), p. 53.

art. The high value placed on recognizing real objects in children's art says much more about our inadequacies than it does about our children's abilities. Parents who recognize the fact that scribbling is hard work for young children and that it is work toward an important goal are helping their children grow and develop.

Ronald Lee Rubin, consultant to the Vermont Department of Education, wrote these six justifications for art education:

1. The arts are basic particularly to the development of sensory perceptual thinking which, in turn, is critical to learning communication skills and developing verbal, mathematical, and reasoning skills.

2. Arts education is necessary for learning conceptual processing skills—sequence, balance, and analogy—required to effectively learn reading, language arts, mathematics, and other basic skills.

3. Arts education provides students opportunities to learn how to understand and use symbolic forms. The concept of nearly every curriculum area is based upon cognitive symbolic forms.

4. Arts education is an effective means of improving students' conceptual development, basic to all types of expressive and receptive communications, and the ability to effectively interpret reality.

5. The arts are a primary means of educating students to be resourceful, self-disciplined, constructive, inventive, self-directed, and critical problem-solvers.

6. And, of course, arts education is a major method by which societies develop and communicate their cultural heritage.*

At a "Fire Museum" I observed a mother with her young son. She told me that he was a frequent visitor and never tired of seeing the fire trucks. His excitement was clear to everyone. At one point, he came up to his mom and said, "When we get home, draw a fire truck for me." Children's natural interests are the best motivation for creative expression. Once Mom draws a fire truck for him, though, he'll almost never draw one for himself. If he stops drawing the thing he loves best, he'll stop drawing altogether. Any child can see the big difference between his or her own and an adult's drawing. It is only natural for that child to assume that the adult's way of drawing, particularly when that adult is his mother,

---

* Ronald Lee Rubin, "Six Basic Reasons," *Arts and Activities*, February 1983, p. 28.

is superior. A child's style of self-expression should never be squelched. I can't think of any justification for drawing for your child. Children who draw for themselves, and who know their parents genuinely appreciate their efforts, are the lucky ones. Drawing for your child reinforces his or her feeling that adult, realistic work is valuable and his or hers childish, but sincere efforts are unworthy. Drawing and the problem-solving exercised within it is as essential to every child's intellectual and emotional development as food is to the physical development. Would you eat for your child just because you are neater and more proficient at it?

Group Art

A few children working together on very large mural paper can receive an invaluable social experience in group interaction and cooperation. Murals present one problem: Who gets to take it home? In one of my son's classes, the children worked on a ten-foot-long group picture in which each child became involved in real creative activity. At the end of the class, however, the children's teacher hastily cut the mural up into equal parts and sent one section home with each child. This is nothing more than a souvenir of the experience, because by cutting up the mural, the teacher was not teaching anything about the real meaning of the group activity. By doing so, it denied the importance of the unified whole reflecting more than the individual parts. Some alternative solutions to the problem: Let the mural stay in the place where it was made, be it school, playground, or one child's home. Or, instead of making a mural, have the group make a giant puzzle, with each child working on a separate puzzle piece and the group as a whole working on the background. Individual children who wish to can take home their puzzle pieces, without destroying the integrity of the experience. Supplement this activity by reading either *The Missing Piece* or *The Missing Piece Meets the Big O*, two books about puzzles by Shel Silverstein.

Materials and Work Space

Fortunately, many interesting art materials cost next to nothing. Save old wrapping paper, sandpaper, ribbons, doilies, and the tissue and colored cellophane that comes wrapped around some items you buy anyway. But do purchase high-quality paint, paper, and brushes. It is difficult to paint with abandon when the bristles fall out of the brushes, or to glue when the background paper keeps curling up.

A child who only recently learned to differentiate between red and blue certainly doesn't need sixty-four different colors. The maximum amount of colors you need to buy of any drawing utensil is eight, and I would not even offer all of these at one session. Even if your child is bright, there is nothing to be gained by offering a confusing number of colors. The child will have to spend more time making choices than drawing or painting. One exception: Do invest in a set of twenty-five Sandford's Craypas or chalks. They include four different shades of several different colors. First, offer one to the child so that he or she can become accustomed to the material. Then, offer all four shades of one color. As the child draws you can talk about light, medium, darker, and darkest.

You can help free your child by providing an appropriate work space. Creativity does not flourish when Mom and Dad carry on about a mess. Don't assume that art means "mess." With careful planning and an understanding of normal development, you can easily avoid any destruction both to your home and to your child's self-esteem.

> I don't think of working with art materials as "messy," although it is very possible that it can be so. When you sit down to a beautifully set meal table, it is impossible to eat without creating some disorder. Forks and knives are rearranged, plates and glasses will need washing, and crumbs may fall. Likewise, as you paint, cut, paste, or use clay, things will get redistributed. But they need not get out of hand if you plan and set up the workspace carefully.*

Set aside an art work space in your home. It can be in the child's room, playroom, corner of the basement, laundry room, kitchen, bath or other area where you can allow the child continual access. Cover the floor with a drop cloth. Set up the materials in a convenient manner and stop worrying. Almost everything is washable. I was even able to remove permanent Magic Marker from my living room rug with Afta-brand cleaning fluid. It is also a good idea to

---

* Muriel Silberstein-Storfer, with Mablen Jones, *Doing Art Together* (New York: Simon and Schuster, 1982), p. 22.

Painting on unusual new surfaces can be a way to rekindle a waning interest in painting. It can also produce mind-boggling visual effects.

keep on hand a large jar of School Paint Remover.* Above all, children are completely washable. It's most sensible to dress them in old clothes, a good smock, or nothing at all.

Tricky Spots and Their Cure

Chewing gum on the bedspread? Poster paint on the walls? Crayon marks everywhere? You must have small children! Take heart. Minor mishaps needn't always become total disasters. Here's a way to deal with them.

• Chewing gum on the bedspread, or the pillow, the rug or just about any place, will be easier to remove if you just run an ice cube over the gum several times, then pick it off. Dab at any remaining stain with cleaning fluid.

• Poster paint on the walls, or finger paint, tempera paint, or watercolors, will be easier to remove if you add one fourth teaspoon of liquid dishwashing detergent to the paint before the child uses it. If the walls are painted, dab at the area with a clean damp cloth, trying to remove as much surface accumulation as possible. Then rub gently with baking soda on a damp cloth. Paint marks on porous wallpaper or unfinished wood are virtually impossible to remove.

• Marker scribblings anywhere present a real problem. So many different types of chemical formulas are used in markers that

* From The Formative Years, Box 130-1, RR #3, Westbrook, CT 06498.

there's no universal remover. Your best bet is to write the manufacturer, giving information about the type of marker and surface scribbled on. The chances of removing marker scribbling from fabric, plaster, wallpaper, and unfinished wood are very slim, however. As a desperate measure, go over the marks with a clean cloth dipped in liquid detergent and lukewarm water. Then dab the stain with rubbing alcohol. (But be extremely careful. This could damage the surface.)

• Crayon marks on a blackboard can be removed by placing a piece of clean blotting paper (tape it on if you like) over the mark and applying a hot iron. Repeat if necessary. Or rub with a clean cloth dampened with hairspray.

• Crayon marks on wallpaper are difficult to remove. First try using a "kneaded eraser," which you can buy in an art supply store. Gently roll the eraser over the marks. It that doesn't work, crush some white chalk and add dry cleaning solvent to make a paste. Apply to the marks without rubbing. When dry, brush off with a clean tissue. If the paper is washable, you might finish the area with mild soap and water. As a last resort on nonwashable paper, gently rub with baking soda on a clean damp cloth.

• Greasy fingerprints on wallpaper needn't be there permanently. To remove, apply a paste of cornstarch and cleaning fluid. Let dry, then brush off. Repeat if necessary. Remove any last traces of grease by gently rubbing the area with a clean cloth dipped in borax.

• Ballpoint pen marks on painted walls and woodwork. Dab (do not rub) the marks with a clean cloth dampened with distilled white vinegar. Blot frequently.

• Ballpoint pen marks on wallpaper. Dab the marks with a damp cloth until the area is barely dampened. Then, holding a dry cloth underneath the marks to catch any dripping, immediately spray the area lightly with hairspray containing alcohol. Wait a minute, then blot with a clean dry cloth.

• Bloody-nose stains on the mattress and pillows. Apply a thick lump of paste made from cornstarch and cold water over the stain. When the starch is completely dry, run a knife under the hardened mass, which will now contain the blood. Vacuum away any residue and finish by wiping the area with a cloth wrung out in cold water. Repeat if necessary.*

* Lois Libien and Margaret Strong, "How," New York Daily News, Feb. 14, 1982.

TWENTY

Movement

The two-year-old is full of energy and bursting with curiosity. Walking is done with fluidity and the child is now ready to really test his or her physical agility. You may want to enroll him or her in an organized gym class. These classes can be an excellent outlet for energy, a vehicle for self-expression, and a wonderful introduction to group play. The best kind of supervision in this kind of class relies on verbal reflection of the child's actions and motivation. A sense of lightness and fun should be used to encourage children to participate. The teacher should recognize the importance of self-discovery and should encourage improvisation and experimentation. Helpful encouragement involves positive comments and an occasional helping hand; it never involves pushing children to do things they are reluctant to do. "Oh, look! You are walking on your toes. That is called walking on tip-toes. That's a quiet way to walk" might be followed with, "Now would you like to try a loud walk?"

The teacher must be flexible and take cues from the interest evidenced by the children. Fun, not skill acquisition, should be stressed. It is premature to have competition of any kind. The best class provides for exploration, and it provides stimulation; it doesn't set goals or provide a set of expectations. An effective teacher helps children understand what their bodies can do and gives them the words to describe it. A child comes away from such a teacher with a strong sense of confidence and a feeling that trying things out is great fun!

Children must always set their own goals. At this age, skills are increasing and children are able to consciously express themselves through movement. It is important now to refrain from "teaching" the child particular dance steps or ways of doing things. Nothing positive will be gained by attempting to teach skills before the child can achieve success. Learning how to feel good about one's body is an excellent goal. So many dancers cannot dance; they can do a plié, relevé, or other specific steps expertly, but are unable to improvise or create dances. The creative urges they were born with have been effectively suppressed.

> I believe that there is a definite relationship be-
> tween starting formal music lessons or formal
> dancing lessons too early and musical inhibi-
> tion. *

Gym fixtures will naturally motivate the child to learn various skills: ladders for climbing, beams for balancing, perches for jump-ing, etc. In addition to gym equipment, there are some props that help motivate children to use their bodies to the fullest, that any home can provide. All of them are more effective when an adult is nearby to provide language and encouragement, and to help the child when it is necessary. It is imperative that adults do not present some preconceived, adult-approved manner of using these props. They are all most effective when their presence inspires the child to try new things and make up new games or dances. Some props can have the effect of adding interest to movement games and opening up new avenues of learning. Ribbons or crepe paper party streamers help expand children's awareness of the space around them, and add a feeling of grace to their movements. Foam balls provide strengthening exercises for hand and finger muscles and can add a new dimension to traditional finger games. Bubbles are a popular stimulant to activity. The child who last year could only watch them float by can now run after a floating bubble, climb on things or bend to reach one, lie on his or her back to pop one with the feet. The adult can make suggestions and also ask, "What else can we pop a bubble with?" (elbows, noses, bottoms, knees, etc.). Of course no self-respecting toddler will watch an adult blow bub-bles without wanting to try it him- or herself. Some liquid will get

---

* Emma D. Sheehy, *Children Discover Music and Dance. A Guide for Parents and Teach-ers* (New York: Henry Holt and Co., 1959), p. 21.

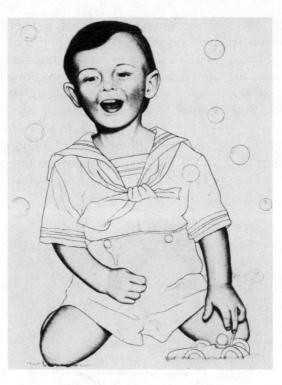

Bubbles are a popular stimulant to activity.

spilled and the necessary breath control takes a lot of practice, but by all means let the toddler try. A little liquid soap mixed with water will make enough bubbles to last an afternoon for pennies. Waiting until the child can do things neatly is waiting too long!

A hoop is a simple-looking object that provides an infinite amount of variety in play. You can jump into a hoop, jump from hoop to hoop, crawl into hoops, pass them to a friend, throw a bean bag into one, do a forward roll through a hoop, etc. Hoops can be used for reaching high and low, crawled through, jumped into and through or up and down in. You can put your ear, hand,

Aren't you grateful no one has figured out how to make a battery-powered hoop?

foot, nose, elbow, and rear end through a hoop. The concept of space can be explored by going inside, outside, or walking around the perimeter of a hoop. Different size hoops help children distinguish sizes, and different color hoops can be used to teach color identification. "Let's jump into the yellow hoop." "Tommy, is this the smallest hoop?" are games that allow for both play and learning. Pretending can be expanded through the use of questions: "How would a frog (kangaroo, snake, bird, etc.) go through a hoop?"

The supervising adult should not be the only one asking these questions. Language is improving by leaps and bounds and children now have the ability to attach word symbols to their activities. Each child should receive positive feedback for whatever movements he or she originates. Children who don't like holding hands in a circle may be willing to join a circle holding hoops. Using the round hoops in a circle reinforces the concept of the round. Aren't you grateful no one has figured out how to make a battery-powered hoop!

Scarves help children more fully explore the range of body movements. Children can actually see the effects of their own body movement reflected in the way the scarf moves. A fast, frenetic arm movement is reflected in the jumpy way the scarf moves, a soft ripple is produced by carefully controlling the pace and arc of the arm's movement. Muscles are stretched to control the movement of the scarf as an understanding of the effects of movement develops. Fantasy play is inspired by the floating quality of scarves, which can remind children of wings and wind.

Songs and music can always be used to stimulate movement. Skating and dancing, for example, are usually accompanied by music and the one is indeed thought of as part of the other. Put on some music and let children improvise. Balls, hoops, scarves, and other props can enrich the experience.

Various water-flotation devices provide parents with a feeling of security around water and are great fun for kids. However, they also provide a false feeling of how the body works in water. Their use should be limited to not more than 50 percent of water time. Your child is ultimately safest when he or she learns how to swim on his or her own.

Water-flotation devices provide a false impression of how the body works in water. Their use should be limited.

TWENTY-ONE

Music

Each of the art forms—the visual arts, music, dance, and movement—provide distinctive ways for the child to express him- or herself creatively. Just as all children can make their own drawings and paintings, so can they improvise their own songs and dances.

> The main purpose of music education in childhood is to provide an effective outlet for feelings. A child's life is so full of restrictions, regulations and frustrations that media of release become essential. Music is one of the best avenues of release: it gives sound to fury, shape to joy, and relief to tension.*

Children who are practicing scales, learning the words to songs someone else wrote, and not making "too much noise" are not being given music as an outlet for their feelings. They are, instead, being robbed of one of the greatest gifts they were born with: the capacity to feel and make music. Children naturally love music. Taking that natural joy away and substituting hard work has turned more children away from music than anything else. Children who, as babies, adored music, find music lessons and practicing a musical instrument the bane of their existence in later years. The fault lies in our adult perception of what children should do rather than expanding on what they already love doing. When did "play" the piano (violin, trumpet, drums, etc.) become "practice" the piano

* Haim G. Ginott, M.D., *Between Parent and Child* (New York: Avon Books), p. 95.

(etc., etc.)? Why have parents and teachers taken the "play" out of music and turned it into "practice" and "work" that seems more like punishment? The unrealistic demands and premature expectations of parents and teachers are the major culprit creating generation after generation of children who refuse to take one more music lesson, only to grow up to regret it. They then repeat the cycle by insisting that their children take music lessons. Somewhere along the way, making music becomes an unpleasant chore instead of the natural joy it started out as and was meant to be. Encourage, don't criticize; expose, but don't force. Children who feel good about the music they are making continue to make music.

In order to appreciate the distinctive sounds each instrument can make and their potential for beauty, a child must hear them. A trip to a local music store can be an exciting musical adventure. If you are lucky, potential customers who are gifted musicians will be trying out instruments. You can show your child that the bigger instruments make deep sounds and the small instruments make high sounds. Showing the child the padded instrument cases will help him or her understand how carefully fragile instruments must

Children who feel good about the music they are making continue to make music.

be handled. As soon as possible, buy real musical instruments rather than toy ones. Consider making a purchase now. A xylophone contains all of the tones of a musical scale. A wooden recorder is a good instrument to start with. Don't expect a child to play melodies or scales. Now is the time for experimentation—seeing what the instrument can do is the best teacher at this point.

Children who are fortunate enough to observe a significant adult making and enjoying music have a head start. This child may not play the sax as well as his father, who is a well-known professional musician, but his dad doesn't want or expect his three-year-old to play like a thirty-year-old.

Watching Dad has its advantages, but children learn by doing far more than they do by observing. If only the grown-ups play the piano or are allowed to touch an instrument, the child is much less likely to develop a real affinity for it. As with painting, if you wait

Exposure to real instruments rather than toy ones helps children to appreciate the distinctive sounds fine instruments can make.

until the child is "old enough" to handle the instrument "properly," you have waited too long. By then the intense curiosity is gone and the spontaneity is lost.

Though the sounds a child produces may not be mellow, the exposure to real instruments is invaluable. Experimentation must include a lot of terrible sounds before a child can recognize beautiful ones. The lesson, when self-taught, will never be lost. This early play that all children delight in engaging in actually provides the fundamentals upon which later music education depends. Do not misinterpret early exposure to mean Suzuki-style classes. The Suzuki method encourages early play of real instruments, but without this very necessary experimentation. The rigid structure of the classes is totally inappropriate for very young children and the directive nature of the instruction can be very frustrating. While Suzuki lessons produce impressive early results, the long-term goal of feeling a very personal relationship with music and musical instruments is ignored.

Your child's vocabulary is expanding, and you should use the

While Suzuki lessons produce impressive early results, the long-term goal of feeling a very personal relationship with music and musical instruments is ignored by the system.

correct musical terms for things whenever possible. For example, "You hit a xylophone with a mallet, not a stick," and "Pitch stands for high and low." Verbalizing for the child helps to provide vocabulary, and it helps clarify and reinforce learning. "When you scratch the drum with your nails, it sounds very different than when you bang on it with your fist." "The smaller keys made higher notes and the big keys made lower notes." "When you bang on the desk, it sounds very different than when you beat on the tom-tom." The scale can be understood as "a flight of stairs, going slowly up, up, up."

With your encouragement, interest can be maintained and the sense of adventure expanded rather than eliminated. "What does the drum sound like if you use a mallet instead of your hand?" "What about if you hit it with your nose, or your shoe?" "What else can you think of to do with a drum?" There is not only one correct way to play an instrument, nor is there only one type of sound that an instrument can make. You can help by providing provocative questions rather than answers, and encouragement rather than control. As always, the limits you set should not intrude too much on the child's ability to experiment freely with the instrument or with sounds. You will be able to recognize the difference between carelessness and curiosity.

> You may find that sitting on drums, throwing drumsticks, hitting others need to be prohibited, but that taking drums to the tree house, putting acorns in a ukelele to hear the sound they make, striking the autoharp strings with drumsticks are legitimate, nonharmful experimentation. . . . Is the child, at this time, being careless or destructive, or is he thoughtfully and imaginatively experimenting?*

Accept the initial noise, because children learn to differentiate sounds by making noise as well as by making music. You must communicate your support of the child's efforts even when those efforts do not produce what you hear as the sound of success. Self-confidence encourages originality.

---

* Elizabeth Jones, *What Is Music for Young Children?* (Washington, D.C.: National Association for the Education of Young Children, 1969), p. 4.

In addition to providing quality music instruments, you will also want to make available other different sound-producing objects for your child to experiment with. A child should own a phonograph, and must be expected to scratch a few records before understanding its proper use. One that operates on batteries instead of electricity eliminates the danger of experimentation with plugs and outlets. If it is a portable, your child can move it to wherever other family members are, since most children don't enjoy playing alone in their rooms now. Continue to help to expand your child's musical taste by buying all kinds of different types of records; not just "children's" songs. Use appropriate music to accompany some activities. Classical is nice for mealtime, marches can speed up clean-up time, and songs about art concepts can inspire art activity. Children love to wear headphones, and this can be a bonus for you if the two of you don't share the same taste in music.

With a tape recorder, you can record your child making music. Listening to it will help him or her understand the process of producing sound in an organized way. If you play an instrument, you

Children learn about music both by listening to it and by making it.

can accompany the child in the performance. The joy of expressing oneself through music comes naturally to all children.

Music games can be played that not only teach music but also reinforce other concepts that the child is learning. When studying the concept of round, you can find round instruments to play. Drums and cymbals are a good start, and your child can make or discover others. Follow this game up with painting on round paper, playing "Ring Around the Rosie," and eating round crackers, as we do in our classes at Young at Art. Learning to appreciate and understand music comes from many varied sources—listening to music and to noise, making both music and noise, playing games, and observing the attitudes of others.

One way to learn about how others feel about music is through books. Some interesting books about music for this age group are listed in Appendix I. See Appendix II for my review of these books.

PART IV

The Child: Age 3-4

TWENTY-TWO

The
Fourth Year

By the time the third birthday comes around, life seems suddenly to become very easy. The child who last year wouldn't ride in his or her stroller even through a hurricane now agreeably hops in whenever asked to. Diapers magically seem to disappear. Cleaning up is a treat instead of a chore. Language improves dramatically, and you'll enjoy real conversations together. "Please," "thank you," and all of the other little pleasantries of life no longer need to be prefaced with a reminder from you.

Don't get too secure. In six months or so, you'll wonder where your little angel has disappeared to. At around three and a half, there is a reemergence of stubbornness that may signal a new sense of insecurity. Your little angel will now say "Oh, shit!" when disappointed and look to see what your reaction is. Language that is sure to shock you will be tried out in crowded elevators and on social visits. If your family speaks politely and with respect to each other, your child will too. Of course, if you occasionally curse, so will your child. This was always a problem for me when I was teaching. It is hard to say, "That is not a nice way to talk," when a child always hears his or her own mom and dad talk that way. Children now begin to use language very creatively, if not politely. For example, outrageous insults are invented. You'll hear: "I hate you," and "You're a dummy" or a "doody head," invariably in front of an audience. It is better not to overreact. You may be more successful countering outrageous language with even more outrageous language (never cursing, though) than you will be by getting

291

angry. A game of "Can you top this?" can be very funny and put the situation in perspective. To "You are a doody head" you might respond, "And you are a roody head, and I'm a toody head, and Daddy is a koody head . . ." etc., which will cause your three-year-old to get a case of the giggles and forget why he or she was angry. When my son said, "Mommy, you're a dum-dum" in front of thirty guests, I responded with "No, I'm not. Yesterday you said I was a dummy. I like being a dummy much better than being a dum-dum." Instead of the reprimand he expected, we got a laugh from the group. Another ploy I used with some success was innocently pretending that I didn't understand a word. The first time he came home with a really foul word I asked him what he meant. Of course he didn't know. I told him I had never heard the word and that maybe it was a foreign word. Not wanting to use a word no one would understand, he dropped it from his vocabulary. The purpose of these words is to shock; if you are not shocked, the words will not be used again. It may seem like an avoidance of the issue, but during this time of seemingly constant battle, a Band-Aid may be more effective than true healing. Your example is the most important teacher in this matter.

One of the biggest mistakes you can make now is to feel that you have to win every issue. And don't turn each encounter into proof that your word is law. Occasionally let the child wear clothes that don't match or eat spareribs for breakfast, if that's what he or she needs to do. If mealtime has become a contest of wills, invite one of the child's friends for one of the daily meals, set out their food, and leave the room. The two of them will probably enjoy eating together and may even eat more than with your coaxing.

Power problems arise mainly at home, and the contest of wills between primary caretaker and child will not usually be a problem in the child's relationship with the nursery school teacher or the baby-sitter. Taking advantage of this fact will greatly ease your life and provide a broadening experience for the youngster. So while I counsel not leaving the clinging ten-month-old with a sitter, I strongly suggest doing exactly that for your three-and-a-half-year-old, especially one who is not in school regularly.

Late in the third year, children begin to understand something about death, pain, illness, and loss. Their feelings of fear and powerlessness are often expressed through an interest in superheros, who live forever and can never be hurt. Perhaps as the child learns

Create an alternative to family mealtime, if you find yourself overly concerned with your child's eating habits.

that parents are not gods, there is a need to replace the fallen idols with new ones. Costumes play a large part in the child's life. Superhero capes, crowns, hats, and other props, often symbols of power or authority, become very important. Respect the child's wishes to wear this symbolic clothing. It is part of a phase that doesn't last terribly long and in no way suggests that your child is eccentric.

The original superhero was Superman, and all others seem to be based on that character. Superman, Batman, Wonder Woman, Aquaman, Flash, and Spiderman all use their special powers to help people and are dedicated to truth and justice. I have found them to be good role models who do not engage in unnecessary violence. The play that they inspire emphasizes rescuing people in distress. They are benevolent, and believing in them is no more threatening than a belief in Santa Claus. There are other hero figures who are not as acceptable to me. If wars, fighting, and power are the character's reason for existing, the play they inspire can become ugly and dangerous. Star Wars, Warlords, and Masters of the Universe characters are all antiheroes, in my opinion. I limit exposure to them, while encouraging exposure to the others. I gave

Children explore the notions of power, authority, and mortality in their play.

my son books, clothes, and toys bearing the symbols of good superheros when he wanted them, and expressed distaste for the
symbols of the blood-thirsty characters. There is always a reason
why generation after generation love the same kind of heros. Parents should not find interest in this kind of play in any way threatening, although they can monitor the types of characters that the
child is exposed to.

We are good at espousing the philosophy that "children are
the future." In reality, we exert the largest amount of energy trying
to fill children's heads with the facts, feelings, and rules of the past.
If children are to grow up to have any influence at all on the future
of the human race, it is only because they will find *new* solutions
to old problems. To be able to do this, children need a lot of
practice solving problems and a lot of praise for the answers they
come up with. Mistakes should be viewed as opportunities for
learning, not cause for criticism or punishment. You have to allow
the child the freedom to experiment with values that are alien to

you. This means that occasionally your child will behave in ways that are unacceptable to you. If the first time this occurs you revert to authoritarian discipline, your child will recognize that his or her freedom is merely an illusion. This will cause even more serious rebellion and difficulty within the family. The three-to-four-year-old is more of an individual than ever. This individual will sometimes have different ideas and feelings than you do. You had a child; not a clone. Be grateful for every difference and don't fall into the trap of being relieved when your child comes around to your way of thinking and feeling threatened when he or she doesn't. A child whose wardrobe, meals, playthings, and schedule are always decided upon by an adult will not be one who grows up making great discoveries, being decisive, or solving the problems of his or her generation.

We often think that in order to guide our children we need to give them answers, but we are better teachers when we ask them questions and let them find their own answers. The child needs to learn that his or her parents respect his or her feelings and needs. It is not harmful if the child learns that by being expressive and persuasive he or she can change Mommy's or Daddy's mind about something. It can be dangerous to set a pattern of acceptance of adult authority at all times, since the child who is accustomed to always following an adult's orders is more likely to obey an adult, even a stranger, when it is not safe to do so. Children who learn not to make their needs known grow up continuing to allow the needs of others to take precedence over their own. Children who were raised to be "seen and not heard" grew up to "simply follow orders" in Nazi Germany.

Adults who are shocked and outraged by this defense of indefensible behavior during World War II nevertheless continue to teach their children that they are never to question the authority of parents and teachers. The sad lament repeated by so many parents of missing children is, "I wish I hadn't taught my child to always obey adults." It is healthy to allow a child to learn that he or she has needs that are of genuine concern to every member of the family. It is equally important to permit a child the thrill of success that comes from occasionally persuading an all-powerful parent to change his or her mind. That, of course, is not the same as parents who are intimidated by whining or tantrum-throwing children, or parents who give in because they really don't care. When parents feel secure in occasionally saying "Okay" to a child's request, it adds enormously to the child's feelings of self-worth.

> What is permissiveness and what is overpermissiveness? Permissiveness is an attitude of accepting the childishness of children. It means accepting "boys will be boys," that a clean shirt on a normal child will not stay clean for long, that running rather than walking is the child's normal means of locomotion, that a tree is for climbing and a mirror is for making faces. The essence of permissiveness is the acceptance of children as persons who have a constitutional right to have all kinds of feelings and wishes. The freedom to wish is absolute and unrestricted; all feelings and fantasies, all thoughts and wishes, all dreams and desires, regardless of content, are accepted, respected, and may be permitted expression through appropriate symbolic means. Destructive behavior is not permitted; when it occurs, the parents intervene and redirect it into verbal outlets and other symbolic channels. Permitted symbolic outlets are painting "mean" pictures, throwing darts at a target, sawing wood, boxing life-size Bobo, recording ill wishes on tape, composing caustic poems, writing murder mysteries, etc. In short, permissiveness is the acceptance of imaginary and symbolic behavior. Overpermissiveness is the allowing of undesirable acts. Permissiveness brings confidence and an increasing capacity to express feelings and thoughts. Overpermissiveness brings anxiety and increasing demands for privileges that cannot be granted.*

One of the dilemmas all parents face with three-year-olds is the emergence of lie-telling. Lying is not, as it sometimes seems to be, a signal that your child is headed for a life of crime. If you ask, "Who spilled the milk?" and your child answers, "A dragon did it!" don't think that a punishment is the only way to end the dis-

---

* Haim G. Ginott, M.D., *Between Parent and Child* (New York: Avon Books, 1965), p. 110.

cussion. Lying is an early expression of creativity. What is great fiction, if not glorious, well-told lies? You can encourage storytelling while still showing the child that he or she must face the consequences of careless or naughty behavior. Stimulating questions can encourage the creative aspect of the story: "What did the dragon look like?" "How did he get in the house?" "What made him spill the milk?" "Where do you think the dragon came from?" Decisive comments may be in order: "Since the dragon didn't wipe up that milk, I guess you'll have to!" Let your child know that you are aware that he or she has told a lie without making that the most important aspect of the exchange. Joint decision-making will help your child see that he or she must face the music without losing face: "Since the dragon left without cleaning up, who do you think should sponge up the milk?" "What can we do now that the dragon is gone and the floor is so dirty?" Help your child expand the idea and write the story down for later retelling. Stress the creative aspects of the lie, not the dishonesty. A child can come away from this experience with a spanking or a strong positive feeling for storytelling that may later lead to the creation of literature. The choice is yours. It is possible to raise a generation of honest, highly moral individuals while being tolerant of early "fibs" and "lies."

Many parents are anxious that their children begin reading early. Some even show flash cards to infants in an effort to assure early reading. It's not how early you read that counts, however, but how much you enjoy doing it. Before long, I.Q. is tested, drawing skills are measured by the amount of details included in a picture, language acquisition is graded, and reading scores precede a child's name on attendance lists. The more testing and drilling that goes on in school, the less likely your child is to enjoy school and learn. Competition for available spaces in some nursery schools can be fierce and often the verbal skills are "tested" when the child is "interviewed" for admission, so some of the anxiety is understandable. I have met many intelligent parents who seriously believe that certain nursery schools are "feeder" schools for "good" private and public grade schools that later are the "feeder" schools to the better universities. Advances of a few percentage points are worried over and boasted about by parents and teachers who seem to forget that this child is a sensitive human being. Forget the scores and numbers; there is only one important factor to consider in judging a child's reading skill and that is: "Does the child love books?" If so, the child will read. If not, why should he or she? Teaching letters too early does more harm than good because children copy the letters when they would be benefiting more from creating and exploring shapes on their own through free scribbling.

> You really can't teach reading as a science. Love
> gets mixed up in it.
> —Theodore Seuss Geisel (Dr. Seuss)*

Children need to learn about literature and there are two important ways to encourage interest in the subject. Children benefit from listening to stories you tell (from books, memory, and your imagination) and they need to have you listen to stories they tell. We will eventually need to teach our children to read, but we also want to teach our children to write. The precursor to later creative writing is creative storytelling. Babies adore looking at picture books and need you to hold them on your lap and point out things in the pictures, and older children need to be read to daily, often wanting to read the same story over and over and over. Your patience will be rewarded years later when your child becomes an avid reader.

Children also need to own some books of their own and to participate in choosing them. Visits to bookstores to make purchases and to libraries to borrow books should be a regular part of the child's schedule. A good nursery school will have a large selection of preschool-level books and a special "story" time daily. My favorite nursery school has its own preschool library and librarian. The children are free to visit it whenever they wish to, to hear stories, look at books, listen to tapes, and participate in other library activities. Children need special "meeting times" both at home and in school during which they are given opportunities to listen and be listened to. At these times, children should not have to worry about being "right" or "wrong." They need to feel free to express their ideas, opinions, and feelings and to have them accepted by their peers. Nurturing parents are essential to the child's ability to be expressive and a sensitive teacher is needed to set the tone of acceptance in school.

* Herbert Kupferberg, "A Seussian Celebration," *Parade Magazine*, 2/26/84, p. 6.

It's not how early you read that counts, but how much you enjoy doing it.

Fostering Security

Feelings of inadequacy and insecurity produce anxiety that prevents a child from fulfilling his or her potential. One of the most common ways to make your child feel unloved at this age is to go off to the hospital and return with a competitor for your time and attention. That doesn't mean that you can't have another child—only that you must, at this exhausting time, devote a lot more energy than usual to assuring your older child of your love. After being the center of the universe in your family, your "baby" now is officially grown-up and must make way for a new baby. Of course, the last thing you need to do is *tell* the child that you love her or him more than the new baby. That means that someday you might love the baby more, and that idea can be very frightening. You can't expect these two siblings to love each other for a very long time, and telling the child how much he or she should, or soon will, love the new baby just increases feelings of guilt and inadequacy. It's best to be accepting of the older child's feelings, even when they are negative. You can admit that you too feel annoyed by the new baby sometimes. We all like to be liked, and every burp can be interpreted as a sign of affection for the older sibling. "Oh look! The baby smiled at you. I think he likes you," will mean a lot now.

Fortunately (unless you have twins), your children will not experience the same needs at the same time. You can give your infant lots of love and attention while big brother or sister is at school or visiting friends—and you can plan special time with the older child during the baby's nap time—when the terrific twos come along. You can help the older child understand the younger one's needs by showing photographs of his or her own adventurous explorations. Help the older child "baby proof" his or her important toys and work-in-progress. The upper level of a bunk bed is a cozy spot to put together a 100-piece puzzle—reassuringly near, yet safe from the baby.

If you will be staying in the hospital, don't let this be the first time you have been away from your child overnight. Do so first in a less threatening situation. Most people agree that it can't hurt to have your spouse, friend, mother, or a baby nurse carry the newborn out of the hospital or into the house where your older child first sees you after this absence, to free your arms for hugging the firstborn. Shortly after the arrival of the new baby, friends will come bearing extravagant compliments and gaily wrapped gifts. This serves to aggravate the older child's feelings of jealousy. Hang a note on your front door telling your visitors where to find a hidden basket of gifts made or purchased by you for your firstborn. The note can ask any friends who may be bringing things for the baby to pick out a small package for your older child, to avoid sibling rivalry. Thoughtful friends will have already brought a gift for the older child if they are giving one to the new baby.

You can't afford to be superstitious about preparing for a second child. You will need any extra time you can find to spend with the older child, so do all of your shopping, washing, folding, and other baby preparations when you are in your seventh month. Don't expect your older child to give up a room, crib, stroller, or any other connection to his or her own babyhood for the new baby. Any moves or changes in your home should take place well in advance of the birth. If you will be taking time off from a job for the new baby, take a few weeks before delivery to spend with your older child, doing special things together.

Promoting a sense of individuality is difficult when you have several children, all clamoring for your attention. Being fair doesn't always have to mean treating them identically. Each family member should have special, different qualities noted and praised. Identical twins present a special problem. They should never be dressed in the same clothes, no matter how adorable. Identifiable differences should be stressed—perhaps one child can have long hair, the other short. Clothes can have names or initials on them because it is demoralizing to always be called "Which one are you?"

TWENTY-THREE

Home Environment

The home provides a greater influence on a child's life than any other place. Many of those influences are subconscious. I have always been an advocate of modern architecture, partly because I do not believe progress is encouraged in an environment that resurrects the past. The materials and decorations of the past also require more care and restrict freedom far more than do the tools of modern designers. Moldings and other decorative additions to walls, furniture, and accessories become hiding places for dirt and germs. When they are used, as they often are, as places to hide telephone wires, they lose all visual appeal anyway. The clean, simple lines of contemporary architects do not clutter our lives with unhealthy objects nor our minds with unnecessary visual junk.

If one's home is like a museum, a child learns to value objects far more than people. If those objects are all from the past, we tend to look back, rather than ahead, for our place in the world.

You will never have to say "don't touch!" in any well-designed home. The clean lines of the ideal contemporary environment do not distract us from the true meaning of our lives. When one is totally surrounded by good design, comprehension of it comes about as if by osmosis. There is no better way to learn about beauty than to live in it. Above all, one shouldn't have to tip-toe through childhood, always afraid of breaking or dirtying something. If your idea of beauty harkens to the past, study your home from a child's eye level and make the most of the advantages of your own special style.

Places to jump from, perch on, hide in, and see the environment from a new vantage point provide enriching experiences.

A child must also know that he or she has one special place in the world that is completely his or hers. Whether this is a bedroom or only a small toy chest doesn't matter as much as the fact that the space is truly one's own. This is the year to pack away the baby things and, as they are packed away, a three-to-four-year-old should have a say in how the space is reorganized and decorated. There is no more worry about drawing or painting on the walls, so this is a good year to repaint. What was thought of as a baby's room recently is now clearly the domain of an individual with strong opinions about how things should look. Wall, floor, and bed covering can be chosen by the child. This inner sanctum may offend your sensibilities and clash horribly with the rest of your home—but it isn't yours! It belongs to the child, and exercising control over it turns it into a physical representation of his or her taste, style, and sense of organization. The space becomes an extension of the child and the child will feel as comfortable in it as he or she feels within him- or herself. No decorating scheme is more important than the autonomy and self-esteem of a child.

If the objects on display in your home are all adult-made, a child begins to feel that as long as childhood lasts, the products he or she produces are valueless. Once a child becomes a member of the family, his or her current art should be as importantly displayed within the home as are purchased paintings and scultpure. The masterpieces you hung in your infant's room three years ago should be replaced with pictures that the child has drawn or painted. Try to hang the pictures that the child feels strongly about, not the ones you like. A bulletin board can hold each day's new products as well as photographs of family and friends, party invitations, circus pictures when an excursion to one is planned, pictures from toy catalogs of things the child has expressed a desire for, and prints from visits to museums. It can work well as an easel also.

TWENTY-FOUR

Excursions

Choosing a Nursery School

The major excursion in the third year will probably be school. The effects of nursery school on the child's future can be profound, so the decision of what school to choose should not be made lightly. Your child's initial nursery school experiences are far more important in shaping his or her future than is the choice of a college, which so many agonize over in later years. People tend to think that education isn't too important now, since they are "just babies." But it is now when attitudes are being formed and work habits established. I remember at a social gathering someone once asked me what kind of work I did and I responded, "I'm chairperson of the art department." "Oh," he replied. "College or high school?" When I told him "elementary school" he involuntarily burst out laughing. All the respect he had had for me after my initial response disappeared when he learned that I "merely" worked with young children. Nevertheless, the play experiences of nursery school affect a child's future far more than do the long hours of test-taking and endless homework of the later school years. A child's first school experience is tremendously important since it will shape a child's approach to learning and affect his or her attitude toward school for many years to come.

Schools should be places where children discover things for themselves and learn how to use their minds. Instead, most have become places where children learn about things that other people have discovered and memorize what year the discoveries were made in. One side effect of this kind of education is that as children are learning facts they are also learning how to learn. If experiences are spoon-fed by the teacher, children quickly learn not to think for themselves. There are many subtle things that teachers do that determine learning methods. Children learn self-esteem by receiving encouragement for doing their own work. When the reward comes for doing only what the teacher says to do, children quickly compromise their own needs in order to win adult approval. This compromise results in children being afraid to answer questions in class for fear of not being "right," children who say they "can't draw" because their own efforts don't look as if they were made by an adult, and children who read only to study, never for enjoyment.

I would not consider sending a child to any nursery school or camp that had on display any projects made by the children that all looked the same. This indicates a total lack of understanding of children's capabilities and suggests unrealistic expectations. I have found that the attitude schools have toward children's art has been very representative of how they think of children in general. Teachers who give patterns to complete to children who are in the scribbling stage don't really understand or respect children and don't realize how important working at one's own rate of development is. As a parent, ultimately your child's education is your responsibility. Since most schools don't encourage parents to spend meaningful time in their children's classrooms, it is difficult to really know much about the quality of teaching going on there. There is only one thing the preschool child regularly brings home: art work. If the teacher respects the child's need to grow and learn through normal development in art endeavors, it is probably true that he or she allows the child to progress in a healthy way in other areas as well. I have found that where children come home with "art" work that looks like it was made by a thirty-year-old rather than a three-year-old, you are likely to find that the teacher doesn't really like or understand children. Those are frequently the teachers who view their jobs as controlling, rather than guiding, children. Children learn through art just as they learn through play experiences. They learn skills they will use throughout their lives, but more importantly they learn approaches to obtaining skills. When interested adults encourage children to participate in the kinds of art experiences that involve no independent problem solving or originality, they produce young minds that soon become unable to think for themselves.

> . . . The public school's problems with non-learners could be greatly reduced through reforms in art education. . . . *

If individual expression in art is encouraged, you will probably find that the teacher listens to verbal cues as well. In many schools, art is misunderstood. It can be the most effective way to teach a child how to think and solve problems. Instead it is treated as a frill. Too often art is viewed as purely decorative, and the children who produce it as little "dolls." Some teachers make pictures of holiday stereotypes for the children to copy or color-in; thirty identical orange pumpkins, green shamrocks, or fluffy Easter bunnies parade across countless school bulletin boards throughout the school year, allowing no room at all for personal expression or individual differences. In some schools, teachers teach by the month; in October the children make orange and black pumpkins, in November they trace their hands to draw turkey tails, December brings triangle Christmas trees, and so on through the school year. Instead of working to enrich lives and moving on as the child develops to do projects requiring increasingly more advanced skills, they mark time on the calendar right up through Father's Day (regardless of how many children have fathers), directing the production of mindless, assembly-line room decorations. This subject-oriented art completely ignores the fact that young children are stimulated to work by seeing materials. (It is adults who are subject-motivated, not young children.) The teacher who treats children as if they were small adults knows very little about good teaching. You don't need to be an expert in children's art to know whether art work was done by a child, or if it is traced from a teacher-made pattern.

When art becomes a teacher-directed, regimented activity, children who are dealing with serious problems in their personal lives miss a crucial opportunity to work their problems through and to express themselves through art. When the product—for example, a green Christmas tree—becomes more important than the child's own self-expression to a teacher, children learn to stifle

* Rhoda Kellogg, *Analyzing Children's Art* (Palo Alto, Calif.: Mayfield Publishing Co., 1969), p. 142.

their own needs. Self-expression may come in less desirable ways
—graffiti, fighting, stealing, etc. Often this kind of antisocial behavior can be avoided if children learn how to express themselves
and channel their anger or disappointments into verbal and graphic
work.

One time I toured a school which is reputed to be one of the
best in New York City. Something bothered me about all the art
work I saw displayed there. Since it didn't appear to be copied or
traced, I had trouble identifying just what was wrong with it. On
bulletin board after bulletin board I saw small, constrained, self-
conscious-looking drawings. I observed a class of seven three-
years-olds and their two teachers in a very small room. At no time
during my one-and-a-half-hour visit did any child choose his or
her own toy or activity. Every three-year-old stayed seated, as did
both teachers. When one scribbling child announced that he had
finished his drawing the teacher replied, "No, you didn't, I want
you to keep drawing," and he did! When another boy accidentally
dropped a box of small toys on the floor, he was reprimanded by
both teachers, blushed crimson, and picked up each little toy with
no help from anyone. One youngster expressed interest in the doll
corner, and teacher's response was, "You know we never play in
the doll corner on Friday." The head teacher informed me that she
alone decided what the children would do each day. As we talked,
she singled out one boy in the class, pointed to him, and said loud
enough for everyone to hear, "Isn't he beautiful? Did you ever see
such a doll?" I never heard any noise at all and no laughter
throughout my visit. Choosing and decision-making were clearly
not part of the curriculum.

On a bulletin board were small collages the children had
made. Each consisted of six teacher-made shapes; they were assembled identically in the shape of a geometrically perfect person:

> One perfect circle
> One upper torso
> Two rectangles for arms
> Two rectangles for legs.

They varied in only one way: Each picture bearing a boy's name
wore pants, each girl's picture had a skirt on the lower torso. Each
shape was clearly made by an adult, and, presumably, assembled
by a child. No paste crept out from behind the pasted shapes. This

project coincided with the time chronologically when normal children are emerging from the stage of making mandalas and beginning to attempt mandala-like humans (see page 17). The easel was nowhere in sight and when I asked about it, the teacher said that she tried to set it up about twice a week.

Work time was followed by a music class with a specialist. The children were seated in a circle on the floor while they waited for her to arrive. Although she was eight minutes late, the three-year-olds waited quietly, hands in their laps. Her lesson included asking the children to make the sounds of various animals and things. As often as not, she corrected the children and let them know that her interpretations of these sounds were the only acceptable answer to her questions.

The art projects alone should have been enough to tell me that the teachers in this school exercised total control over the class. They had no respect for young children as people and viewed them as "pretty dolls" with no real feelings and no real understanding of their own needs. According to the teacher, what children needed was to be the same as all of their classmates and more like adults. I might add that the school catalog made no mention of this and at the interview I had with the director, she assured me that free art expression was encouraged. One quick look at the bulletin board proved that she and I had very different definitions of "freedom."

On the very same day that I visited the above school, I also visited another. I walked into a very large room which opened out onto an outdoor play area. The classroom was at least four times the size of the classroom I had visited earlier that day, but the children had full run of it. The size of a classroom often suggests just how restrictive the atmosphere is. Some children played at a sand table, others painted at an easel, worked with play dough, blocks, and housekeeping toys. In a reading corner one of the teachers was reading to some children. One boy was not engaged in any activity and the second teacher was trying to get him interested in something. One child left the sand table, went into the bathroom, and returned with a bucket of water which he proceeded to pour into the sand. The teacher immediately noticed it, looked at me, and rolled her eyes. I asked her if she was going to permit it and she said, "Yes, it makes a mess, but the children can do so many new things in wet sand." She went on to say that it seemed to her that no child had ever done this early in the year, but that by spring each year someone invariably discovered it. She saw it as a sign of sound, healthy, innovative thinking and was willing to put up with the mess. "It must be spring," she said as she went off to ask a child painting at the easel to confine his painting to his own large paper and please not move off onto his neighbor's paper.

That easel, incidentally, was one of two permanent fixtures in the room. The paint and paper were set up on it before school and children were free to use it, or not, during play time every day. The term *play time* was in strong contrast to the term *work time* used in the other school to describe similar activities. All of the art work on display was appropriate for the age of the children. It was all quite large and free looking. I spotted a big bin of pictures divided into sections labeled for each child in the class. As I started to flip through it the teacher came over to me and asked what I was looking for. I replied that I was just curious to know whether the art included pumpkins, Christmas trees, and bunnies, and she replied, "I really don't see the value of that kind of activity for three-year-olds." She also informed me that they stored the art work in school until the bin was full, before sending it home. This was to avoid overemphasis on art as a product to take home to mommy every day and to keep the focus of all art projects on the process of working. The children were all talking quietly whenever they wished to and a lot of laughing was going on. The teachers knew where each child was and what he or she was doing. They obviously were in control of the situation, even though each child was doing his or her "own thing." Children also had the option of leaving the room to go next door to the library, fully stocked with books, records, and tapes appropriate to the level of the children. There a librarian supervised children in the activities they chose to participate in. Later on in the morning the class (including the teachers) sat in a circle on the floor and talked about how they helped their parents at home. Every child was given a chance to talk and each job a child described received a positive comment from the teacher. It was clear that there was no "right" answer to the teacher's questions and that she was genuinely interested in what each child had to contribute to the discussion.

Just because children are not under the total control of an adult doesn't mean that things are out of control. Establishing the habit of freedom within a basic structure provides the environment in which creativity and independence are most likely to be fostered. The basis of the founding of our country was freedom of choice. You cannot hope to teach the concept of democracy to children who have been raised and educated only in environments of adult dictatorship. Total adult control is like fascism—it invites rebellion.

> . . . the adult offering art must provide a frame-
> work or structure within which the child can be
> free to move and to think and to fantasize, not a
> structure which imposes, controls, and makes a
> child dependent . . . *

Although I saw little positive teaching going on in the first school and quite a lot of it in the second school, the first school has a much better reputation in New York City than the second school. I can only believe that the reason the school is so widely regarded is that parents want their children to be controlled. They *want* them to be clean and quiet and just like everyone else. Too often, I think, our criteria for judging educational programs are based on how well the children are controlled, rather than how well they are learning to live in the world. In a school where children don't know what to do or think until the teacher tells them, confusion and even chaos occur as soon as the teacher does not provide the answer. This is part of the reason why children frequently behave so poorly when their regular teacher is absent and a substitute is in charge. In classrooms where children have some control over their activities and behavior, that control does not break down if the teacher is away. Since it comes from within, not from the teacher, it does not rely on the teacher's presence to continue. Children learn through play, so if most play is teacher-directed, the children learn to rely on adult approval rather than to think for themselves.

> The finest inheritance you can give to a child is to
> allow it to make its own way, completely on its
> own feet.†

It is impossible to judge a school just by statements in the

---

* Judith Rubin, *Child Art Therapy* (New York: Van Nostrand Reinhold Co., 1978), p. 30.

† Isadora Duncan, *My Life* (New York: Liveright Publishing Corp., 1927, renewed 1955), p. 21.

school catalog, appearance, discussion with directors, or conversations with parents of children in attendance. It is important to ask to observe a class and to compare at least two or three schools before choosing one. The most obvious thing to look for is whether the children are happy. But children love being with other children so many seem happy in very bad schools. Check also to see if they seem relaxed and comfortable. Are they permitted choices in their play? You can learn an awful lot about a school's general approach to dealing with children by looking at art projects on display. School fairs, performances, and bazaars also reflect the philosophy of the school. One time I saw a fund-raiser for a private school in which an entire city block was devoted to one child-involving activity after another, each booth using children's interests to help raise money, right around the corner from a fund-raiser for another school in which adult-produced products were sold. At the first the activities included: decorate your own cake, make a pin, paint a balloon, polish and decorate your nails, and put on your own face makeup. At the second, slick clothing, plants, books, and records were sold. I imagine that the administrators and parents did not set out to present activities that would reflect their school's educational philosophy—nevertheless they did. The first school appeared to place a high value on children, the second on worldly goods.

Although it is impossible to recommend for or against specific schools, I would say that Montessori schools should be avoided since Maria Montessori found scribbling an unacceptable acitivity and felt that schools should teach children "how to draw."* Her influence is, unfortunately, still reflected in the art projects offered in many schools today, despite the fact that most educators recognize that this approach was a mistake. The Montessori method stresses doing various tasks in very specific ways as demonstrated by the teacher. The Montessori classroom is described thusly:

> There was always one correct way to approach
> each problem, and no piece of apparatus was to
> be manipulated by the child in a free or playful
> way. Nor was free dramatic play or fantasy play
> encouraged in any way in the program.

* Claudia Lewis, Ph.D., *The Montessori Method: Education Before Five,* A Handbook on Preschool Education developed by the Bank Street College of Education (New York: Bank Street College of Education, 1977), p. 7.

There is periodically a so-called back-to-basics movement in education. Parents demand reading, writing, and arithmetic in earlier-than-ever grades in hopes that these subjects, introduced early enough, will make their children somehow smarter. We forget that children learn so much from play and that the real basics include those activities which are fun and make children want to learn. Playing, pretending, squishing, painting and scribbling, daydreaming, developing friendships—all are activities that lay the foundation for and provide readiness to do later schoolwork and to function in the world. As we eliminate time for these real basics to make time for premature introduction of advanced work, we are robbing our children of time they would otherwise use to develop a firm base for coping with information. We are compounding the problem by assuring loss of interest and motivation. Reading scores get lower and lower and schools add even more time for the drilling and testing that turn children away from reading. Yet we fail to recognize that we have forgotten to give our children a sense of excitement and to fill them with a joy for learning. The very same children who two years ago were so eager to learn that they had tantrums when we wouldn't let them stop to look at or touch something now begin to mark time until they can drop out of school.

> Avoid compulsion and let your children's lessons
> take the form of play.
>
> —Plato*

When looking at schools for your child, find out what the administration feels are the basics. "Reading, writing, and arithmetic" is an unrealistic foundation for learning for very young children. Well before children acquire these skills, they acquire approaches to thinking. Will the written word be used for writing, or copying? A child who copies the teacher's words from the blackboard all day long is not learning how to write. In most schools that I have worked in, the first writing skills were taught in exactly that way. The teacher writes a story on the blackboard and every child in the class copies it. Neatness and accuracy are graded. Not only does this method teach copying instead of writing, but it is a sure way to bore a child to death! One of the main reasons that I chose the school to which I sent my son was that when I visited

* Quoted by Reed Herbert in *Education Through Art* (New York: Random House, 1948), p. 6.

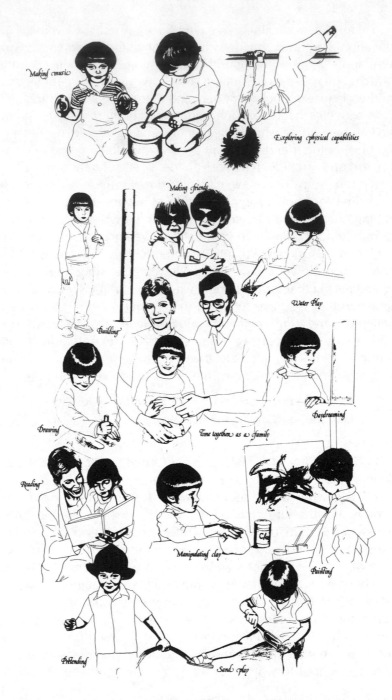

Making music

Exploring physical capabilities

Making friends

Building

Water Play

Drawing

Time together as a family

Daydreaming

Reading

Manipulating clay

Painting

Pretending

Sand play

The real basics.

the first-grade class, the children had all written their *own* stories. That, I feel, is the only way to capture a child's interest and motivate him or her to learn about the great potential of the written word.

Ask how many teachers take the time to read to their classes every day—not as a prelude to a quiz, but as a relaxing and enjoyable part of the day. One of the most exciting and stimulating teachers I ever knew dramatically read one chapter of a children's classic to her class every afternoon, although this activity appeared nowhere in the educational curriculum and her class included eleven-year-olds, not nursery school children. The children adored it and could hardly work fast enough to get to "story time." Once, when a fight had broken out in the lunchroom, she punished the class by canceling story time for that day. One of the toughest boys in the class told me, with tears in his eyes, how "mean and unfair" he found that punishment. He had been so eager to find out what happened next in the story!

Who talks more, the teacher or the children? Remember, from your own schooling, how little you learned from teachers who were in love with the sound of their own voices? Teachers who listen to their students are the more effective teachers.

In my many years of teaching, I discovered that even in the best schools there are both good and bad teachers. I have seen a warm, competent teacher right next door to a bellowing, screaming teacher who intimidated the children all day long and ran her classroom of very young children like a Marine boot camp. I know of one teacher, in a generally excellent school, who punished a rambunctious youngster by keeping him in the trash can for a whole afternoon and telling him in front of the entire class that he was "a piece of garbage." Another stopped a usually well-behaved child who was running in the hallways and told him to "get into my class, fold your hands, and wait for me." The teacher forgot all about him, and went home. The tearful child was found in the locked school building, hands still folded, at 6 p.m. Please don't assume that when you send your child off to school, he or she will be in good hands. There are many fine, dedicated teachers, but there are some "bad apples" as well. It is unwise to assume that it is impossible for your child to be in a bad situation in a good school. If you care about your child, you must stay informed about what goes on in the classroom. If your child is put in a class that you don't approve of, seek a change. School principals will usually accommodate you if such a request is made. Ultimately, you are responsible for your child's education. His or her future is in *your* hands, not some teacher's.

Early schooling should introduce your child to the fun and challenge of learning. It should not be patterned after higher education. Cramming information down throats is counterproductive. Too many teachers hand out dittoed sheets to be underlined, circled, and colored-in when they could instead be filling chidren with a love for literature, music, art, science, and history. Learning to organize thoughts (in story-telling) or objects (like toys after play time) helps give children far more of a headstart in acquiring math skills than does pushing numbers on a too-young child. Counting steps as you walk, counting cookies at snack time, counting backward as an elevator descends, are all games that children love, as well as a way of preparing children for later math. It is important not to become overly concerned with accuracy; "one-two-three-eleven" shows an admirable familiarity with the numerical system for a three-year-old and deserves support, not criticism.

When choosing a school for your child, stop by to look around on the first day of school. How separation is handled is immensely important to your child. I visited a summer program for three-year-olds where the lobby was predictably noisy and confusing on the first day. I heard the director say to mothers, "Don't worry about your children, we'll take them up to the classroom in the elevator." With no more preparation than that, a three-year-old was put on the crowded elevator. As the doors closed, she began screaming for her mother. It turned out that there was no teacher on the elevator who knew where the child belonged. This kind of beginning school experience causes irreparable harm. My son went to a program for two mornings a week when he was only two. Although the catalog went on and on about easing separation, the director suggested that I leave him the very first day. I refused! Many parents left screaming children on the flimsy advice: "Don't worry, we know what we're doing, he'll be fine," but I saw one girl who cried for at least two and a half hours, and her mother was never contacted. I stayed all morning for three weeks (six sessions), long after all of the other mothers had gone. In the third week my little boy came over to me and said, "Mommy, go." I did, and never stayed again. He would be in school for another twenty years or

so. I wanted him to feel good about school from the very beginning. At this age, the reassuring presence of the child's primary
caretaker is the best way to ease the transition from home to
school.

When looking for a regular nursery school, choose one where
teachers do not feel threatened by a child's attachment to his or
her parents. The school I chose sent the teacher to visit the child at
home a few days before school started, since they felt that the child
would feel more comfortable getting to know this important new
stranger in his or her own home. On the first day of school, the
child already had spent some time alone playing with the teacher,
and also had more quality time because only one half of the class
was scheduled to come at one time. The school also insisted that
at least one parent stay in school with each child for the first ten
60-120-minute school days. Parents were encouraged to stay in
the background and to let the teachers gain the children's trust by
playing with them, helping them get along with the others, and
meeting their physical and emotional needs. When a mother or
dad left to "get a cup of coffee," the teacher would take the child
down the hall to see the "coffee room" and say something like,
"While Mommy is drinking her coffee, you can come to me if
there is anything you need." If a child whose parent was out of the
room asked about him or her, the parent was immediately sum-
moned. Not one child cried throughout the entire two-week transition period.

After a week or so, all sixteen children in the class came to
school at the same time. With all parents present, it was anything
but ideal for the teachers, but everyone agreed that it was clearly
best for the children. They were getting to know each other, and
their teachers, and adjusting to a new environment, under the
reassuring gaze of their moms or dads. The parents were also re-
assured by seeing how competent the teachers were. The following
year, each four-year-old had a thirty-minute appointment the day
before school with the new teacher. She spent that time playing
with and getting to know the child in the new classroom. School
started on an abbreviated schedule with no more than half of the
class coming at one time so that relationships could be worked on
and no child could get lost in the shuffle. Parents were required to
stay in the building for the first two ninety-minute school days and
after that each child's needs were individually assessed. Parents

were expected to stay if their children needed them. The time some parents had to take away from their jobs, or from other family members, was a very small investment in their child's attitude toward the very place he or she would be spending the next twenty or so years.

The alternatives are many, ranging from schools where parents never set foot in the classroom to schools that require a parent's presence for two weeks—to schools that expect parents to take turns assisting the teacher. My feeling on the subject is that the school must realize the importance of the parent-child relationship and do everything possible to ease the separation for the child. The child must feel comfortable, safe, and secure in the environment before the parent leaves. If you invest two weeks of your time now to stay with your child in school, it will help your child feel good about the school experience for many years. Don't be surprised if after an illness or long holiday, your child again has to be eased into the transition from home to school. A child this age should never be left in school—or anywhere else—crying for his or her mother.

There are some other ways that you, as a parent, can help to ease the transition from home to school for your child. We respond positively when people call us by name. As a fellow teacher, I appreciated how difficult it was to learn the names of so many children at one time, but as a parent I knew that I wanted my child to feel that he was important enough for the teacher to remember his name. I therefore always dressed him in shirts that had his name on them for the entire first week of school, as well as for birthday parties and other unfamiliar situations. You can use fabric paint to paint it on, or permanent "magic markers," press-on letters, or embroidery.

Some schools require children to wear uniforms. It is a safe bet that where all of the children look alike, they are being encouraged to think alike as well. This goes against human nature. David K. Shipler tells us that in Russia, schoolgirls who all wore brown uniforms and ribbons in their hair expressed their individuality by wearing subtly patterned stockings with their uniforms "as a faint form of rebellion into individual expression."* Some schools don't require uniforms, yet the children develop them themselves, as a

---

* "Russia, A People Without Heroes," The New York Times Magazine, October 16, 1983.

reflection of their habit of confirmity. In a school that truly nurtures individual expression, the children's clothing and hairstyles show variation and reflect individual personal taste more than peer pressure or authoritarian rules.

I found that summer camps are even more likely to be offering negative programs than schools are. The pervasive philosophy seems to be that children's minds are on vacation for the summer. Even camps that are affiliated with schools that do have sound art programs dispense with their positive creative curriculum and send the children home with Snoopys fashioned from Styrofoam cups and Miss Piggy figurines made from molds. Young counselors with absolutely no training in art or creativity regularly "teach" arts and crafts, a euphemism for "quiet time." The idea of a piano or violin teacher who didn't know how to play an instrument would be positively laughable, yet we accept this in the area of art quite regularly, both in schools and camps. As soon as it rains, out come the coloring books, as if children turned into mindless robots with the first raindrop.

Quite often in camps, we also find an undue emphasis on competition. "Color wars" pit child against child and take all of the fun out of games. Physical activity is rife with unhealthy competition. Children who adore playing games, and get essential physical exercise while doing so, suddenly discover that they are "losers," and often lose interest in the game. Although their skills may be steadily improving, clearly making them "winners," they stand sadly by while another child is awarded a medal or certificate. Why must well-meaning adults take all of the fun out of being young, when children learn so much more, and with so much more fun, when we get off their backs?

One very athletic four-year-old child told me he "always lost" at camp. He had a certificate proving that he was "junior olympic swimming champion" of his division in camp, but he still felt like a loser. Despite having won some contests, he had lost some too. The losses stood out in his mind far more than the wins because constant losers lose incentive. In contests, even the winners lose. They get an unrealistic idea of their own abilities accompanied by a tendency to "rest on their laurels."

> Self-esteem is the constant winner in cooperative
> games whose purpose is to attain a common goal

rather than to defeat an opponent.*

I have prepared this checklist for you to take with you as you look at schools and camps:

1. Is the work on display typical adult stereotypes or child-made art that reflects normal development?

2. Is all the art "pretty" or is some also expressive?

3. Do children make decisions about play activities or do what they are told?

4. Do all questions have one "correct" answer?

5. Can children do things that are messy, if they need to?

6. Are art materials, especially paint and easel, accessible to children and used at will?

7. Is reading a pleasurable or a painful activity?

8. Does dress vary and reflect the children's personalities?

9. What provisions are made to ease separation?

10. Are there specialists for music, art, and physical education?

11. Are children encouraged to compete with each other, or do they work toward their own goals?

12. Are letter or number concepts being introduced prematurely?

13. Does it look like fun?

* Susan D. Shilcock and Peter Bergson, *Open Connections: The Other Basics* (Bryn Mawr, Pa.: Open Connections, 1980), p. 67.

TWENTY-FIVE

Toys, Playthings, and Playmates

Children learn in a variety of ways; alone, together, and with adults. Fine motor skills are developed through manipulation of varied materials. Activities can be specific or open-ended, with the latter contributing more toward self-confidence, self-direction, independence, and creative thinking. Building with blocks, for example, works toward this end, while putting together puzzles teaches that there is always a "correct" answer to every problem. The set of blocks you bought for your one-year-old should be added to, as building becomes more elaborate and structures begin to be named and to play an increasing role in pretend play.

Pretending constitutes a big part in the play time for a three-to-four-year-old. It helps develop symbolic and abstract thinking and provides a richer, more meaningful understanding of the world around us. Fantasy play takes on greater importance than ever now, and it is an early manifestation of true creative thinking. An active imagination is the most wondrous gift, to be nurtured and encouraged at every turn. Toys and games that discourage it should play a very limited part in your child's life. *Let's Pretend,* by Julie Hagstrom, (New York: A&W Visual Library, 1982) offers some very helpful ideas on games you can play with your child to encourage fantasy play. There are also several books that you can read to the child that deal with imaginative play. My reviews of these books appear in Appendix III.

Important relationships develop between your child and his or her dolls and stuffed animals. You can encourage this by inviting a doll to dinner, bringing treats for it, accepting the role your child has assigned it, and generally treating it with a sense of importance. When Jason's "Kitty" was returned after being accidentally left behind in a museum, we bought a cake, lit candles, and sang, "Welcome home, Kitty." Needless to say, it was returned because I had sewn a name and address label to it just as soon as I realized how much Jason loved it. These meaningful symbols of people and animals can be so useful in working out problems and trying to understand the world.

When you notice that your child has turned every pencil, stick, and candy bar into an airplane, accompanying it with sound effects, don't decide it's time to run out and buy a shiny silver airplane. These other objects representing the airplane signal the start of abstract thinking and a creative use of pretending that is so important in developing the child's ability to be resourceful and creative. You can help by "seeing" the pencil as an airplane, "buying" an imaginary ticket, and "going" for a ride with the child. Expand the child's thinking with relevant questions such as: "Where will the plane land?" "What are they serving for lunch on board today?" "What does it look like from your window?" You'll need fewer toys now than you did for the last two years, since between the ages of three and four the child becomes increasingly involved in imaginative play. He or she will find a stick in the park and turn it into a magic wand, a sword, a cane, or dozens of other wonderful toys within the course of a day. By believing in each new assigned role the stick plays, and expanding the child's thinking through questions, you help enrich the child's play.

You can enrich your child's fantasy play through active participation and stimulating questions.

You can help encourage creative thinking through pretend play. Just about everything you do at home can become a game. Mealtime can be turned into an imaginary visit to a restaurant, with you and your child exchanging the roles of waiter and patron. While brushing your child's hair, pretend that you are a hairdresser in a salon; tying sneakers can become a "visit" to a shoe store, a ride in an elevator can be a trip on a rocket. A new addition to the family always inspires a child to revert to baby ways. You can be very helpful now by joining the game, offering to change a diaper, fix a bottle, and spoon-feed mush. This game will serve to remind the child that infants can't talk, eat cookies, play, or go to school and will probably make your child very satisfied about being "grown-up."

Dressing up, often in Mom's or Dad's old clothes, is something that children this age love to do. Costumes become an extension of children's bodies and help them to expand their understanding of it. The role playing that costumes encourage broadens a child's understanding of the adult world. Children do some sex role exploration in this manner and need to have an opportunity to try on

Try to obtain open-ended objects for a "dress up" collection.

adult clothes of both sexes. Dress-up time should be a time for fantasy, so don't lock your child into sex roles. Little boys may want to try on lipstick or nail polish, while girls need to see how they look in neckties. You can be absolutely certain that a three-year-old boy who wants to wear red nail polish will not want to wear it when he's twelve! Save some old clothes and accessories for a "dress-up" box or corner. You can also find some very interesting things in thrift shops that your child will love. Keep your eyes open for old bridal veils, uniforms, attaché cases, and feather boas, and remember:

A hat transforms the wearer as nothing else can.*

When securing objects for the "dress-up" box, try to keep them as open-ended as possible. A blue jacket with a little gold trim can be a uniform for a police officer or a soldier, while a G.I.

* John and Elizabeth Newson, *Toys & Playthings* (New York: Pantheon Books, 1979), p. 111.

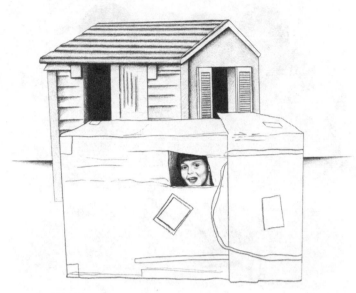

A cardboard box can be more exciting to play in than an expensive playhouse.

Joe suit is limited to that character. A yard of fabric can be a superhero's cape, a bridal veil, or a turban, while a child quickly becomes bored with a Superman cape and in no time will be asking for Batman, Spiderman, and Aquaman capes to play with. After all, every self-respecting child knows that Batman, Spiderman, and Aquaman don't wear Superman capes. Buy one only if you are willing to wind up with four.

Open-ended, nontoy playthings often can inspire the most creative play. In fact, a collection of old cartons and boxes makes a wonderful gift! When your child is interested in trains, brown cardboard boxes from the supermarket are as loved and used as any expensive, self-propelled train that catches one's eye in the toy store. The boxes are really much more valuable, however, because the train can only be a train, while the boxes can be rearranged tomorrow to become a truck, a building, an airplane, or a rocket to the moon. Here is a photo of a child playing in his own cardboard house, which he did incessantly for days—right in front of a $300 playhouse! His mother had bought the playhouse; the carton was his own discovery. It is easy to give children all of the wrong things. Expensive toys are advertised and children beg for them,

but these toys rarely fulfill a child's needs for extended, growing, and ever-changing play experiences.

We need to give our children time—our time. When we observe them at play and expand their horizons with tantalizing questions, we are stretching their minds. We also need to show interest in their play, since interest gives validity to what they are doing and increases self-confidence. I am not recommending that you sacrifice your whole life to your child; but neither can you be a weekend parent, nor always expect your child to play alone or with other children.

It also takes time to help children develop friendships with other children, but through these friendships their horizons are expanded. We often inadvertently insulate children from people who are very different from us and try to teach them with words about tolerance and understanding. These meaningless lectures are merely boring, while children of vastly different cultural roots and family structures need only to be introduced to each other in order to understand their lesson.

It is most effective if your child has time alone with you, time with friends (closely as well as loosely supervised), time alone, and time with other significant adults. A child who is exposed only to your ideas and value system will hardly grow up to be an individual with broad horizons.

TWENTY-SIX

Art Experiences

By now, your child has already developed a strong attitude about art. If it has been encouraged at home and has been an enjoyable experience, your child is well on his or her way to possessing a lifelong interest as well as a style of thinking that will contribute to many other areas of endeavor. If scribbling and smearing paints have met with parental disinterest or reprimands for messiness, the child will be already turning away from art, and it will be difficult, if not impossible, to reverse the trend.

The three-year-old is showing increasing interest in doing things correctly; whereas last year you heard "I want to do it myself," now you'll hear "Show me how" and "Is this the right way?" For this reason, it is important to be aware of the fact that there is not a "correct" way to draw. Let your child know that you heartily approve of his or her efforts. Provide time to work and materials to work with, but do *not* provide specific direction about what will be made. Now is the time when curiosity and creativity can be so easily crushed. The child who is now using coloring books and assembling adult-made art projects is not the child who will grow up with confidence in his or her own art abilities. Try to set a good example yourself. If you do needlepoint, do you stitch over someone else's guidelines? Your own lack of confidence provides a significant role-model for your child. If a lifetime of insecurity about your own art ability is too hard to overcome, why not try using your child's scribble as a pattern? It will save your own anxiety while becoming a great source of pride to the child.

Never give your child three triangles to paste in the "correct" spots on a pumpkin, or circles to paste on a car for wheels. These trite art projects perpetuate insecurity in one's own abilities, primarily because they are not what art is about for a three-year-old. If your own background makes it seem necessary for you to insist that your child tie in art projects with holidays, give him or her black paint and orange paper in October. Hang the resulting painting on your door—not some store-bought jack-o'-lantern or scarecrow—and never suggest that the child paint a pumpkin, skeleton, etc. When Christmas comes around, let your child freely cut shapes out of construction paper ("freely" doesn't mean they will look like traditional Christmas ornaments—they will look like a three-year-old's cutouts). Punch holes in the tops and hang them on your tree! Colorful scribbles, particularly when they are done on good-quality card-stock paper, make delightful greeting cards.

Appropriate art projects at this age level are never adult-directed. Give the child time to learn through manipulation of materials. Be very suspicious of any daycare, camp, scout, or school program that sends the children home with pictures that look like pumpkins, turkeys, robots, Easter baskets, and Christmas trees. Any project made up of noodles, macaroni, lentil seeds, or

the like pasted on a teacher-made shape has a negative effect on your child's artistic development. These teacher-pleasing experiences turn your child further and further away from the true meaning of art.

Too many parents and nursery school teachers offer these kinds of activities because of their own insecure feelings about their art expertise. This anatomically "correct" skeleton was made by three-year-old Jeffrey at Halloween. Each part of the skeleton was actually made by Jeffrey's teacher, and it was assembled by the child under very close supervision. Teachers often are encouraged to do these kinds of projects by parents who expect too much too soon from their bright offspring. Jeffrey's first rendering of his own human came a full six months later and was clearly not affected at all by this "anatomy" lesson. Jeffrey had many of these "anatomy" lessons in school; Jason had none. You can see by comparing their first drawings of a human that the lessons had no effect on his drawing development, though they probably did have an effect on his self-esteem. It was so clearly inappropriate for the child at this age that the skeleton was done correctly, probably to please the teacher, and quickly forgotten. At the same time, if a child's drawing experiments evolve naturally to include a human, the drawing techniques learned then are added to the child's memory bank, retained forever, and slowly built upon and expanded.

Jason's first human.

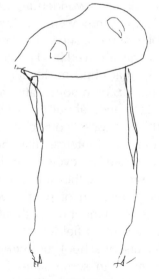

Jeffrey's first human.

One friend of mine who really didn't like the "mess" her two-year-old son's art projects created in her home told me, "He'll have enough time to paint in nursery school." Of course, since a child learns a full 50 percent of everything he or she will learn by age four, the total lack of art until age three teaches him or her a great deal as it is. In this case, the very same mother told me, two years later when her child had entered nursery school, that at the first parent/teacher conference in November, the one problem his teachers reported to her was that her child never expressed any interest in doing any of the art activities. When it was suggested that he try one, he refused. That mother finally realized, too late, that by taking her child to the playground each day she was encouraging physical activity and by offering no art and by punishing when the child made a mess or drew on her walls, she had taught him that art was not important in their lives. Not making provisions for art activities, of necessity, requires that children draw on the walls; yet few parents are willing to take responsibility for this when it happens. Instead, they punish the child, who soon has only negative associations with art. That mother inadvertently not only robbed her child of the world of art, but also deprived him of an important means of learning. That child was not born predisposed to shun art. I can personally attest to the fact that he was not born with any lack of talent or interest. I well remember him and Jason doing a wonderfully free chalk drawing on my living room wall when they were eighteen months old. When his mom came to pick him up, she said I "must be crazy" to allow such behavior. I not only allowed it—I photographed it for posterity. Within a year or so, that child no longer engaged in art activities, even in my home. His own home, after all, was the major influencing factor.

Ignorance about art is no excuse. You can't wait for an "expert" to expose your child to it. Fundamentally, a child forms attitudes and interests like those of his or her parents. Now is the time to end the cycle of art-illiterate parents raising children who are exactly like they are, and who will go on to produce generation after generation of people who have a great void in their lives where enjoyment of art should be, as well as a handicap in learning many other fields.

Nursery school, unfortunately, is no guarantee of valid art experiences. In some states it is possible for teachers to become certified without taking even one art education course. Add to that the fact that the teacher has to deal with ten or more painting three-year-olds at a time, and it's very likely that the child will have only negative art experiences in nursery school. I visited scores of nursery schools as part of my work or in connection with my child. In the entire city of New York I visited only two schools that I could say had solely age-appropriate art on display (I sent my child to one of them).

Many schools misuse art in the guise of ineffectively teaching counting or letter recognition, while effectively stifling creativity. In one school that I visited with my child when he was two and a half, he sat at a table, picked up a red crayon, and began to scribble. The teacher came over to him and ignorantly asked: "What are you drawing?" He thought for a minute and said, "A number two." "That's not a two," she said. She then picked up a blue crayon and drew a number two right over his picture. He came over to me and said, "I'm ready to go home now," and we did! That teacher clearly didn't know that *how* a child is drawing is far more important than *what* a child is drawing. Added to that was an insensitivity to the child's feelings.

What, you may well ask, should preschool art look like? It consists of the various stages of scribbling shown on page 105 and combinations of the following:

If it looks just like a real object, it is not age-appropriate art.

The leaf and turkey that follow are typical of the non-art projects forced on scribblers by overstructured nursery school programs. The leaf was freely painted by the child in school, only to be then cut out into a more "acceptable" shape by the teacher, who also drew and wrote all over it, in total violation of the integrity of the work. Both pictures were done by the same child within a month of his third birthday. His own art development was otherwise normal. His teacher told me that she had never taken a course in the art of young children. Nevertheless, she daily presented art projects to impressionable young children at a crucial time in their artistic development—the time when they are just beginning to understand that their scribbles can become pictures. Here is a free collage the child made on his own contrasted with a flag collage he made under his teacher's supervision. Both utilize similar types of materials; one is recognizably teacher-directed, the other free.

At one nursery school late in November, I saw a picture of a five-foot-high turkey, obviously drawn by the teacher. The children had painted over it, completely ignoring the teacher's outline. For

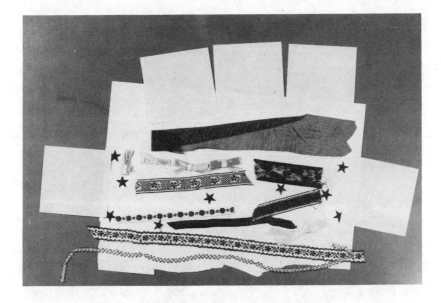

Turkeys are not what Thanksgiving is all about.

children who recognized that they were supposed to stay within the lines but couldn't, it was an introduction into feelings of inadequacy relating to art. Furthermore, turkeys are not what Thanksgiving is all about, thankfulness is. This holiday "art" time so many teachers feel compelled to have could be put to much better use doing age-appropriate projects, while the meaning of holidays can be expanded through personal experience and discussion. Personal reflection, and comparison of comments made by classmates, help children understand their privileges and give them an idea of how much they have to be thankful for.

> Watchful and well-meaning teachers who coax young children to draw real-life objects are not being helpful; indeed, their efforts may stifle the pride, the pleasure, the confidence so necessary to the growth of the creative spirit.*

* Rhoda Kellogg and Scott O'Dell, *The Psychology of Children's Art* (San Diego: CRM-Random House, 1967), p. 17.

If your child is already in a school that does inappropriate art projects, let your child's teacher know that you value your child's own work—indeed, you prefer it to teacher-made patterns. Parents' expectations are very important, and you can help by communicating your wishes to your child's school. Parents do have influence in schools. I know of one teacher whose students did wonderful, free, age-appropriate art who was told by her school director that, although she understood what the teacher was doing, parents expected realism and so she had better send home a few Christmas trees!

Neither parents nor teachers should ever consider giving adult-drawn maps or other pictures to children to be colored-in in the guise of teaching math, reading, or history. I have seen many nursery school children given coloring book pages and teacher-drawn art to color-in, which shows total ignorance of what a preschooler is all about. All preschool, nursery school, and kindergarten teachers have an obligation to their students to take some courses in early childhood art before embarking on their careers.

Some teachers may try to suggest that they are teaching "number or letter concepts," or that old standby "encouraging eye-hand coordination" when they give children coloring books or dots to connect to form letters or numbers. This is pure garbage! It is easy to see why children whose teachers are so insensitive to their art give up drawing after a while. It has long since been shown that coloring books work against, not toward learning, and similar paint-by-number, paint with water, and connect the dots are equally damaging to a child's development and self-esteem.

> . . . a thesis by Johnson (1963) indicated that tracing over a letter up to ten times was of no value in recognizing that letter later. There is no evidence that these laboriously colored balloons and kites actually help to develop either number concepts or reading abilities. Although no one will admit it, one of the main reasons for using these workbooks may well be that they give the classroom teacher a chance to have some rest while the youngsters fill in the appropriate number of birds or color the kites green.*

* Viktor Lowenfeld and W. Lambert Brittain, *Creative and Mental Growth*, 6th ed. (New York: Macmillan, 1975), p. 110.

In this illustration, Jeffrey's teacher wrote the number three and drew three symbols for strawberries. Jeffrey, as is appropriate for his age, scribbled freely all over the page. Even if he had colored in each strawberry neatly, the only thing he would have learned is how to suppress his own needs in order to please adults. Any teacher trying to introduce the concept "three" and familiarize children with strawberries need only bring three fresh, delicious strawberries for each child to eat. The number concept "three" is quickly learned as the child chews one, then two, then the third. The motivation to count is high when the child wants "just one more," not when the child mindlessly moves his or her hand back and forth within the confines of an adult's drawing. These "art" activities create dependency responses that, all too quickly, become habit forming. Children who experience too many of these kinds of activities go through life sitting meekly, awaiting instructions when offered crayons, and repeating the phrase: "I can't draw."

In an effort to counteract the poor art activities Jeffrey had in school, his parents made special efforts to encourage his creativity at home. One of the more interesting things that they did was to arrange an art exhibit of Jeffrey's original work at a prestigious New

Three-and-a-half-year-old Jeffrey poses with his art work.

York art gallery when he was three and a half. Invitations were sent out to family and friends, most of whom came bearing gaily wrapped gifts for him. The drawings and paintings were all framed and displayed to their best advantage. Needless to say, none of the pictures made by Jeffrey's teacher were displayed; but at no time did Jeffrey, while choosing pictures for the show, suggest that any of that work be included.

This is an opportunity that is not available to most of us, but there are many other ways for you to encourage your child in his or her creative endeavors.

It is difficult to find a play group, nursery school, daycare center, or camp that doesn't offer some coloring-in of adult drawings. When my son was three and a half the inevitable happened. He came home from day camp on a rainy day with a coloring book page he had scribbled over, if not colored-in. All of his previous efforts at producing his own art had always met with positive comments and encouragement. I was faced with the dilemma of showing pleasure at his efforts and displeasure over the counselor's choice of project. What I said was: "The counselor must not know

Adults who give children coloring books communicate their preference for adult art and their disdain for children's endeavors.

what a good artist you are. Maybe she thinks that you aren't smart enough to do your own drawings so she gave you this to color. But we know better. Shall I write her a note to let her know that you already know how to draw, or would you rather tell her yourself?"

Sometime during the third year, your child's scribbles will become outlined shapes. The same shapes that have been automatically included in scribbles up to now will be singled out and consciously repeated. There is a change in the look of the scribbles done now, since they are no longer as linear as they were and have become enclosed shapes. The beginning of symbolization comes as the child looks at what he or she has drawn and notices similarities to objects. Many of these shapes have lines radiating from them. It is possible that by the end of the year, realistic objects will appear in the drawings, and they are derived directly from these mandala-like circles with radiating lines—the lines become arms

Sometime during the third year, your child's scribble will become outlined shapes.

and legs which radiate from the body, which is represented by the basic circle or oval. People are the most popular first attempts at realism, closely followed by animals, buildings, and vehicles.

I hope that the event will not be marked by significantly greater enthusiasm than has been shown for the child's art achievement so far. The fact that you understand and relate to representational drawing doesn't make it more important. All stages of art are important and require your interest and support. After discovering that they can make an image, children go back and forth between image-making and design. If you have expressed a clear preference for realism, you discourage this very necessary movement back and forth. Children need to explore and understand each stage totally before they abandon it. It is terribly important to support children in their efforts to master lines and shapes. Children need a solid foundation of these abstract design experiences before they can move to representation. If they abandon personal experimentation and move right into copying stereotypes, they miss an im-

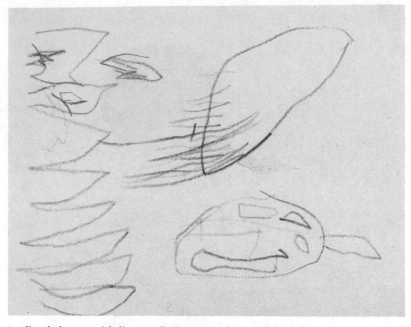

Outlined shapes with lines radiating from them will later become body shapes with arms and legs radiating from them.

portant stage of mental development.

So many parents have proudly shown me early art work their grown children had done years before. Invariably these pictures depict the human figure—something not done until about age four. No one remembered what had happened to three years' worth of drawing before the inevitable picture of a human showed up. Many parents don't seem to really become interested and appreciate their children's work until they can understand it and relate to it themselves. Even art educators rarely recognize the significance of this early stage of art. Early scribbles are a language unto themselves and reveal a lot about the individual as well as something about development. It therefore behooves parents to learn their child's graphic language just as they understand baby talk. Mothers understand the language of their children long before the children are speaking like adults. In order to keep the lines of communication open and to help our children reach their potential, it is just as important for mothers, fathers, and teachers to understand the visual language of scribbles, which children use for the many years

Animal

Building

Vehicle

People are the most popular first attempts at realism, closely followed by animals, buildings, and vehicles.

before they can draw representationally or write. It is counterproductive for you to make representational interpretations of a child's scribble designs.

Your child has now outgrown the urge to draw on walls (unless it's become a perfect act of rebellion in your home). Art materials should be readily available and in view. The easel should be permanently set up in a special area with drawing utensils, paints, paper, and brushes all ready to use. Paper should still be at least 14" x 17". Crayons, markers, paper scraps, and paste can be kept on a shelf, on the child's work table, or together in a box that the child has access to. A sponge or paper towels should be part of the art box so that the child can take responsibility for any spills. He or she should always be secure in the knowledge that Mom won't be angry to see a little paint on the floor if it got there in the creation of a masterpiece.

At this age, simple materials and limited colors are still the most effective learning tools. The most important projects to stimulate creativity and intellectual development remain free scribbling experimentation, independent painting, and working with three-dimensional manipulative materials.

Art Contests

The quickest way to rob your child of the true value of art as exploration and self-expression is to create competition between children by having contests. In order to have a "winner," you must have "losers," and there are a lot more losers than there are winners in any contest. What purpose is served by telling a child that his or her art work, which represents so much of the child's development and feelings, "lost"? Most judges of these contests know nothing about children's art and judge the work by adult standards anyway. The winner invariably is the picture that looks most like an adult drew it. When my sister was young, her favorite radio show sponsored a drawing contest, the winner to receive a camera. Our mother sat down, did a perfect rendition of Donald Duck, and entered it in my sister's name. Gail won, proving to herself that her own age-appropriate art was worthless and that adults value children who are most like themselves—adults.

Art contests are not the only way that harmful competition is forced on children. Often adults single out one child for the honor of being "class artist," or "the best artist in the family." That child's work is most often praised and displayed and becomes the barometer by which other children judge their own work. Often they will stifle their own needs and imitate these favored artists! This doesn't help the children learn and turns many away from art permanently.

TWENTY-SEVEN

Movement

Three-year-olds are secure in their bodies, and can explore the qualities of movement and find their own ways of doing things. Since imagination is at its richest now, you can incorporate it into the child's movement repertoire. Pretending inspires body use when presented properly. Movement specialists Cynthia Olivera and Patty Caplan use some of these ideas with their classes of three- and four-year-olds: "Be a lump of clay" (one child is the clay, another the sculptor), "Do the Jell-O jiggle" (making your feet, legs, hips, arms, etc., move just like Jell-O). They ask their students to crawl into a tunnel as one object or creature, then crawl out the other side as another, or to "look out the window at the city street and pretend to be the very first thing you see." Put up a sheet, shine a light behind it, and let your children entertain each other with silhouette shows. The exaggerated shadow encourages experimental body movement.

Other stimulating ideas might be: "How would an orange move?" "What if you were a balloon?" "Pretend you are a bubble!" "Move as if you were sad, tired, or happy." "How does a kangaroo look to you?" Since animals also represent human characteristics, such as power or gentleness, enacting the roles of animals helps children understand and accept these characteristics in themselves. Be careful that these dance exercises don't lose their spontaneity, however. Creative dance teacher and author John Wiener cautions: "It's quite possible for an overly structured teacher to use 'Be a horse, flower, train, etc.' as an excuse for

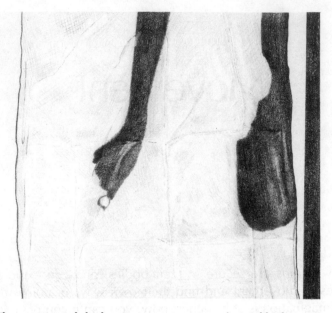

The exaggerated shadow can encourage experimental body movement.

creative activities and turn them into exercises in skills." There is
never any reason to correct the child. The individual's personal
expression must always be respected, even when it differs from our
own. The point here is not being "correct," it is simply a way of
getting a child to use and enjoy his or her body. Through these
experiments in movement, children are able to develop confidence
and find some personal mastery of movement in the physical universe.

Sometimes music is all that is needed to inspire movement.
Three-year-olds can easily use movement to interpret music or
express feelings. Play "happy" or "sad" music and let your child
make up dances. Next time life is miserable in your home, turn a
tantrum into a "war dance"—probably its real origin! Use props
like tom-toms to emphasize the rhythm and let your child apply
"scary makeup" to heighten the effect and increase awareness of
his or her angry face. Any activity that your child has feelings about
can be expressed through the vehicle of dance. There is nothing
more stifling to an interest in dance than most dance classes for
young children. Movement should help children to feel good about
their bodies and use their new-found physical skills expressively.
Teaching three-year-olds specific dances or basic steps provides

answers for questions as yet unasked. These lessons are movement equivalents of coloring books. The adorable recital at the end of the course traditionally marks an end to the careers of many potential ballerinas. The rare child who continues will eventually have to unlearn bad habits and work on rediscovering his or her personal physical relationship with rhythm and music. Ideally, a classroom should create an environment for learning. When movement is taught from a creative point of view, the emphasis is on developing individual potential and using dance to discover and express inner feeling. All of the arts best serve the child when taught from this personalized point of view. John Wiener has no mirrors in his dance studios. "We're not so concerned with how movement *looks,* as with how it *feels.* . . . I call it the mirror within." Eurhythmics, moving to and feeling rhythms, encourages children to experience music on a direct, physical level.

Why, in these liberated times, when every newspaper and magazine you pick up talks about changing sex roles and careers, was my son the only boy in a creative dance class for three-year-olds? Despite our voiced concern, we are perpetuating antiquated stereotypes. As a parent, I want my child to grow up feeling good about his body. Even if you are old-fashioned enough to think that dance is an unsuitable career for a man, I don't think you need to worry that doing some creative dance will force a boy into an early career choice. Depriving boys of a chance to use their bodies expressively robs them of much more than a possible future career. Boys are frequently more physically active than girls are and need opportunities to channel their energy usefully. Because of society's expectations, it is frequently difficult for males to express their feelings. If we can help our sons to do so through their natural physical abilities, we will all benefit. There is, of course, safety in numbers. One day my little boy may look around and realize he's the only boy in a class full of girls. He'll probably join the ranks of males the world over in thinking that dance is only for girls— despite all of my efforts.

Books about dance that will be enjoyed by the young dancer are listed in Appendix II and are reviewed in Appendix III.

Sports for young children are often handled in the same stifling way that dance is. I know that there are specific rules in each sport and correct ways to hold or use equipment, but age three, or even four, is not the time to introduce these rules. Lots of rules only

make a child self-conscious. Don't expect children this age to approach a sport as an adult does any more than they should be drawing, making music, or thinking like an adult. Just wearing skis and being out in the snow or running after balls on a tennis court with racquet in hand is usually enough to whet a child's appetite for mastering a sport.

You really don't have to teach a child the "right" way to do something. They'll watch you and learn what they are ready to learn. Their questions will alert you to their level of readiness. Responding to the child's questions will ultimately be the most effective way to teach the rules. The child will ask them when he or she is most ready to learn. Before then, leave the rule books at home and let the child have some fun! Sometimes children have

Galloping

Skipping

Hopping

so much energy they only want to run. Provide a big enclosed space for running and channel the movement into games such as Statue, Red Light-Green Light, or Freeze, if the children seem to be getting too "wild."

Music, too, can inspire certain predictable kinds of activities, such as hopping (like a frog or a rabbit) and skipping. The song "Skipping" alternates a "run" eighth-note with a "walk" quarter-note. Children this age won't have the necessary coordination to skip from one foot to the other, but even if they skip with only one foot, they are hearing the rhythmic sound of the skipping song and are moving their bodies according to the rhythm and connecting the sound to the rhythm. Praise the effort at skipping, even if it is not "accurate."

TWENTY-EIGHT

Music

It is not unusual for some four-year-olds to be starting to read, and some recognize many letters of the alphabet and express a desire to write them. Exposure to books, educational television, and seeing adults read have all gradually lead to an interest in reading, and scribbling helps provide a foundation for writing. We don't want to push children to read too early, but we can provide many age-appropriate preliminary activities that naturally stimulate an interest in reading. After interest in reading is evidenced, we show children that each letter is a symbol for a sound. The same is true in music notation! Even infants understand that pictures of things represent those objects, and young children look at picture books for several years before they are able to understand the alphabet. The most effective techniques for introducing music notation to very young children are very similar to those used in reading readiness.

A child who was never exposed to the written word would grow up illiterate—as most do, unfortunately, in the area of music. Children don't only learn to read what others have written, but they must learn to express themselves in writing as well. Music notation is the basic alphabet of music. Being literate in music means being able to both read and write music. Early, pleasant exposure to the concept of "reading" music notes will form the foundation for later literacy. It would be preposterous to expect a young child to understand and read an alphabet before he or she was old enough to understand the concept of abstraction, so we

must begin by first showing children realistic-looking symbols for objects in picture books and later move on to introduce the abstract symbols for sounds. Recent research has proven that children learn much more, much earlier, than we ever imagined. But this must never be translated as meaning that they should read or write letters, play instruments like adults do, or memorize the music notes. What it means is that children are learning many diverse things that ultimately culminate in their being able to do some of these things. Skipping stages of development may show impressive early results, but it does not provide an effective foundation for building further learning upon. Children must hear sounds before they can speak, and must speak before they can write. So too, we begin by hearing music, then we make music, and we must develop a personal feeling for music before moving on to learning music skills. The desire to learn these skills should come from the child and should not be imposed by an adult. And only then are we ready to see the connection between the music and the symbols.

In music notation, the concept of doing age-appropriate preliminary activities before introducing the staff and music notes translates to showing children realistic "pictures" of rhythm. The

"beat" is the easiest thing to hear, and all children begin by expressing music through rhythm, just as primitive peoples do. It is logical, therefore, to first introduce pictures of symbols of rhythmic patterns before moving on to symbols for melodic notes. Such pictures remind me of the pictures of toys you paste on a toy box to indicate what is inside and later replace with a word label. In her book *Threshold to Music*, Mary Helen Richards (Palo Alto, Calif.: Fearon Publishers, 1964) gives these samples of pictures that represent rhythms. A young child can easily understand that when the sticks are depicted touching the drum they represent a beat, and when the sticks are up in the air it means "rest." Then the large flower, elephant, or bird represents a long sound, while the smaller versions represent short sounds. In no time, children can follow the pictures and "read" rhythm, a precursor to reading music.

Just as hearing will precede language acquisition, so is it the first introduction to music. Simple, enjoyable games can be devised to provide an introduction to music. Since children do so much of their learning through physical movement, these games will naturally allow for a lot of movement. They also must always allow for the child to make music. You can begin by hiding something and making louder and louder sounds on a musical instrument as the child gets closer to finding it. A variation may involve playing an increasingly fast tempo or a more melodic tune as the child nears the goal. Then change places and let the child figure out a way to clue you in on how well you are doing at finding what he or she hid. You can play off-key notes to signify humor, high- or low-pitched notes to represent size.

When the public begins to recognize the importance of music as a basic life skill, toy companies will devise games and toys that introduce music notation in play activities. Schools must consider music one of the basics, and all children should be able to read music, as they can now read books, by third grade. In Hungary, Zoltan Kodaly's methods of teaching music to young children have achieved exactly that, without the too-early introduction of the abstract symbols of music notation.

Every baby loves and responds to music; most ten-year-olds find music "lessons" a chore. Music-making as a form of early play can provide much of the learning that seems so boring to the older child. Children do not need to be taught to scribble, only encouraged at it and provided with appropriate materials. Adults observing a child scribbling learn a lot about the process of learning to create symbols, and how best to help their child progress. Like all effective education, music education must also take its cues from children. It is as inappropriate for young children to play songs well as it is for them to draw pictures that look like adult art. However, that does not mean that children must wait until they can play like adults do before they are given instruments.

Even the simple chants all children do form a foundation for understanding, and making, fine music. According to Kodaly, these chants use only the basic portions of the musical scale that children hear and can sing: do, re, mi, so, and la. Bank Street preschool music teacher Nancy Montgomery provided chants you may remember from your own childhood and can share with your child, including:

Bill Grogan's Goat	Candyman
Bim Bom	Che Che Koolay
Brush Your Teeth	Chicken and a Chicken
Cadima	Did You Feed My Cow?

Dulce
Flea!
Hey, Little Boy
I Saw
Jambo
John the Rabbit
Moon Don't Go
My Mama Told Your Mama
No More Pie
Peanut Butter and Jelly

Popcorn
Red Light, Red Light
Sheenasha
Telephone Song
Three Little Monkeys
Tongo
What's Your Name?
Who Built the Ark?
Who Fed the Chickens?
Who Took the Cookie?

One important way to support the blossoming of creativity in this imaginative age group is encouraging the child to make up chants and songs. "Na, Na, Na, Na, Na, I go first," which grates on the nerves of so many adults, is actually a very simply composed song that is easy for a child to repeat and remember. As much of an emphasis should be made on creating music as on learning or playing music. Quite often, creative endeavors in other areas stimulate music or lyric creation. Once when my son was working on a collage he spontaneously burst into this song:

(To the tune of "Skip to My Lou")

Glue, glue, stick to my glue,
Glue, glue, stick to my glue,
Glue, glue, stick to my glue,
Stick to my glue my paper.

An excellent source of children's chants is *Chants for Children* compiled by Mary Louise Colgin (Colgin Publishing, Manlius, New York, 1982).

Two little ducks that I once knew,
Fat ones, skinny ones, there were two
But the one little duck with the feathers on his
    back,
He led the others with a quack, quack, quack.
Down to the river they would go,
Wibble, wobble, wibble, wobble, to and fro.
But the one little duck with the feathers on his
    back,
He led the others with a quack, quack, quack.
He led the others with a quack, quack, quack.

Teddy Bear, Teddy Bear, turn all around.
Teddy Bear, Teddy Bear, touch the ground.
Teddy Bear, Teddy Bear, read the news.
Teddy Bear, Teddy Bear, shine your shoes.
Teddy Bear, Teddy Bear, go upstairs.
Teddy Bear, Teddy Bear, say your prayers.
Teddy Bear, Teddy Bear, turn out the light.
Teddy Bear, Teddy Bear, say GOOD NIGHT!

I never saw a purple cow.
I never hope to see one.
But I can tell you anyhow
I'd rather see than be one.

It's raining; it's pouring,
The old man is snoring.
He went to bed with a pain in his head
And didn't get up until morning.

Five little monkeys, jumping on the bed.
One fell off and bumped his head.
Mama called the doctor, and the doctor said,
"No more monkeys jumping on the bed."

Four little monkeys . . . three . . . two . . . one.

Five little ducks went swimming one day,
Over the pond and far away.
Mother Duck said, "Quack, quack, quack."
But only four little ducks came back.

Four little ducks . . . three . . . two . . . one.

There were five in the bed and the little one said,
"Roll over, Roll over."
So they all rolled over and one fell out —(pause).
There were four in the bed and the little one said,
"Roll over. Roll over."
So they all rolled over and one fell out —(pause).
(Continue with numbers three and two.)
There was one in the bed and the little one said,

"GOOD NIGHT!"

Who stole the cookies from the cookie jar?
    (Name) stole the cookies from the cookie jar.
Who, me?
    Yes, you.
Couldn't be.
    Then who?

(Another child's name) stole the cookies from the
    cookie jar.
    Who, me?
Yes, you.
    Couldn't be.
Then who?

(Repeat, using each child's name.)

Writing new words to old songs is one easy way to begin. A nursery class wrote these lyrics to an existing song, "B-I-N-G-O":

Four-Year-Olds' Song
1. There was a class of four-year-olds
And everyone was different.
Chorus.
We are four-year-olds, we are four-year-olds,
We are four-year-olds, and everyone is different.
2. Everybody's face is different
And everybody's eyes.
Chorus.
3. Favorite colors are different, too.
And hair color, too.
Chorus.
4. Our names are special, our shoes are different,
And we wear different clothes.
Chorus.
5. Some have brothers, some have sisters,
And some of us have cousins.
Chorus.

Children learn much more about painting by painting than by copying or coloring pictures from a museum, and ultimately assimilate more about music by creating music than by parroting it.

Educational television has done so much to help children learn to read letters and numbers. It is far more effective than traditional methods of education because it recognizes that learning can be enjoyable and natural and that teaching doesn't have to be force-feeding some information to unwilling children. If their expertise were applied to music notation, the world would be greatly enriched, through the addition of a whole generation of literate music makers. It is up to us as parents to see to it that educational television, nursery schools, and toy companies recognize how necessary music is to our society.

Appendix I

Books About Art, Music, Dance, and Creativity for Young Children, Arranged by Subject

Activity Books
The Anti-Coloring Book®, by Susan Striker and Edward Kimmel
The Second Anti-Coloring Book®, by Susan Striker with Edward Kimmel
The Third Anti-Coloring Book®, by Susan Striker
The Fourth Anti-Coloring Book®, by Susan Striker
The Fifth Anti-Coloring Book®, by Susan Striker
The Sixth Anti-Coloring Book®, by Susan Striker
The Anti-Coloring Book® of Masterpieces, by Susan Striker
The Anti-Coloring Book® of Red Letter Days, by Susan Striker
Build a Better Mousetrap, An Anti-Coloring Book®, by Susan Striker
Exploring Space on Earth, An Anti-Coloring Book®, by Susan Striker
The Superpowers™ Anti-Coloring Book®, by Susan Striker
Young at Art®, The First Anti-Coloring Book® for Preschoolers, by Susan Striker
. . . And How to Draw Them, by Amy Hogeboom
The Metropolitan Museum of Art Activity Book, by Osa Brown

Amorphic Shapes
The Little Red Ant, by Yvonne Hooker

Art
The Anti-Coloring Book® of Masterpieces, by Susan Striker
Going for a Walk with a Line, by Douglas and Elizabeth MacAgey
A Painted Tale, by Kate Canning

Artists
An Artist, by M. B. Goffstein
Ernie's Work of Art, by Valjean McLenighan
Jackson Makes His Move, by Andrew Glass
Leonardo da Vinci, by Ibi Lepscky
Liang and the Magic Paintbrush, by Demi

Lives of the Artist, by M. B. Goffstein
Pablo Picasso, by Ibi Lepscky
The Painter's Trick, by Piero and Marisa Ventura

Beauty
Everybody Needs a Rock, by Byrd Baylor
Miss Rumphius, by Barbara Cooney

Black
Black Is Beautiful, by Ann McGovern

Blue
New Blue Shoes, by Eve Rice

Building
Changes, Changes, by Pat Hutchins
Exploring Space on Earth, An Anti-Coloring Book, by Susan Striker
I Can Build a House, by Shiego Watanabe
My Hands Can, by Jean Holzenthaler

Camouflage
Brown Bear in a Brown Chair, by Irina Hale

Children Drawing
A Picture for Harold's Room, by Crockett Johnson
The Scribble Monster, by Jack Kent

Children Painting
Ernie's Little Lie, by Dan Elliot
Francie's Paper Puppy, by Achim Broger and Michelle Sambin
The Goodbye Painting, by Linda Berman
Liang and the Magic Paintbrush, by Demi

Circles
Fly Hoops Fly, by Yutaka Sujita
A Kiss Is Round, by Blossom Budney
Round and Round and Round, by Tana Hoban
Round in a Circle, by Yvonne Hooker
Round Things Everywhere, by Seymour Reit

Clay
Maria Making Pottery, by Hazel Hyde
When Clay Sings, by Byrd Baylor

Multiple Color Differentiation
Blue Hat, Green Hat, by Sandra Boynton
Brown Bear, Brown Bear, What Do You See?, by Bill Martin, Jr.
The Color Kittens, by Margaret Wise Brown
Color Wheel, by Peter Robinson
Colors, by Peter Curry
Colors, by Jan Pientowski
Colors, by John J. Reiss
Colors, by Peter Schaub
Colors, Colors, All Around, by Rochelle Scott
The Colors That I Am, by Cilla Sheehan
Feeling Blue, by Robert Jay Wolff
Follow Me!, by Mordicai Gerstein
The Great Blueness and Other Predicaments, by Arnold Lobel
Green Says Go, by Ed Emberly
Hailstones and Halibut Bones, by Mary O'Neill
Is It Red? Is It Yellow?, by Tana Hoban
I Want to Paint My Bathroom Blue, by Ruth Krauss
Let's Paint a Rainbow, by Eric Carle
Look at Rainbow Colors, by Rena K. Kirkpatrick
Mabel and the Rainbow, by Carol Niklaus
Magic Monsters, by Jane Bilk Moncure
May Horses, by Jay Wahl
My Very First Book of Colors, by Eric Carle
Open Your Eyes, by Roz Abisch
Orange Is a Color, by Sharon Levy
The Rainbow, by Mike Thaler
Red and Blue, by Janet Martin
Richard Scarry's Color Book, by Richard Scarry
Roses Are Red, Are Violets Blue?, by Alice and Martin Provenson
What Is the Color of the Wide, Wide World?, by Margaret Friskey

Color Mixing
Adventures of Three Colors, by Annette Tison and Talus Taylor
The House of Four Seasons, by Roger Duvoisin

Little Blue and Little Yellow, by Leo Lionni
The Strawberry Book of Colors, by Richard Hefter

Color Mood
Color Seems, by Ilma Haskins
Feeling Blue, by Robert Jay Wolff
Hello Yellow, by Robert Jay Wolff
Seeing Red, by Robert Jay Wolff
What Is the Color of the Wide, Wide World?, by Margaret Friskey

Creative Thinking
Daydreamers, by Eloise Greenfield
Good Junk, by Judith A. Enderle
If I Weren't Me . . . Who Would I Be?, by Pam Adams
Imagine That! Exploring Make-Believe, by Joyce Strauss
Regards to the Man in the Moon, by Ezra Jack Keats

Creativity
I Wish I Had a Computer That Makes Waffles, by Dr. Fitzhugh
    Dodson
Oh, Were They Ever Happy, by Peter Spier
Suzuki Bean, by Sandra Scoppettone

Dance
Angelina Ballerina, by Katherine Holabird
At Every Turn! It's Ballet, by Stephanie Riva Sorine
Dance Away, by George Shannon
The Dancing Class, by Helen Oxenbury
The Dancing Man, by Ruth Bornstein
Imagine That! It's Modern Dance, by Stephanie Riva Sorine
I'm Dancing, by A. McCarter and G. Reed
Our Ballet Class, by Stephanie Riva Sorine
That's Jazz, by Stephanie Riva Sorine

Dark
A Dark, Dark Tale, by Ruth Brown

Diagonals
The Slant Book, by Peter Newell

Easter Eggs
The Easter Egg Artists, by Adrienne Adams

Finding Pictures in Shapes
It Looked Like Spilt Milk, by Charles G. Shaw
Splodges, by Malcolm Carrick

Finger Painting
Finger Paint and Pudding Prints, by Ann Sayre-Wiseman
Fingerprint Owls and Other Fantasies, by Marjorie Katz

Five Senses
Faces, by Barbara Brenner
My Five Senses, by Aliki
Five Senses, by Tasha Tudor

Green
The Big Green Book, Robert Graves (illustrated by Maurice Sendak)
Spring Green, by Selkowe/Bassat

Hoops
Fly Hoops Fly, by Yutaka Sujita
Holes and Peeks, by Ann Jonas

Imaginative Thinking
A Picture for Harold's Room, by Crockett Johnson
Regards to the Man in the Moon, by Ezra Jack Keats

Line
The Dot and the Line, by Norton Juster

Listening
The Country Noisy Book, by Margaret Wise Brown
The Indoor Noisy Book, by Margaret Wise Brown
Listen! Listen!, by Ann and Paul Rand
Listen to That, by H. Klurfmeier
The Listening Walk, by Paul Showers
The Noisy Book, by Margaret Wise Brown
Old MacDonald Had a Farm (pictures by Moritz Kennel)

Long and Thin
Do You Want to Be My Friend?, by Eric Carle
Magic Shoelaces, by Audrey Wood

Looking
Bird's Eye, by Judy Graham and Michael Ansell
Do You See What I See?, by Helen Borten
Everybody Needs a Rock, by Byrd Baylor
Guess What?, by Roger Bester
I Am Eyes, Ni Macho, by Leila Ward
I See, by Rachel Isadora
Max the Artlover, by Hanne Turk
Take Another Look, by Tana Hoban
The Turn About, Think About, Look About Book, by Beau Gardner
What Is It? A Book of Photographic Puzzles, by Joan Loss
Where Is It? A Hide-and-Seek Puzzle Book, by Demi

Movies
Ida Makes a Movie, by Kay Chorao

Museums
Child's Play Museum, by P. Adams
A Tale of Two Williams, by D. Goldin and I. Heckel
Visiting a Museum, by Althea

Music
Journey into Jazz, by Nat Hentoff
A Little Schubert, by M. B. Goffstein
Max, the Music Maker, by Miriam B. Stecher and Dr. Alice S. Kandell
Miranda, by Tricia Tusa
Music, Music for Everyone, by Vera B. Williams
The Old Banjo, by Dennis Haseley
Pet of the Met, by Lydia and Don Freeman
The Philharmonic Gets Dressed, by Karla Kushkin
Something Special for Me, by Vera B. Williams
The Troll Music, by Anita Lobel

Painting
Begin at the Beginning, by Amy Schwartz

Francie's Paper Puppy, by Achim Broger and Michelle Sambin
The Painter's Trick, by Piero and Marisa Ventura

Paper
Let's Make Rabbits, by Leo Lionni
Paper, Paper Everywhere, by Gail Gibbons

Photography
The Photographer and the Pony, by Fred Gurner
Simple Pictures Are Best, by Nancy Willard
Snapshot Max, by Hanne Turk

Pink
First Pink Light, by Eloise Greenfield

Printing
Finger Paint and Pudding Prints, by Ann Sayre-Wiseman
Fingerprint Owls and Other Fantasies, by Marjorie P. Katz

Progressive Shapes
Fuzzy, What-Was-He?, by Peter Saymour
The Little Red Ant, by Yvonne Hooker

Purple
Harold and the Purple Crayon, by Crockett Johnson
Tobo Hates Purple, by Gina Calleja

Puzzles
The Missing Piece, by Shel Silverstein
The Missing Piece Meets the Big O, by Shel Silverstein
Where Is It?, by Demi

Red
Big Bird's Red Book, by Rosanne and Jonathan Cerf
Clifford the Big Red Dog, by Norman Bridwell
Clifford the Small Red Puppy, Norman Bridwell
The Little Red Balloon, by Iela Mari
The Red Balloon, by A. Lamorisse
Red Is Best, by Kathy Stinson
Seeing Red, by Robert J. Wolff

Reflections
If I Weren't Me . . . Who Would I Be?, by Pam Adams

Sculpture
Faces on Places, by Suzanne Haldane
I Carve Stone, by Joan Fine
Norman the Doorman, by Don Freeman

Self-Expression Through Art
The Goodbye Painting, by Linda Berman
The Trip, by Ezra Jack Keats

Shadows
Dreams, by Ezra Jack Keats
Nothing Sticks Like a Shadow, by Ann Tompert
Shadow, translated by Marcia Brown from the French of Blaise
    Cendrars
Shadow, by Taro Gomi
Shadows Here, There and Everywhere, by Ron and Nancy Goor

Shapes
Circles, Triangles, and Squares, by Tana Hoban
The Dot, by Cliff Roberts
Shapes, by Peter Curry
Shapes, by John J. Reiss
Shapes, by Gillian Youdon
Shapes and Things, by Tana Hoban
Spaces, Shapes, and Sizes, by Jane Jonas Srivastava

Smell
Follow Your Nose, by Paul Showers

Spirals
Spirals, by Larry Kettelkamp

Square
The Box Book, by Cecilia Maloney
Boxes! Boxes!, by Leonard Everett Fisher
Draw Me a Square, by Robyn Supraner
Square Is a Shape, by Sharon Lerner

Texture
The Blind Men and the Elephant (illustrated by Paul Galdone)
Find Out by Touching, by Paul Showers
Fuzzy, What Was He?, by Peter Saymore
Is It Rough? Is It Smooth? Is It Shiny?, by Tana Hoban
Pat the Bunny, by Dorothy Kunquist
What Is Your Favorite Thing to Touch?, by Myra Tomback Gibson

Triangle
Shapes and Colors, #3, published by Price/Stern/Sloan

Ugly
The Ugly Book, by Arthur Crowley and Annie Gusman

Water
Rain Drop Splash, by Alvin Tresselt
The Rain Puddle, by Adelaide Holl
Splish, Splash, by Yvonne Hooker
Water Is Wet, by Penny Pollock and Barbara Beirne

White
Stopping by Woods on a Snowy Evening, by Robert Frost

Yellow
The Big Yellow Balloon, by Edward Fenton
Hello Yellow, by Robert Jay Wolff
Marmalade's Yellow Leaf, by Cindy Wheeler
Who Has the Yellow Hat?, by Shinobu Ariga
Yellow, Yellow, by Frank Asch

Appendix II

Capsule Reviews of Books About Art, Music, Dance, and Creativity

*   indicates book is in print
?   print status unknown
•   book is out of print

* *Adventures of Three Colors*
by Annette Tison and Talus Taylor
Charles E. Merrill Publishing Co.
This book uses acetate overlays and is the most effective tool for teaching color mixing, except, of course, for actually working with paints. First in a series of four books; the others are *Animals in Color Magic, Hide and Seek,* and *Inside and Outside.* The stories and cute effects in the last three detract from what was originally an excellent idea. The first book is, by far, the best.

* *. . . And How to Draw Them*
by Amy Hogeboom
Vanguard Press
This is a series which includes nine books, each with a theme such as forest animals, dogs, cats, horses, familiar animals, wild animals, boats, birds, and sea animals. In addition to giving information about each subject, the author gives specific directions and formulas for drawing one view of the subject. This is a prime example of what is wrong with art education in our society. Exposure to this kind of simplistic "art" instructions turns so many children away from real creative exploration and makes them feel insecure about their own age-appropriate drawings. Training like this makes children rely on adult directions and stop using their own eyes and begin to see only others' views of things.

* *Angelina Ballerina*
by Katherine Holabird
illustrated by Helen Craig

Crown Publishers
Angelina is so obsessed with dancing that she cannot concentrate on anything else. She dances when she is supposed to be doing other things. When her parents allow her to take ballet lessons she is so busy in dance class that she is able to think about other things when she is finished dancing. She does her chores at home, works very hard in dance class, and grows up to be a famous ballerina.

The Anti-Coloring Books®
by Susan Striker
  * *The Anti-Coloring Book®*
  * *The Second Anti-Coloring Book®*
  * *The Third Anti-Coloring Book®*
  * *The Fourth Anti-Coloring Book®*
  * *The Fifth Anti-Coloring Book®*
  * *The Sixth Anti-Coloring Book®*

A series of thirteen books. Each of the above contains forty-five ideas to stimulate creative thinking and self-expression in children ages six and up. Each page consists of a mind-tingling suggestion and a partial drawing to get the reader started. After that, anything goes. Questions include: "Have you ever had a dream come true?" "What does the tooth fairy look like?" "What does it look like inside your stomach after you eat a big meal?" and "What will a newspaper look like in a thousand years?"

  * *The Anti-Coloring Book® of Exploring Space on Earth*
  by Susan Striker
  Holt, Rinehart and Winston
  The theme of this book is architecture and interior design. "What does the inside of your spaceship look like?" "What do you imagine a house in heaven looks like?" and "Build a tree-house where you can go to be alone."

  * *The Anti-Coloring Book® of Masterpieces*
  by Susan Striker
  Holt, Rinehart and Winston
  This book departs from the usual Anti-Coloring Book format by providing black and white and full color reproductions of par-tially reproduced masterpieces of art to inspire creativity. A faceless Mona Lisa allows you to draw your own idea of a

beautiful woman, and Roy Lichtenstein's triptych about the machine age is presented minus the center panel.

* *The Anti-Coloring Book® of Red Letter Days*
by Susan Striker
Holt, Rinehart and Winston
Children's favorite holidays, year-round and worldwide, are the subject of this book. Instead of the usual stereotypes we see representing these occasions, this book gives children an opportunity to express their feelings and excitement. "What do you wish for when you blow out the candles on your birthday cake?" "Design your own Halloween mask," and "What are you thankful for this Thanksgiving?" are some of the ideas designed to help children explore the real meaning of each holiday.

* *Build a Better Mousetrap, An Anti-Coloring Book®*
by Susan Striker
Holt, Rinehart and Winston
This book was written for the computer wizards, science buffs, and inventors among us. Twenty-eight partial drawings include "Design a new ride for the amusement park" and "Invent a way to combat weightlessness in space."

The Superpowers™ Anti-Coloring Book®
by Susan Striker
Grosset & Dunlap
Superman, Batman, Wonder Woman, and their allies join forces to encourage problem solving and inspire creativity.

* *Young at Art®, The First Anti-Coloring Book® for Preschoolers*
by Susan Striker
Fireside Books/Simon & Schuster
This book is aimed at the scribbling set. Information for parents and teachers on the significance of children's art and a full curriculum in early art education is included, as are activity pages for children to work.

* *An Artist*
by M. B. Goffstein

Harper & Row
If you can believe that "an artist is like God" and tries to make
paint "sing," this lyrical, religious approach to the work of an artist
will speak to you.

* *At Every Turn! It's Ballet*
by Stephanie Riva Sorine
photos by Daniel S. Sorine
Alfred A. Knopf
This book shows us that ballet is really in every movement we
make. Fine photographs of boys and girls dancing and at play help
us to see the beauty of bodies in action.

* *Begin at the Beginning*
by Amy Schwartz
Harper & Row
Sara feels pressured when her teacher gives her the assignment of
doing the class picture. Nothing she tries seems worthy, until she
finally decides to paint a picture of her favorite tree. For children
ages seven or eight, at least.

* *Big Bird's Red Book*
by Rosanne and Jonathan Cerf
illustrated by Michael J. Smollen
Little Golden Books/A Sesame Street Book/Western Publishing Co.
As Big Bird searches in his bag for a sample of something red, he
doesn't notice all of the red things that are passing right under his
nose.

* *The Big Green Book*
by Robert Graves
illustrated by Maurice Sendak
Macmillan
Jack finds a big green book of magic spells, which he quickly uses.
Unfortunately Mr. Sendak's illustrations are only in black and
white, so the fact that the book is green is incidental.

* *The Big Yellow Balloon*
by Edward Fenton
illustrated by Ib Ohlsson

Doubleday & Co.
An exciting adventure begins when young Roger buys a big yellow balloon. He is followed by a cat, who is followed by a dog, who is followed by the dogcatcher, who is followed by a lady trying to protect the dog, who is followed by a thief, who is followed by a police officer. When the balloon pops, there is havoc.

* Bird's Eye
by Judy Graham and Michael Ansell
The Green Tiger Press
This book chronicles the journey of two pigeons on their way to find two elderly friends, humans who have moved down south. It is stunningly calligraphed, and presents the reader with a new perspective on viewing the world.

* Black Is Beautiful
by Ann McGovern
photographs by Hope Wurmfeld
Four Winds Press
This is one of the very rare books to focus on one color. Sensitive black and white photographs illustrate black objects, although unfortunately the author occasionally focuses on things such as jelly beans or paint, which can be any color. The beautiful black face will also confuse a toddler who recognizes that "black" is really brown.

? The Blind Men and the Elephant
John Godfrey Saxe's version of the famous Indian legend
illustrated by Paul Galdone
McGraw-Hill Book Co.
This old Indian legend, retold with Paul Galdone's pictures, makes children aware of texture as well as how our senses inform us about the world.

* Blue Hat, Green Hat
by Sandra Boynton
Little Simon/Simon & Schuster
A silly book that twelve- to eighteen-month-old children love to giggle over, it mentions all of the colors.

? *The Box Book*
by Cecilia Maloney
illustrations by Carolyn Bracken
Golden Books/Western Publishing Co.
This inexpensive paperback describes all of the things that are
shaped like a box. Good for babies. Save it to look at when your
older child does box sculpture.

* *Boxes! Boxes!*
by Leonard Everett Fisher
The Viking Press
Colorful paintings and rhymes explore all of the things that boxes
can be used for.

* *Brown Bear, Brown Bear, What Do You See?*
by Bill Martin, Jr.
pictures by Eric Carle
Holt, Rinehart and Winston
Every animal sees another animal that is a new color. Charming
illustrations include a brown bear, redbird, green frog, yellow
duck, blue horse, purple cat, white dog, black sheep, goldfish.

* *Brown Bear in a Brown Chair*
by Irina Hale
Atheneum Publishers
A brown bear gets sat on all the time because no one can see him
in the brown chair. A new set of clothes seems to be a good
solution, but in the end his new outfit is made from the same fabric
as the chair's new slipcover, so again no one notices the bear.

* *Changes, Changes*
by Pat Hutchins
Macmillan
A brightly colored, charmingly illustrated picture book demonstrating how blocks can become anything the child can imagine.

? *Child's Play Museum*
by P. Adams
Child's Play
This book is a brief introduction to science and history museums,

with no mention at all of art museums. Bones, coins, armor, and pottery are shown in relation to history.

* *Circles, Triangles, and Squares*
by Tana Hoban
Macmillan
The child who already knows these shapes will enjoy finding them in Tana's artistic photographs.

* *Clifford the Big Red Dog*
story and pictures by Norman Bridwell
Four Winds Press
Emily Elizabeth describes her big, red, lovable dog Clifford. Simple illustrations in black, white, and red help a toddler recognize the color red.

* *Clifford the Small Red Puppy*
story and pictures by Norman Bridwell
Scholastic
Black, white, and red illustrations help the young viewer identify red while listening to the silly story of a dog who grew to be huge. Toddlers who love Clifford from other books in the series will also learn about the concept big.

? *The Color Kittens*
by Margaret Wise Brown
Golden Books/Western Publishing Co.
Hush and Brush, two kittens, have color-mixing adventures.

* *Color Seems*
by Ilma Haskins
Vanguard Press
A beautiful book about the nature of color, with illustrations that leave a lot to the imagination of the child. One of my favorites on this topic.

* *Color Wheel*
by Peter Robinson
Platt & Munk/Grosset and Dunlap
One page is devoted to each color in the color wheel, giving examples of objects that are that color.

* *Colors*
by Peter Curry
Price/Stern/Sloan Publishers
With one color per double page, this is a whirlwind of color information, including color-mixing facts. Best as a review for the experienced child.

* *Colors*
by Jan Pientowski
Little Simon/Simon & Schuster
One very simple graphic illustrates each color. The black cat will be confusing to the very young audience of this book, since they are learning that cats can be many different colors. The colors are luscious, but the drawings are based on stereotype formulas.

* *Colors*
by John J. Reiss
Bradbury Press
A beautifully illustrated book about color, which devotes one double page to each color.

? *Colors*
by Peter Schaub
illustrated by children from Lionel Road Primary School
Bowmar/Noble Publishers
This little paperback is enchantingly illustrated with children's paintings.

* *The Colors That I Am*
by Cilla Sheehan
illustrated by Glen Elliott
Human Sciences Press
A book that is simple yet sophisticated. It deals with the relationships between feelings and colors.

* *The Country Noisy Book*
by Margaret Wise Brown
Harper & Row
This book is designed to sensitize toddlers to the sounds we hear in the country.

* *Dance Away*
by George Shannon
Greenwillow Books
Rabbit's great dancing distracts the wolf's attention and saves his friends.

* *The Dancing Class*
by Helen Oxenbury
Dial Press Books for Young Readers/E. P. Dutton
Simple drawings depict a very young child's first dance class.

* *The Dancing Man*
by Ruth Bornstein
The Seabury Press/A Clarion Book
The dancing man gives the gift of dance to a sad, lonely boy. The boy finds all the ways that the world dances, and he brings happiness to others, as well as to himself, through dance. He grows up to become the dancing man, and gives his gift to a boy, as it was once given to him. Lovely.

* *A Dark, Dark Tale*
by Ruth Brown
Dial Press Books for Young Readers/E. P. Dutton
A slightly scary, very simple story that focuses on the dark, but has a silly surprise ending.

* *Daydreamers*
by Eloise Greenfield
illustrated by Tom Feelings
The Dial Press
Illustrations of black children caught daydreaming. The text points out what an important, growth-inducing activity daydreaming is.

* *Do You See What I See?*
written and illustrated by Helen Borten
Abelard-Schuman
The old (1959) book deals with line, shape, and color with surprisingly contemporary illustrations and fairly simple text.

* *Do You Want to Be My Friend?*
by Eric Carle
Thomas Y. Crowell Co.
This book is fun to have around when your child begins to roll clay
into a long coil and label it a snake. It has no words, but tells a
story with pictures. Your eyes follow along the very long snake
shape throughout the book, from left to right.

• *The Dot*
by Cliff Roberts
Franklin Watts
In a charming, simple way, this book traces the beginning of a
shape which started as a dot, was stretched to become a line, and
enclosed to form a shape—which later became the whole world.
Toward the end of the third year, when children are discovering
enclosed shapes for themselves, this book helps clarify and reinforce the learning. It ends with corny stereotypes of realistic drawings, ruining an otherwise wonderful book.

? *The Dot and The Line*
by Norton Juster
Random House
This book explores the qualities of line with a sophisticated sense
of humor.

? *Draw Me a Square*
by Robyn Supraner
pictures by Evelyn Kelbish
Nutmeg Press/Simon & Schuster
Describes all of the square things we see all around us, including
the confusing "walk around the block is square."

* *Dreams*
by Ezra Jack Keats
Macmillan
A young boy made a paper mouse and put it on his windowsill
when he went to sleep at night. In the middle of the night he was
awakened by a noise and found that a big dog had cornered his
cat and was threatening it. Just then the little paper mouse fell out

of the window. As it falls, the shadow that it casts on the wall gets bigger and bigger. It looks so ominous that it scares away the dog.

* *The Easter Egg Artists*
by Adrienne Adams
Charles Scribner's Sons
This family of bunnies are in the business of painting Easter eggs, but they also decorate houses, bridges, flagpoles, airplanes, and anything else they can think of.

* *Ernie's Little Lie*
by Dan Elliot
illustrated by Joe Mathieu
Random House/Children's Television Workshop
Ernie is so eager to win the beautiful box of paints that is the prize in Mr. Hooper's art contest that he allows his cousin's picture to be submitted as his own. When he wins the contest, he just cannot let everyone believe his lie. He admits that his cousin painted the picture and decides to send the paints to his cousin, the real winner.

* *Ernie's Work of Art*
by Valjean McLenighan
illustrated by Joe Mathieu
A Sesame Street Book featuring Jim Henson's Muppets
Western Publishing Co. in conjunction with Children's Television Workshop
Ernie is painting a view of Sesame Street, to the great interest of all of his Sesame Street friends. When Big Bird comes along on a unicycle and knocks down everything in sight, the picture is ruined. Oscar the Grouch loves the ruined painting and Ernie gives it to him as a gift.

* *Everybody Needs a Rock*
by Byrd Baylor
pictures by Peter Parnall
Charles Scribner's Sons
Ten rules for choosing your very own special rock because "everybody needs a rock for a friend." The size, shape, and texture are all important in deciding which rock you will choose for your own.

I like to read this book to my students at Young at Art before we paint on rocks.

* Faces
by Barbara Brenner
photos by George Ancona
E. P. Dutton
This beautifully photographed book deals with four of the five senses. It makes children aware of how we learn about the world through our senses.

* Faces on Places
by Suzanne Haldane
The Viking Press
Although intended for somewhat older children, this book will be enjoyed by toddlers who live in the city and enjoy looking at the gargoyles and other stone creatures that dwell on old buildings.

• Feeling Blue
by Robert Jay Wolff
Charles Scribner's Sons
Very simple, abstract illustrations deal with the effects of the color blue, alone and in combination with other colors.

• Find Out by Touching
by Paul Showers
illustrated by Robert Galster
Thomas Y. Crowell Co.
Provides vocabulary for texture exploration experiences and suggests a game for children to play that will help them distinguish between textures. This is not a captivating book.

* Finger Paint and Pudding Prints
by Ann Sayre-Wiseman
Addison-Wesley Publishing Co.
This book will inspire parents and children to get out the chocolate pudding and finger paint! It is a great idea, although it makes more specific suggestions about what to do than kids want or need. Such suggestions as "draw a serpent" make it more for an older child than the activity would normally appeal to. When I read it to my

classes, I make changes that render it more suitable for the toddlers it appears to be intended for.

? *Fingerprint Owls and Other Fantasies*
by Marjorie P. Katz
M. Evans and Co.
Realistic drawings to make out of fingerprints. The book misses the point of the fun of making fingerprints for themselves, and for the fun of mushing around in paint.

* *First Pink Light*
by Eloise Greenfield
illustrated by Moneta Barnett
Scholastic
Black, white, and pink illustrations focus on the color pink and tell a heartwarming story of a little boy waiting for his daddy, who has been away for a month. The child wants to wait up all night to welcome him home. He settles into a chair and, while watching out of the window for the first pink light of dawn, he falls asleep. Daddy does come home with the dawn. Illustrations depict a black family.

* *Five Senses*
by Tasha Tudor
Platt & Munk/Grosset & Dunlap
Sally lives on a farm and uses all of her five senses to enjoy life there. The illustrations are a bit too sweet for my taste.

* *Fly Hoops Fly*
by Yutaka Sujita
Barron's Educational Series
This book mentions many different uses of one hoop, encouraging creative thinking. Nice illustrations.

* *Follow Me!*
by Mordicai Gerstein
William Morrow & Co.
A simple tale of ducks, each of which is a different color to help teach the reader color identification. There is an awful lot of information for the age child it will appeal to—three and under.

* *Follow Your Nose*
by Paul Showers
illustrated by Paul Galdone
Thomas Y. Crowell Co.
Mr. Showers suggests that children "follow their noses" to learn about things. He suggests experiments and games to help them use this sense. Somewhat pedantic.

* *Francie's Paper Puppy*
by Achim Broger and Michelle Sambin
Picture Book Studio USA
In this beautifully illustrated book, Francie loses herself experimenting with her paints. Quite accidentally, she paints a picture of a dog. When she notices it, she cuts it out of the picture and makes it into her special friend and pet. One morning when she awakens, the dog has come alive. A delightful book, which I recommend highly.

* *Fuzzy, What-Was-He?*
by Peter Saymour
illustrated by Karen Acosta
Price/Stern/Sloan
A book for very young "readers," it features successively larger fabric cutouts from a fuzzy egg to a large fuzzy imaginative creature. Children enjoy the tactile quality of the fabric and learn about progressive sizes.

• *Going for a Walk with a Line*
A Step into the World of Modern Art
by Douglas and Elizabeth MacAgey
Doubleday & Co.
Just about the only book about modern art for young children. It was very popular in its day, and it is a shame that it is out of print. Nowadays, publishers seem to feel that preschoolers are "too young" to be interested in art, but preschoolers are interested in everything! We owe it to them to introduce them to the finer things in life.

* *The Goodbye Painting*
by Linda Berman

illustrated by Mark Hannon
Human Sciences Press
A wonderful book that deals with painful feelings, and how art can help us deal with them. It will bring tears to your eyes. I recommend it very highly.

? *Good Junk*
by Judith A. Enderle
illustrated by Gail Gibbons
Elsevier/Nelson Books
Young Kirby finds innovative and creative uses for what everyone else thinks of as junk.

? *The Great Blueness and Other Predicaments*
by Arnold Lobel
Harper & Row
A lovely fantasy of how the great Wizard gave color to a dismal, all-gray world. One color is dealt with at a time. It is not just about blue, as the title suggests.

• *Green Says Go*
by Ed Emberly
Little, Brown & Company
Explains color facts from a scientific standpoint as well as touching on what colors stand for.

* *Guess What?*
By Roger Bester
Crown Publishers
Close-up photographs promote visual discrimination.

* *Hailstones and Halibut Bones*
by Mary O'Neill
illustrated by Leonard Weisgard
Doubleday & Co.
Two pages of illustrations and verse effectively describe each of these colors: purple, gold, black, brown, blue, gray, white, orange, red, pink, green, and yellow. This is one of the best books of its type.

* *Harold and the Purple Crayon*
by Crockett Johnson
Harper & Row
Harold's drawings come to life, and kids really enjoy that notion.
The drawings are a little bit like stereotyped formulas but the ad-
ventures they provide seem to make up for that.

• *Hello Yellow*
by Robert Jay Wolff
Charles Scribner's Sons
A beautifully illustrated book about yellow and its relationship to
other colors.

* *Holes and Peeks*
by Ann Jonas
Greenwillow Books
This book deals with holes and openings, both the kind that sometimes frighten children and the decorative kind that children sometimes make. I always read this to my classes at Young at Art before
giving them paper with holes cut out of them to paint on, since the
book encourages children to think about holes.

? *The House of Four Seasons*
by Roger Duvoisin
Lothrop, Lee & Shepard Books
This is a book about color mixing, in which each member of a
family contributes to the final decision of how their home should
be painted.

* *I Am Eyes, Ni Macho*
by Leila Ward
pictures by Nonny Hogrogian
Greenwillow Books
A small girl awakens in Kenya and says "Ni macho," which means
"I am eyes" in Swahili. She continues to describe the wonderful
things that she sees in the world.

* *I Can Build a House!*
by Shigeo Watanabe
pictures by Uasuo Ohtomo

Philomel Books/The Putnam Publishing Group
A bear decides to build a house and experiments with several possible ways to do so: with blocks, pillows, and an old carton. Unfortunately, the book seems to suggest that the final solution was the best one, while actually all were creative solutions to the problem.

* *I Carve Stone*
by Joan Fine
photographs by David Anderson
Crowell Junior Books

* *I See*
by Rachel Isadora
Greenwillow Books
A baby sees things throughout the day from her first look at a teddy bear when she wakes up until it is time for her to see her crib at night. Sweet illustrations.

? *I Want to Paint My Bathroom Blue*
by Ruth Krauss
illustrations by Maurice Sendak
Harper & Row
A child fantasizes about how he would use colors to change his house.

* *I wish I had a computer that makes waffles*
by Dr. Fitzhugh Dodson
illustrated by Al Lowenheim
Oak Tree Publications
Modern nursery rhymes for contemporary children who are more interested in cars than cows and more familiar with rocket ships than horses and carriages. It is written by a noted child psychologist who clearly understands the needs of preschool children. This book is a far better investment than any anthology of Mother Goose. I can't remember ever doing a play dough activity with young children without having delighted them by reading the rhyme about play dough. This book also has a lot of information for parents on how to stimulate creativity. It is a "must have" for every home or school that has children one through seven.

* *Ida Makes a Movie*
by Kay Chorao
The Seabury Press/A Clarion Book
Ida's film wins a contest, but for all of the wrong reasons. This book should remind us how much contests interfere with a child's creativity, though I don't think that was the author's intention.

* *If I Weren't Me . . . Who Would I Be?*
illustrated by Pam Adams
Child's Play
Reflective paper allows children to see themselves as a wolf, a bat, a butterfly, a gnome, a giant, a snake, St. George, or the dragon. I wish the book had a higher quality mirror-like substance capable of producing a sharper reflection.

* *Imagine That!!! Exploring Make-Believe*
by Joyce Strauss
illustrations by Jennifer Barrett
Human Sciences Press
Encourages children to think about imaginary situations.

* *Imagine That! It's Modern Dance*
by Stephanie Riva Sorine
photographs by Daniel S. Sorine
Alfred A. Knopf
A companion to *At Every Turn! It's Ballet,* this book combines spirited photographs with simple text. The author is a sculptor and the photographer recorded her at work transforming a block of marble into a piece of modern sculpture over a period of three months. While at work the author describes what she is doing and how she feels about her work.

* *I'm Dancing*
text by Alan McCarter and Glenn Reed
photographs by Michael Spector
Charles Scribner's Sons
Describes what dance classes frequently are: only for girls, with lots of hard work and steps to learn. This book will turn many away from dance.

* *The Indoor Noisy Book*
by Margaret Wise Brown
One of the Ms. Brown's popular series that sensitizes children to sounds.

* *Is It Red? Is It Yellow? Is It Blue?*
by Tana Hoban
Greenwillow Books
Photographer Tana Hoban's photographs of brightly colored things in the environment delight the eye. No text.

* *Is It Rough? Is It Smooth? Is It Shiny?*
by Tana Hoban
Greenwillow Books
Excellent photographs without text concentrate on texture.

* *It Looked Like Spilt Milk*
by Charles G. Shaw
Harper & Row
This book is a classic story children love, about finding different objects in a changing puddle of milk.

* *Jackson Makes His Move*
by Andrew Glass
Frederick Warne & Co.
I hope this rare, sensitively told biography of a great painter, told on a child's level, becomes a classic. It is a thinly disguised, captivating version of the life of Jackson Pollock. A delightful, insightful story about how to paint with feeling. No child's library should be without it. We read it at Young at Art before experimenting with throwing and dripping paint.

? *Journey into Jazz*
by Nat Hentoff
drawings by David Stone Martin
Coward-McCann
The story of a very musical boy who learns about jazz.

• *A Kiss Is Round*
by Blossom Budney

pictures by Vladimir Bobri
Lothrop, Lee & Shepard Books
"A kiss is round and so is a hug," begins this delightful rhyming text about circles. This classic book about round remains one of the best on the subject.

* *Leonardo da Vinci*
by Ibi Lepscky
Barron's Educational Series
Curious Leonardo had his family worried. It seemed as if he did not stay interested in one thing for very long. Actually, Leonardo was interested in everything and was multi-talented. He grew up to be an engineer, architect, botanist, inventor, and painter.

* *Let's Go to the Art Museum*
by Virginia Levy
artwork by Patricia Campau
Veejay Publications
A pedantic book designed to help children six through twelve appreciate a visit to an art museum. Does not make the trip sound like a lot of fun.

* *Let's Make Rabbits*
by Leo Lionni
Pantheon Books
This book doesn't have the same appeal of Lionni's *Little Blue and Little Yellow* (reviewed on page 389) because the characters are a lot like the stereotypical bunny drawings children see too much of. The paper bunnies do come alive and suggest that art can become real (something children already know).

* *Let's Paint a Rainbow*
by Eric Carle
Philomel Books/Putnam Publishing Group
More about counting than colors, this rainbow is painted one color at a time, with each color being given a name and number. Could be confusing for children who don't know their colors yet.

* *Liang and the Magic Paintbrush*
by Demi

Holt, Rinehart and Winston
This is a charmingly illustrated story of a boy who loved to paint. He is given a magic paintbrush and everything that he paints with it becomes real. Unfortunately, when a greedy Emperor tries to take the brush from him, Liang paints a storm and drowns the whole royal family. Like many of the old-fashioned fairy tales, the unnecessary violence teaches children simplistic, violent solutions to problems, which I think have no place in literature for children.

• *Listen! Listen!*
by Ann and Paul Rand
Harcourt Brace Jovanovich
Brief rhymes that describe the sounds children hear.

* *Listen to That*
by H. Klurfmeier
Golden Books/Western Publishing Co.
A board book of photographs and simple text that encourages toddlers to listen to the sounds in their environments.

? *The Listening Walk*
by Paul Showers
illustrated by Aliki
Thomas Y. Crowell Co.
Dad, the dog, and a young boy take a walk and listen to footsteps, lawnmowers, cars, and other things, and imitate them with mouth sounds.

? *Little Blue and Little Yellow*
by Leo Lionni
An Astor Book
One of the most charming books on the subject of color mixing ever written. Little Blue and Little Yellow are presented as living characters who are best friends. When they hug so tight that they merge and become green, their families don't recognize them. All turns out well in the end, of course. All subjects can be taught to children in this delightful manner, if we could learn from Mr. Lionni's positive style and up-beat, charming approach to a subject. I recommend it highly. We always read this at Young at Art before introducing color mixing.

* *The Little Red Ant*
English text by Yvonne Hooker
illustrations by Giorgio Vanetti
Grosset & Dunlap
A red ant finds a series of progressively smaller, amorphically shaped cut-outs which it mistakes for an ant nest. After each is tried and found to belong to another breed of animal, the ant finally locates the smallest hole of all which does turn out to be the ant nest. This book helps children explore amorphic shapes.

* *The Little Red Balloon*
by Iela Mari
Barron's Educational Series
A child's bubble turns into a balloon, an apple, a butterfly, and then returns to the child as an umbrella. There are no words and the black, white, and red illustrations focus interest on the color red. Nice to have when the very young child is concentrating on drawing and painting with the color red.

* *A Little Schubert*
story and pictures by M. B. Goffstein
Harper & Row
Makes the life of the composer more human. An accompanying record by Peter Schaaf is a nice idea.

* *Lives of the Artists*
by M. B. Goffstein
Farrar, Straus & Giroux
A biographical poem and a color illustration of each of five artists.

? *Look at Rainbow Colors*
words by Rena K. Kirkpatrick, science consultant
pictures by Anna Bernard
Raintree Publishers
A scientific explanation of colors precedes some discussion of what objects are certain colors.

• *Mabel and the Rainbow*
by Carol Niklaus

Platt & Munk
This fantasy about a rainbow is a color identification book.

Magic Monsters
by Jane Bilk Moncure
illustrated by Dianna Magnuson
The Child's World/Distributed by Childrens Press
Creatures look for and find green, yellow, red, and blue things. They then spot purple and orange things in a rainbow. After devoting three pages for some colors, the book seems to run out of enough room to adequately cover other colors.

Magic Shoelaces
by Audrey Wood
Child's Play
The problem shoelaces present may not seem like an art concept, but I use this book when I talk about long and narrow with my four- to seven-year-old students at Young at Art, although Velcro shoe fastenings are rapidly making this issue obsolete.

Maria Making Pottery
by Hazel Hyde
Sunstone Press
Photographs of Maria, a famous Indian potter, at work.

Marmalade's Yellow Leaf
by Cindy Wheeler
Alfred A. Knopf
A cat keeps track of a yellow autumn leaf as it flies to the ground amid the other autumn leaves. A perfect book for helping very young children learn about the color yellow. We read this to our 1–2-year-olds on "yellow day" at Young at Art.

Max the Artlover
by Hanne Turk
Neugebauer Press USA/Distributed by Alphabet Press
Max the Mouse visits a museum in this wordless, charmingly illustrated book.

* *Max, the Music Maker*
by Miriam B. Stecher and Dr. Alice S. Kandell
Lothrop, Lee & Shepard Books
Little Max explores sounds and improvises with music in creative,
child-directed play. The photographs follow Max as he experiments with sounds and music.

• *May Horses*
by Jan Wahl
illustrated by Blair Lent
A Seymour Lawrence Book/Delacorte Press
The two May horses in this book are blue and orange. This fantastic
tale is beautifully illustrated and deals in imaginative ideas as well
as color identification.

* *The Metropolitan Museum of Art Activity Book*
by Osa Brown
Random House
Although intended for older children, I know many teachers and
parents of preschoolers will be tempted to buy this. The activities
are all modeled on great works of art from history, but a copy book
is a copy book. Children benefit far more from creating their own
work than they do from imitating someone else's, even when that
someone else was a great artist.

* *Miranda*
by Tricia Tusa
Macmillan
An absolutely "must have" book that gives a full course in music
while celebrating the spirit of individuality in each child.

* *Miss Rumphius*
by Barbara Cooney
Viking Penguin
A little girl sets a goal of making the world a more beautiful place.
The book follows her into old age and tells the story of how she
decided to fulfill her goal.

* *The Missing Piece*
by Shel Silverstein

Harper & Row
The Missing Piece is the perfect book to read to a child who is interested in puzzles. Shapes that fit together are the theme, but these shapes have real personalities.

* The Missing Piece Meets the Big O
by Shel Silverstein
Harper & Row
While looking for a proper fit, the Missing Piece meets the Big O, who suggests that it can roll by itself by simply changing shapes. How the shape changes, loses its sharp corners, and becomes round is the story. You'll have a good laugh when the Missing Piece tries to make itself flashy and attractive.

* Music, Music for Everyone
by Vera B. Williams
Greenwillow Books
A beautifully illustrated book full of feelings for family and love of music.

? My Five Senses
by Aliki
Lists the five senses and describes, in very simple terms, how we use them.

* My Hands Can
by Jean Holzenthaler
illustrated by Nancy Tafuri
E. P. Dutton
Some of the things a child can do with his or her hands, including making music, pasting, building, and shaping clay.

* My Very First Book of Colors
by Eric Carle
Thomas Y. Crowell Co.
One picture and one color swatch of each color to be matched by the reader. Not very interesting.

* New Blue Shoes
story and pictures by Eve Rice

Puffin Books
Rebecca's mom seems to be fully in charge of Rebecca's life until
Rebecca states quite emphatically that she wants "nice new blue
shoes," not the brown ones her mother had planned to buy for
her. After being assertive, Rebecca worries about whether she has
done the right thing. She and her mother both agree that Rebecca,
and her new blue shoes, are okay.

• *The Noisy Book*
by Margaret Wise Brown
illustrated by Leonard Weisgard
Harper & Row
Muffin, a lovable dog, hears the sounds of his town while his eyes
are covered with a bandage. The cooperation of an adult to imitate
the sounds makes this an all-time favorite of the under-three set.

* *Norman the Doorman*
by Don Freeman
Viking Penguin
A mouse who lives in a museum makes a sculpture out of found
objects. It wins first prize in the sculpture contest and Norman can
choose his own prize. His choice is to have a tour of the museum
without fear of being caught.

* *Nothing Sticks Like a Shadow*
by Ann Tompert
illustrated by Lynn Munsinger
Houghton Mifflin Co.
Rabbit and Woodchuck have a very interesting argument about
whether or not you can escape from your shadow. While following
their argument, and its outcome, children understand the nature of
shadows.

* *The Old Banjo*
by Dennis Haseley
drawings by Stephen Gammell
Macmillan
On a farm that has many old, unused musical instruments, a hard-
working farmer tells his son that they have no time for dreams and
music. No one plays the instruments anymore and they soon be-

come enchanted and begin to make music themselves. The book has lovely illustrations.

* *Oh, Were They Ever Happy*
by Peter Spier
Doubleday & Co.
When their baby-sitter fails to show up, three children decide to surprise their parents by painting the house for them. Charming illustrations show quite interesting results as the dog turns purple, plants are knocked over, and paint footprints and fingerprints cover everything in sight. The bright, multicolor results please the children, who ask at the end, "Won't they be happy when they come home and see what we've done!" The ending states, "OH, WERE THEY EVER HAPPY!" There are some who may interpret the ending as sarcastic, but those would not be the people who read *my* books!

? *Old MacDonald Had a Farm*
pictures by Moritz Kennel
Golden Press/Western Publishing Company
This illustrated version of every toddler's first favorite song teaches children the sounds each animal makes and helps them discriminate sounds.

• *Open Your Eyes*
by Roz Abisch
illustrated by Boche Kaplan
Parents Magazine Press
"Let's play red," "let's play blue," and "let's play yellow" begin searches for objects in the environment that are either red, blue, or yellow. Unfortunately, the objects depicted are likely to be things like pajamas, drums, birds, trains, and other objects that can be any color at all.

* *Orange Is a Color*
by Sharon Lerner
Lerner Publications Company
Shapes of color that look like torn paper teach color facts in a straightforward, no-nonsense way. This book takes all of the magic out of color mixing.

* *Our Ballet Class*
by Stephanie Riva Sorine
Harper & Row
This book combines photographs of young dancers (by Daniel S. Sorine) with easy-to-understand text.

* *Pablo Picasso*
by Ibi Lepscky
illustrated by Paolo Cardoni
Barron's
Moody young Pablito is described as being very naughty and destructive. When no one else is able to cope with him anymore, his father is told about the boy's bad behavior. He soon realizes that Pablito is really extraordinarily talented and gives him all of his artist's materials. Pablito grows up to be one of the "greatest and most original artists of modern times."

* *A Painted Tale*
by Kate Canning
Barron's Educational Series
A tiger from a Henri Rousseau painting, which hangs in an art gallery, leaves the picture. He wanders out of the museum and goes to a zoo. Upon returning he tries to find the painting he belongs in. He tries out a Picasso, with interesting visual effects, before finding his way back to his own place in his picture. This book is what children's books should be, but usually aren't: imaginative, informative, and lovely to look at.

* *The Painter's Trick*
by Piero and Marisa Ventura
Random House
A traveling painter stops at a monastery and tricks the monks into giving him food and wine because each of them envisions that the painter will use him as a model for his painting of St. George slaying the dragon. None of these immoral characters are likable.

* *Paper, Paper Everywhere*
by Gail Gibbons
Harcourt Brace Jovanovich
More about a commonly used art material than about art, this book

will interest children who have worked with paper and want to know about how it is made.

* *Pat the Bunny*
by Dorothy Kunquist
Golden Press/Western Publishing Co.
This book is well loved for its tactile qualities by one-year-olds who love to touch everything. The book has furry, wood-like, and other interesting textures pasted into it. Unfortunately, the illustrations are very poor quality.

* *Pet of the Met*
by Lydia and Don Freeman
Viking Seafarer Books
Maestro Petrini, a white mouse, and his family, Madame Petrini and Doe, Ray, and Mee, live in a harp case at the Metropolitan Opera House. Maestro acts as a page turner for the prompter until one day he gets carried away by the music and leaps onto the stage. Mefisto the cat joins him. They both fall under the spell of the music and dance together.

* *The Philharmonic Gets Dressed*
by Karla Kushkin
illustrations by Marc Simot
Harper & Row
As the men and women of the orchestra prepare for a concert, we are reminded of the fact that they are people just like you and me.

• *The Photographer and the Pony*
by Fred Gurner
illustrated by Benjamin Levy
Bobbs-Merrill Co.
A photographer takes pictures of children who pose sitting on his pony. Unfortunately, all of his pictures come out very badly and soon no one comes to have their picture taken. When it turns out that the pony is a great photographer, people come from all over to be photographed.

* *A Picture for Harold's Room*
by Crockett Johnson

Scholastic
Harold's drawings become real and suggest the real power of an
artist. Too bad the drawings themselves are so trite. Sequels: *Harold's ABC's, Harold's Circus, Harold and the Purple Crayon* (reviewed on page 384), *Harold's Trip to the Sky.*

? *The Rainbow*
by Mike Thaler
pictures by Donald Leake
Harlin Quist/Distributed by Crown
This is a charming story that begins when there was no color in the
world. After a big rain, a rainbow came to bring us color.

* *Rain Drop Splash*
by Alvin Tresselt
pictures by Leonard Weisgard
Lothrop, Lee & Shepard Books
I always pull this old book out when children start splattering paint
and making "rain" on their paintings.

* *The Rain Puddle*
by Adelaide Holl
pictures by Roger Duvoisin
Lothrop, Lee & Shepard Books
Deals with reflections.

? *Red and Blue*
by Janet Martin
illustrated by Philippe Thomas
Platt & Munk
Not just about red and blue, this book looks at many objects and
names their colors.

* *The Red Balloon*
by A. Lamorisse
Doubleday & Co.
The story of a little boy and a magic, red balloon will help make a
child aware of the color red.

• *The Red Horse and the Bluebird*
by Sandy Rabinowitz

Harper & Row
The red horse and the bluebird help each other and become friends. The red and blue creatures show up beautifully in the black and white plus one color format. We like to read this story at Young at Art before exploring these colors.

* *Red Is Best*
by Kathy Stinson
art by Robin Baird Lewis
Annick Press
This book focuses on the color red, which is the narrator's favorite. A charmingly told story of almost every child's favorite color. Of all of the books about the color red, this one is my favorite, as well as the favorite of many of my students.

* *Regards to the Man in the Moon*
by Ezra Jack Keats
Four Winds Press
A beautifully illustrated book which glorifies the wonders and points out the possibilities of a good imagination. No library of children's books should be without this one.

* *Richard Scarry's Color Book*
by Richard Scarry
Random House
Richard Scarry is an enormously popular illustrator with the very young, and he knows how to fill a page with lots and lots of things to be named. This book is a failure, however, as a tool for teaching color. Red airplanes, green trains, brown tractors, and blue boats are the worst possible examples of color identification. Who has ever seen a red airplane? With the multitude of things that are *always* red to choose from, this is a confusing selection. Mr. Scarry has illustrated some of the worst examples, such as red airplanes, mixed them with the best, like orange oranges, to thoroughly confuse toddlers. Given his popularity, I think he has a responsibility to do better by his fans.

• *Roses Are Red, Are Violets Blue?*
by Alice and Martin Provensen
Random House

Asks some confusing questions, such as, "What color are the blue-eyed girl's eyes when she is wearing her rose-colored glasses?" More confusing than thought provoking.

* *Round and Round and Round*
by Tana Hoban
Greenwillow Books
This wordless book concentrates on photographs of circles. Children can look at it alone or discuss it with an adult. I have always been a fan of Ms. Hoban's fine photographs.

* *Round in a Circle*
English text by Yvonne Hooker
Grosset & Dunlap
This should have been three books, since it covers circles, squares, and triangles; not just circles. This board book is sturdy enough to encourage children to run their fingers along the shapes to get the feel of them. Bright, cartoon-style illustrations.

• *Round Things Everywhere*
by Seymour Reit
photographs by Carol Basen
McGraw-Hill Book Co.
This excellent old book focuses on only round things like balls, balloons, buttons, and the like. The photographs are not great art, but they are simple and easy to understand.

* *The Scribble Monster*
by Jack Kent
Harcourt Brace Jovanovich
Two children ignore the "No Graffiti" sign and draw pictures all over a wall. The pictures come alive and are angry. They chase the boy and girl and are a little scary. When the children begin to wash the drawings, the pictures become happy again and a drawing of a girl kisses one child just before she disappears. This lesson about not drawing on inappropriate places also recognizes the power and importance of a child's drawing.

• *Seeing Red*
by Robert Jay Wolff

Charles Scribner's Sons
This attractively illustrated book deals with the effects the color red
has on us and how it affects the appearance of other colors.

* *Shadow*
translated and illustrated by Marcia Brown
from the French of Blaise Cendrars
Charles Scribner's Sons
This beautifully illustrated book of collages tells the haunted, enchanted story of the Shadow. It is a little scary in places and will
probably be appreciated by children who are over six (though my
four-year-old loved it). A fine complement to art projects that make
use of silhouettes and shadows.

* *Shadows*
by Taro Gomi
Froebel-Kan Co., Ltd./Distributed by Heian International
Cute illustrations depict shadows in a way that is easy to understand.

* *Shadows Here, There, and Everywhere*
by Ron and Nancy Goor
Thomas Y. Crowell Co.
This artistically photographed book studies and explains the reasons why shadows look the way they do. This is a beautiful book
that belongs in every library. Toddlers, who are fascinated with
shadows, will love the pictures, and as they grow older the text
will take on more meaning for them.

* *Shapes*
by Peter Curry
Price/Stern/Sloan Publishers
Formula art is used to illustrate the basic shapes.

* *Shapes*
Jan Pientowski
Harvey House
One page, sterotypical graphic illustrations devoted to each shape.

* *Shapes*
by John J. Reiss

Bradbury Press
John Reiss describes and defines one shape on each double page
and has included brightly colored, stylized illustrations.

• *Shapes*
by Gillian Youldon
Franklin Watts
Bright, simple illustrations of a circle, a square, a rectangle, triangle, and an irregular shape.

* *Shapes and Colors*
no author
Price/Stern/Sloan Publishers
A board book of four simple pictures, each with a triangle cut out
of it. Not very interesting, even for the youngest child. It is a
shame, because it is very difficult to find books about triangles.

* *Shapes and Things*
by Tana Hoban
Macmillan
Ms. Hoban's photographs never disappoint, although more concentrated focus would help teach shapes to her very young audience.

* *Simple Pictures Are Best*
by Nancy Willard
Harcourt Brace Jovanovich
A couple try too hard to make their anniversary photo interesting
by including far too many things.

* *The Slant Book*
by Peter Newell
C. E. Tuttle
A book in the shape of a parallelogram, it follows the adventures
of a baby whose carriage is rolling down a hill by itself.

* *Snapshot Max*
by Hanne Turk
Neugebauer Press/Distributed by Alaphabet Press
Max works very hard at taking some photographs, but winds up

with only little portions of things in them.

* *Something Special for Me*
by Vera B. Williams
Greenwillow Books
A little girl looks in all of the stores but has trouble deciding just
what would be special enough to choose as a birthday present that
her mother has promised to buy her. After hearing a street musician
play an accordian, she finally knows just what would be special
enough to receive for this special occasion. This story lends a
lovely magical quality to musical instruments.

* *Spaces, Shapes, and Sizes*
by Jane Jonas Srivastava
illustrated by Loretta Lustig
Thomas Y. Crowell Co.
Spaces, Shapes, and Sizes deals with comparative volumes. It is
about how volume stays the same even when a shapes changes.
Although it is more science than art, it does increase awareness of
shapes. Not a lot of fun to read.

* *Splish, Splash!*
English text by Yvonne Hooker
illustrations by Nadia Pazzaglia
Grosset & Dunlap
A nice precursor or follow-up to water play, this book's puddle-
shape cutouts also introduce the free-form, or amoebic, shape.

• *Splodges*
by Malcolm Carrick
The Viking Press
Surprising shapes to find in "splodges" of colors. Look for this in
the library, since it is out of print.

* *Spring Green*
by Valerie Selkowe and Jenny Bassat
Lothrop, Lee & Shepard Books
A duck is on his way to a party and has to bring something green
as part of a contest. He eliminates many green things that seem
inappropriate to him, and finally gives up, since he can't think of

anything to bring to the party. He invites his friend the frog to go with him. Since the frog is green, the duck wins the contest.

* *Stopping by Woods on a Snowy Evening*
by Robert Frost
illustrated by Susan Jeffers
E. P. Dutton
Susan Jeffers' lovely illustrations of this classic poem are a beautiful way to make a child think about snow and concentrate on the color white. I always follow up reading it with a white paint and gray paper art project.

* *The Strawberry Book of Colors*
by Richard Hefter
Larousse & Co.
Three painters produce new colors and havoc. This is a nice book on color mixing.

• *Suzuki Bean*
by Sandra Scoppettone
drawings by Louise Fitzhugh
Doubleday & Co.
This somewhat dated story is nevertheless a charming revelation of the real meaning of individuality.

* *Take Another Look*
by Tana Hoban
Greenwillow Books
Artistic photos show children how the close-up view changes our perception of objects.

* *A Tale of Two Williams*
by Diana Goldin and Inge Heckel
photographs by Carl Mydans
The Metropolitan Museum of Art
Rhyming text and photographs taken of a boy visiting the museum tell the story of a boy who meets a reproduction of an ancient Egyptian hippopotamus in the museums's gift shop. The figure, known as William, takes the boy, named William too, on a visit to some of the museum's exhibits. It seems unduly commercial for

the hippo to be a reproduction, when the original lives at the Met anyway, and for three photographs to show the museum's shop while only four are devoted to the Egyptian exhibits. Savvy children want to know why the child left the gift shop without telling his mother where he was going and why none of the museum guards prevent the boy from taking the animal from the shop without paying for it. These issues can interest children so much that they detract from the book.

* *That's Jazz*
by Stephanie Riva Sorine
Random House
Photographs by Daniel S. Sorine are combined with simple text that is appealing and informative.

* *Tobo Hates Purple*
by Gina Calleja
Annick Press
A story about a little purple boy who hates being purple but learns, by trying out the other colors, that purple really is his color.

* *The Trip*
by Ezra Jack Keats
Greenwillow Books
Greenwillow seems to have cornered the market on beautifully illustrated books, and this is no exception. Mr. Keats's work never disappoints. In this book the main character builds a diorama of his old neighborhood, using an old shoe box and some paper, paste, and paint. The experience helps him accept the fact that his family had to move. This book is the best example of how art can be used to help children adjust to the world, rather than just to make "pretty decorations."

* *The Troll Music*
story and pictures by Anita Lobel
Harper & Row
After a spell is cast by a troll, musicians who make the "best music in the land" now find that their instruments make animal sounds when they play. The story and illustrations are enhanced by the introduction of mouth sounds, which youngsters can imitate.

* *The Turn About, Think About, Look About Book*
text and graphics by Beau Gardner
Lothrop, Lee & Shepard Books
This book presents graphics that can be viewed in four different ways and appear to be a different picture from each view. Your child can be encouraged to think up still more things the pictures can be.

* *The Ugly Book*
by Arthur Crowley and Annie Gusman
Houghton Mifflin
The Ugly Book makes fun of the real meaning of ugly and beautiful. If you and your child can enjoy taking the position that flowers, butterflies, meteorites, and the moon are all ugly, you'll enjoy the tongue-in-cheek approach of this book.

* *Visiting a Museum*
by Althea
illustrated by Maureen Galvani
Dinosaur Publications Ltd.
Straightforward facts about things we see in museums and what they tell us about the people who made them.

* *Water Is Wet*
by Penny Pollock and Barbara Beirne
G. P. Putnam's Sons
Delightful photographs capture the essence of wetness. This is a most appealing book for children under five.

? *What Is It?*
A Book of Photographic Puzzles
by Joan Loss
Doubleday & Co.
The reader is challenged to identify the objects shown in magnification from ten to thirty times larger than they really are. An identifiable photograph backs each mind boggler to confirm your answer. This lovely book really encourages children to appreciate the close-up.

? *What Is the Color of the Wide, Wide World?*
by Margaret Friskey

illustrated by Mary Gehr
Regensteiner Publishing Enterprises
Animals discuss their ideas on what color the world seems to appear to them.

* *When Clay Sings*
by Byrd Baylor
illustrated by Tom Bahti
Charles Scribner's Sons
This book describes the deep reverence for the magic of clay that the Indians felt.

* *Where Is It?*
A Hide-and-Seek Puzzle Book
by Demi
Doubleday & Co.
This attractive book helps your child concentrate on details.

* *Who Has the Yellow Hat?*
by Shinobu Ariga
Price/Stern/Sloan Publishers
Yellow objects are hidden under flaps for the reader to lift up.

• *Yellow, Yellow*
by Frank Asch
illustrations by Mark Allan Stomaty
McGraw-Hill Book Co.
Black, white, and yellow illustrations focus the reader's attention on the color yellow. The story line stresses creative thought through innovative uses of mundane things and resourcefulness. Although this book is out of print, it is one of the best on the list and a "must have." If your library doesn't have a copy, try second-hand bookstores. I don't know any self-respecting art teacher of young children who didn't beg, borrow, or steal a copy of this book. I got mine by contacting someone who searches for old children's books. A friend found her copy for $.50 while I paid $15.00 for my copy. The book sold for $3.95 when it was new in 1971. What a pity the authors didn't follow up with books about red and blue, and that the publisher let it go out of print.

Appendix III

Records That Teach Art and Music Concepts

Are You Ready for . . . Red was recently reissued under the title
There's Music in the Colors
by Willy Strickland and James Earle
Kimbo Educational
P.O. Box 477
16 North Third Avenue
Long Branch, New Jersey 07740
Includes one song about each color, describing things we usually
see in that color. Be sure to throw away the accompanying color-
ing book before giving it to your child!

Big Bird Discovers the Orchestra
Starring Carroll Spinney as Big Bird
Sesame Street Records
1 Lincoln Plaza
New York, New York 10023

Can You Fool Your Shadow?
Folkways Records
43 W. 61st Street
New York, New York 10023
Two songs on this album are related to art concepts: "Mr. Mud"
and "Can You Fool Your Shadow?"

Color Me a Rainbow
Color Concepts for Early Childhood
Melody House Recordings
819 N.W. 92nd Street
Oklahoma City, Oklahoma 73114
Songs about colors.

Shapes in Action
by Georgiana Liccione Stewart

Kimbo Educational
P. O. Box 477
16 North Third Avenue
Long Branch, New Jersey 07740
Movement activities that relate to shapes.

Tubby the Tuba (and other songs about music for children)
narrated by Annette
Walt Disney
A Disneyland Record
Introduces young children to the orchestra.

Appendix IV

Children's Museums and Museums with Children's Activities

ALABAMA

Anniston Museum of Natural
History
4301 McClellan Boulevard
Anniston, AL 36201
(P.O. Box 1587
Anniston, AL 36201)
205-237-6766

Cooks Museum
412 13th Street
Decatur, AL 35601
205-350-9347

Discovery Place
1320 22nd Street S.
Birmingham, AL 35205
205-939-1176

The Exploreum
1906 Spring Hill Ave.
Mobile, AL 36602
205-476-6873

ARIZONA

Museum for Youth
35 N. Robson
Mesa, AZ 85201
602-898-9046

ARKANSAS

Museum of Science and Natural
History
MacArthur Park
Little Rock, AR 72202
501-371-3521

CALIFORNIA

Alexander Lindsay Junior Museum
1901 1st Avenue

Walnut Creek, CA 94596
415-935-1978

California Academy of Sciences
Golden Gate Park
San Francisco, CA 94118
415-221-5100

Coyote Point Museum
Coyote Point Drive
San Mateo, CA 94596
415-342-7755

The Discovery Center
1944 North Winery Avenue
Fresno, CA 93703
209-251-5531

Exploratorium
3601 Lyon Street
San Francisco, CA 94123
info. 415-563-3200
adm. 415-563-7337

Ft. Roosevelt Natural Science and
History Museum
870 W. Davis
P.O. Box 164
Hanford, CA 93230
209-584-7685

Josephine D. Randall Junior
Museum
199 Museum Way
San Francisco, CA 94114
415-863-1399

Junior Arts Center
4814 Hollywood Boulevard
Los Angeles, CA 90027
213-485-4474

Kidspace: A Participatory Museum
700 Seco Street
Pasadena, CA 95821
818-449-9143

La Habra Children's Museum
301 S. Euclid
La Habra, CA 90631
213-694-1011

Lori Brock Junior Museum
3801 Chester Avenue
Bakersfield, CA 93301
805-395-1201

Los Angeles Children's Museum
310 North Main
Los Angeles, CA 90012
213-687-8800

The Oakland Museum Preschool
    Program
1000 Oak Street
Oakland, CA 94607
415-273-3402

Palo Alto Junior Museum
1451 Middlefield Road
Palo Alto, CA 94301
415-329-2111

Sacramento Science Center
3615 Auburn Boulevard
Sacramento, CA 95821
415-485-4471

Youth Science Institute
16260 Alum Rock Avenue
San Jose, CA 95127
408-258-4322

COLORADO

Children's Museum of Denver, Inc.
2121 Crescent Drive
Denver, CO 80211
303-433-7444

CONNECTICUT

Connecticut Children's Museum
567 State Street
New Haven, CT 06510
203-777-8002

Lutz Junior Museum
247 S. Main Street
Manchester, CT 06040
203-753-0381

The Mattatuck Museum of the
    Mattatuck Historical Society
119 W. Main Street
Waterbury, CT 06702
203-753-0381

Monument House-Children's
    Museum
Park Avenue
Groton, CT 06430
203-643-0949

Museum of Art, Science and
    Industry
4450 Park Avenue
Bridgeport, CT 06604
203-372-3521

The Museum for Children
Stamford, CT
(Scheduled to open spring 1986.
Phone to obtain exact location.)
203-329-0150
203-372-3521

New Britain Youth Museum
30 High Street
New Britain, CT 06051
203-225-3020

Science Museum of Connecticut
950 Trout Brook Drive
West Hartford, CT 06119
203-236-2961

Thames Science Center
Gallows Lane
New London, CT 06320
203-442-0391

DISTRICT OF COLUMBIA

Capitol Children's Museum
800 3rd Street N.E.
Washington, DC 20002
202-543-8600

The Children's Museum of
    Washington
4954 MacArthur Boulevard
Washington, DC 20007
202-337-4954

Rock Creek Nature Center
5200 Glover Road N.W.
Washington, DC 20015
202-426-6829

FLORIDA

Discovery Center
231 S.W. Second Avenue
Fort Lauderdale, FL 33301
305-462-4115

Jacksonville Museum of Arts and
   Sciences
1025 Gulf Life Drive
Jacksonville, FL 32207
904-396-7062

The Junior Museum of Bay County
1731 Jenks Avenue
Panama City, FL 32401
904-769-6128

The Metropolitan Museum and Art
   Centers
1212 Anastasia Avenue
Coral Gables, FL 33134
305-442-1448

St. Petersburg Historical Museum
335 Second Avenue, N.E.
St. Petersburg, FL 33701
813-894-1052

Tallahassee Junior Museum
3945 Museum Drive
Tallahassee, FL 32304
904-576-1636

Tampa Museum
601 Doyle Carleton Drive
Tampa, FL 33602
813-223-8130

GEORGIA

Museum of Arts and Sciences
4182 Forsythe Road
Macon, GA 31200
912-477-3232

Cobb County Youth Museum
649 Cheatham Hill Drive
Marietta, GA 30064
404-427-2563

Georgia Southern Museum
Box 8061
Rosenwald Building
Statesboro, GA 30460
912-681-5444

IDAHO

Herret Museum
1220 Kimberly Road
East Five Points
Twin Falls, ID 83301
208-733-9554

ILLINOIS

Blazekas Museum of Lithuanian
   Culture
4012 S. Archer Avenue
Chicago, IL 60632
312-847-2441

Chicago Children's Museum
1807 Lincoln Park West
Chicago, IL 60614
312-664-5529

INDIANA

The Children's Museum
3000 N. Meridan Street
Indianapolis, IN 46208
317-924-5431

Hannah Lindahl Children's
   Museum
1306 South Main
Mishawaka, IN 46544
219-259-0013

Mishawaka Children's Museum
410 Lincoln Way East
Mishawaka, IN 46544
219-258-3056

Muncie Children's Museum
306 South Walnut Plaza
Muncie, IN 47305
317-286-1660

IOWA

Des Moines Center of Science
4500 Grand Avenue
Greenwood Park
Des Moines, IA 50312
515-274-4138

Maxwell Community Historical
   Society Children's Museum
Maxwell, IA 50161
515-387-8685

KANSAS

Fellow-Reeve Museum of History
  and Science
2100 University
Wichita, KS 67213
316-261-5800

Wichita Public Schools
Office of Museum Programs
640 North Emporia
Wichita, KS 67214
316-268-7752

KENTUCKY

Living Arts and Science Center
362 Walnut Street
Lexington, KY 40508
606-252-5222

Louisville Art Gallery, Inc.
301 West York Street
Louisville, KY 40203
502-583-7062

LOUISIANA

Contemporary Arts Center
The Ice Cream Factory
900 Camp Street
New Orleans, LA 70130
504-523-1216

Education Department
Friends of the Cabildo
Young Explorers Program
701 Chartres Street
New Orleans, LA 70116
504-523-3939

Grindstone Bluff Museum and
  Environmental Education Center
501 Jenkins Road
P.O. Box 7965
Shreveport, LA 71107
318-425-5646

Louisiana Arts and Science Center
100 S. River Road
P.O. Box 3373
Baton Rouge, LA 70821
504-344-9463

Louisiana State Museum/Children's
  Museum
751 Chartres Street
P.O. Box 2458
New Orleans, LA 70176
504-568-6968

New Orleans Recreation
  Department
Children's Museum
1218 Burgundy Street
New Orleans, LA 70116
504-587-1909

Old U.S. Mint
400 Esplanade Avenue
New Orleans, LA 70116
504-568-6968

Storyland Village
City Park
Victory Avenue
New Orleans, LA 70116
504-488-8906

The Zigler Museum
411 Clara Street
Jennings, LA 70546
318-824-0114

MAINE

Children's Museum of Maine
746 Stevens Avenue
Portland, ME 04103
207-797-5483

MARYLAND

Ann Arundek Community College
101 College Parkway
Arnold, MD 21012
301-269-7335

Cabin John Regional Park Noah's
  Ark
7400 Tucker Lane
Potomack, MD 20854
301-299-4555

Cloister's Children's Museum
P.O. Box 66
10440 Falls Rd.
Brooklandville, MD 21022
301-823-2550

Clyburn Museum
Clyburn Mansion
4915 Greenspring Avenue
Baltimore, MD 21209
301-396-0180

Howard B. Owens Science Center
9601 Greenbelt Road
Lanham-Seabrook, MD 20706
301-577-8718

Old Princess Anne Days
Mansion Street
Princess Anne, MD 21853
301-651-1705

Rosehill Manor Children's Museum
1611 N. Market Street
Frederick, MD 21701
717-694-1648

MASSACHUSETTS

Children's Art Centre
36 Rutland Street
Boston, MA 02118
617-536-9666

Children's Museum
Museum Wharf
300 Congress Street
Boston, MA 02210
617-426-6500

Children's Museum
276 Gulf Road
South Dartmouth, MA 02748
617-426-6500

Dartmouth Children's Museum
P.O. Box 98
Russells Mills
Dartmouth, MA 02714
617-993-3361

Thornton W. Burgess Museum
4 Water Street
Sandwich, MA 02563
617-888-4668

Wistariahurst Museum
238 Cabot Street
Holyoke, MA 02537
413-536-6771

MICHIGAN

The Ann Arbor Hands-On Museum
219 East Huron Street
Ann Arbor, MI 48104
313-995-5437

Children's Museum
Detroit Public Schools
67 East Kirby
Detroit, MI 48202
313-494-1210

Hackley Art Museum
296 West Webster Street
Muskegon, MI 49440
616-722-2600

Impressions 5
200 Museum Drive
Lansing, MI 48933
517-485-8115

Kingman Museum of Natural
    History
West Michigan Avenue at 20th
    Street
Battle Creek, MI 49017
616-965-5117

Your Heritage House
110 East Ferry Street
Detroit, MI 48202
313-871-1667

MINNESOTA

A. M. Chishom Museum
506 West Michigan Street
Duluth, MN 55802
218-722-8563

The Children's Museum, Inc.
1217 Bandana Boulevard North
St. Paul, MN 55108
612-644-3818

Science Museum
Omni Theater
10th and Wabasha
St. Paul, MN 55108
612-221-9488

MISSOURI

Eugene Field House and Toy
    Museum

634 South Broadway
St. Louis, MO 63102
314-421-4689

Historic Hermann Museum
4th and Schiller Streets
Box 88
Hermann, MO 65041
314-486-2017

The Nelson-Atkins Museum of Art
4525 Oak Street
Kansas City, MO 64111
816-561-4000

NEBRASKA

Children's Museum
P.O. Box 3393
Omaha, NE 68102
402-342-6163

Omaha Children's Museum
551 South 18th Street
Omaha, NE 68102
402-342-6164

NEW HAMPSHIRE

The Arts and Science Center
14 Court Street
Nashua, NH 03060
603-883-1506

NEW JERSEY

Cora Hartshorn Arboretum
324 Forest Drive South
Short Hills, NJ 07078
201-376-3587

Gloucester County Historical
    Society-Children's Museum
58 N. Broad Street
Woodbury, NJ 08096
609-845-4771

Liberty Village
P.O. Box 161
Flemington, NJ 08822
201-782-8550

Monmouth County Historical
    Association Museum-Junior
    Museum
70 Court Street

Freehold, NJ 07728
201-462-1466

Monmouth Museum
Lincroft, NJ 07738
201-747-2266

Montville Township Historical
    Museum
84 Main Street
Montville, NJ 07045
201-334-0012

Morristown Museum of Arts and
    Sciences
Columbia Road
Morristown, NJ 07960
201-538-0454

Newark Museum/Junior Museum
49 Washington Street
Newark, NJ 07101
201-733-6600

NEW YORK

Brooklyn Children's Museum
145 Brooklyn Avenue
Brooklyn, NY 11213
212-735-4400

Cayuga County Agricultural
    Museum
P.O. Box 309
Silver Street Road
Auburn, NY 13021
315-252-7994

Children's Museum of History,
    Natural History and Science at
    Utica, New York
311 Main Street
Utica, New York 13501
315-724-6128

Children's Museum of Manhattan
314 West 54th Street
New York, NY 10019
212-765-5904

History Center and Museum
Children's Museum
Main and Portage Streets
Center of Village Park
P.O. Box 7
Westfield, NY 14787
716-326-2977

Metropolitan Museum of Art/Junior
   Museum
Fifth Avenue at 82nd Street
New York, NY 10028
212-879-5500

New York Aquarium
Boardwalk and West 8th Street
Brooklyn, NY 11224
718-266-8500

Rensselaer County Historical
   Society
59 2nd Street
Troy, NY 12180
518-272-7232

Rensselaer County Junior Museum
282 Fifth Avenue
Troy, NY 12182
518-235-2120

Science Museum of Long Island
1526 North Plandome Road
Manhasset, NY 11030
516-627-9400

Scotia-Glenville Children's
   Museum
15 Beach Street
Scotia, NY 12302
518-374-2262

Staten Island Children's Museum
15 Beach Street
Staten Island, NY 10304
212-273-2060

NORTH CAROLINA

The Catawba Science Center
234 Third Avenue N.E.
Hickory, NC 28601
704-322-8169

Charlotte Nature Museum
1658 Sterling Road
Charlotte, NC 28202
704-372-6261

Community Council for the Arts
111 East Caswell Street
Kinston, NC 28501
919-527-2517

The Health Adventure
501 Biltmore Avenue

Asheville, NC 28801
704-254-6373

Historic Bethabara Park
2147 Bethabara Road
Winston-Salem, N.C. 27106
919-924-8191

Natural Science Center of
   Greensboro
4301 Lawndale Drive
Greensboro, NC 27408
919-288-3769

Nature Science Center
Museum Drive
Winston-Salem, NC 27105
919-767-6730

North Carolina Museum of Life
   and Science
433 Murray Avenue
Durham, NC 27704
919-477-0431

Pick Shin Farm Living Museum and
   Nature Center
Surry Central High School
Dobson, NC 27017
919-386-8211

Rocky Mount Children's Museum
   Inc.
1610 Gay Street
Sunset Park
Rocky Mount, NC 27801
919-972-1167/8

OHIO

Lake Erie Nature and Science
   Center
28728 Wolf Road
Bay Village, OH 44140
216-871-2900

Little Red Schoolhouse
80 South Main Street
Oberlin, OH 44074
216-774-8003

Milan Historical Museum
Children's and Junior Museum
10 Edison Drive
Milan, OH 44846
419-499-2968

OKLAHOMA

Oklahoma Art Center
3113 Pershing Boulevard
Oklahoma City, OK 73107
405-946-4477

OREGON

Portland Children's Museum
3037 SW, 2nd Avenue
Portland, OR 97201
503-248-4587

Wonderworks—A Children's
  Museum
Rt. 4, Box 253
The Dalles, OR 97058
503-296-4964

PENNSYLVANIA

The Children's Museum of
  Northeastern Pennsylvania
1710 Wyoming Avenue
Forty Fort, PA 18704
717-288-3107

Parkway Program of Franklin
  Institute
20th Street and Parkway
Philadelphia, PA 19103
215-266-4957

Please Touch Museum
210 North 21st Street
Philadelphia, PA 19103
215-630-0660

Quiet Valley Living Historical Farm
R.D. 2
Box 2495
Stroudsburg, PA 18360
717-992-6161

PUERTO RICO

Museo Infantil
Instituto de Cultura
  Puertorriqueña
Box 4184
San Juan, PR 00905
809-723-6246

RHODE ISLAND

Children's Museum
58 Walcott Street
Pawtucket, RI 02860
401-726-2591

SOUTH CAROLINA

Children's Nature Museum of York
  County
Route 4, Box 211
Rock Hill, SC 29730
803-329-2121

TENNESSEE

Children's Museum of Oak Ridge
461 Outer Drive
P.O. Box 3066
Oak Ridge, TN 37830
615-482-1074

Cumberland Museum and Science
  Center
800 Ridley Avenue
Nashville, TN 37210
615-259-6099

Estelle Carmack Bandy Children's
  Museum
Jackson Street
Kingsport, TN 37660
615-245-7211

Memphis Museum—Pink Palace
232 Tilton Road
Memphis, TN 38111
901-454-5600

Netherland Inn House Museum
  and Boatyard Complex
Box 293
Kingsport, TN 37660
615-247-3211

Students' Museum
516 Beaman
Chilhowee Park
P.O. Box 6108
Knoxville, TN 37914
615-637-1121

TEXAS

Brazos Valley Museum
3232 Briarcrest Drive

Bryan, TX 77801
409-779-2195

Dallas Museum of Natural History/
    Dallas Aquarium
First and Forrest Avenue
P.O. Box 26193
Fair Park Station
Dallas, TX 75226
214-421-2169

Fort Worth Museum of Science
    and History
1501 Montgomery Street
Forth Worth, TX 71607
817-732-1631

Gateway Gallery
Dallas Museum of Art
1717 North Harwood
Dallas, Texas 75201
214-922-0220

McAllen International Museum
1900 Nolana Street
McAllen, TX 78504
512-682-1564

Youth Cultural Center
815 Columbus Avenue
Waco, TX 76702
817-752-9641

UTAH

Children's Museum of Utah
840 North and 300 West
Salt Lake City, Utah 84103
801-322-5268

VERMONT

The Children's Place
143 Main Street
Brattleboro, VT 05301
802-254-8707

Discovery Museum
51 Park Street
Essex Junction, VT 05452
802-878-8687

VIRGINIA

Chesapeake Planetarium
300 Cedar Road

P.O. Box 1520
Chesapeake, VA 23320
804-547-0153

Children's Museum
400 High Street
P.O. Box 850
Portsmouth, VA 23704
804-393-8717

Peninsula Nature and Science
    Center
524 J. Clyde Morris Boulevard
Newport News, VA 23601
804-595-1900

Richmond's Children's Museum
7101 Geen Parkway
Richmond, VA 23219
804-643-5436

Roanoke Valley Science Museum
1 Market Street
Roanoke, VA 24011
703-342-5710

Tidewater Children's Museum
601 Court Street
Portsmouth, VA 23704
804-393-8393

Valentine Museum
1015 East Clay Street
Richmond, VA 23219
703-342-5710

WASHINGTON

Pacific Science Center
200 2nd Avenue North
Seattle, WA 98109
206-625-9333

Paul H. Karshner Memorial
    Museum
426 4th Avenue N.E.
Puyallup, WA 98371
206-593-8748

WEST VIRGINIA

The Huntington Galleries
Junior Art Museum
2033 McCoy Road
Huntington, WV 25701
304-529-2701

Sunrise Museums
746 Myrtle Road
Charleston, WV 25314
304-344-8035

Youth Museum of Southern West
   Virginia
Box 1815
Beckley, WV 25801
304-252-3730

WISCONSIN

Ripon Historical Society
508 Watson Street
P.O. Box 274

Ripon, WI 53271
414-748-5354

WYOMING

Lander Conservation Center
863 Sweetwater Street
Lander, WY 82520
307-332-5460

Washakie County Museum
   Children's Museum
1115 Obie Sue Avenue
Worland, WY 82401
307-347-4102

Appendix V

Toy and Doll Museums

ARKANSAS

Gay Nineties Button and Doll
Museum
Route 1 Box 788
Eureka Springs, AR 72632
501-253-9321

Geuther Doll Museum
188 North Main Street (Route 23N)
Eureka Springs, AR 72632
501-253-8501

CONNECTICUT

Cornwall Historical Society
P.O. Box 115
Cornwall, CT 06753
203-672-6958

GEORGIA

Museum of Antique Dolls
505 President Street East
Savannah, GA 31401
912-233-5296

Toy Museum of Atlanta
2800 Peachtree Road North East
Atlanta, GA 30305
404-266-8647

KANSAS

Thomas County Historical Society
and Museum
1525 West 4th Street
Colby, KS 67701
913-462-6972

MAINE

Boothbay Railway Village
Route 27
Boothbay, ME 04537
207-633-4727

MISSOURI

Eugene Field House and Toy
Museum
634 South Broadway
St. Louis, MO 63102
314-421-4689

Patee House Museum
1202 Penn Street
St. Joseph, MO 64502
816-232-8206

MONTANA

House of a Thousand Dolls
P.O. Box 136
Loma, MT 59460
406-739-4338

NEBRASKA

Burt County Museum
114 South 13th
Tekamah, NE 68061
402-374-1505

Old Brown House Doll Museum
1421 Avenue F
Gothenburg, NE 69138
308-537-7596

NEW JERSEY

Buccleuch Mansion
Buccleuch Park-George Street
New Brunswick, NJ 08901
201-846-1063

NEW MEXICO

Gadsen Museum
Barker Road and Highway 28
Mesilla, NM 88046
505-526-6293

NEW YORK

Aunt Len's Doll and Toy House
6 Hamilton Terrace
New York, NY 10031
212-926-4172

Homeville Museum
49 Clinton Street
Homer, NY 13077
607-749-3105

Town of Bethlehem
Clapper Road and Route 144
Selkirk, NY 12158
518-767-9432

Town of Yorktown Museum
1974 Commerce Street
Yorktown Heights, NY 10598
914-962-2970

NORTH DAKOTA

Fort Seward Historical Society
503-15th Street South East #3
Jamestown, ND 58401
701-252-6741

OHIO

Milan Historical Museum
10 Edison Drive
Milan, OH 44846
419-499-2968

OKLAHOMA

Eliza Cruce Hall Doll Museum
Grand at East Northwest
Ardmore, OK 73401
405-223-8290

PENNSYLVANIA

Perelman Antique Toy Museum
270 South 2nd Street
Philadelphia, PA 19106
215-922-1070

Toy Train Museum of the Train
    Collector's Association
Paradise Lane
Strasburg, PA 17579
717-687-8976

SOUTH DAKOTA

Enchanted World Doll Museum
615 North Main
Mitchell, SD 57301
605-996-9896

Ledbetter Antique Car Museum
2½ West Highway 16
Custer, SD 57730
605-673-4762

TENNESSEE

Chattanooga Museum of Regional
    History
176 South Crest Road
Chattanooga, TN 37404
615-698-1084

WASHINGTON

Henry Art Gallery Textile
    Collections
BH-30, University of Washington
Seattle, WA 98195
206-543-1739

Appendix VI

Zoos

ALABAMA

Birmingham Zoo
2630 Cahaba Road
Birmingham, AL 35253
205-879-0409

Montgomery Zoo
329 Vandeiver Boulevard
Montgomery, AL 36109
209-832-2637

ARIZONA

Arizona Zoological Park
5810 East Van Buren
Phoenix, AZ 85010
602-273-1341

ARKANSAS

Little Rock Zoological Gardens
1 Jonesboro Drive
Little Rock, AR 72205
501-666-2406

CALIFORNIA

Applegate Park Zoo
Corner of 25th and R
Merced, CA 95340
209-385-6855

Hi Desert Nature Museum
57117 29 Palms Highway
Yucca Valley, CA 92284
619-365-9814

Living Desert Reserve
47-900 Portola Road
Palm Desert, CA 92260
619-346-5694

The Los Angeles Zoo
5333 Zoo Drive

Los Angeles, CA 90027
213-666-4650

Marine World-Africa U.S.A.
Marine World Parkway
Redwood City, CA 94065
415-591-7676

Micke Grove Zoo
11793 North Micke Grove Road
Lodi, CA 95240
209-369-4635

Oakland Zoo
9777 Golf Links Road
Oakland, CA 94605
415-632-9523

Palo Alto Junior Museum
1451 Middlefield Road
Palo Alto, CA 94301
415-329-2111

Roeding Park Zoo
894 West Belmont
Fresno, CA 93728
209-488-1549

Sacramento Zoo
3930 West Land Park
Sacramento, CA 95822
916-447-7383

San Diego Wild Animal Park
1500 San Pasqual Valley Road
Escondido, CA 92027
619-747-8702

San Diego Zoo
P.O. Box 551
Zoo Drive
San Diego, CA 92112
619-231-1515

San Francisco Zoological Gardens
Zoo Road and Skyline Boulevard
San Francisco, CA 94132
415-661-2023

Santa Barbara Zoological Gardens
500 Niños Drive
Santa Barbara, CA 93103
805-962-5339

COLORADO

Cheyenne Mountain Zoological
   Park
Cheyenne Mountain Highway
Colorado Springs, CO 80906
303-475-9555

Denver Zoological Gardens
City Park
Denver, CO 80205
303-575-2432

CONNECTICUT

Herbert F. Moran Nature Center
   and Zoo
Chester Street
New London, CT 06320
203-443-2861

Stamford Museum and Nature
   Center
39 Scotfieldtown Road
Stamford, CT 06903
203-322-1646

DISTRICT OF COLUMBIA

National Zoological Park
3001 Connecticut Avenue N. W.
Washington, DC 20008
202-673-4800

FLORIDA

Jacksonville Zoological Park
8605 Zoo Road
Jacksonville, FL 33177
305-251-0401

Metro Zoo
12400 South West 152nd Street
Miami, FL 32602
904-378-9768

Santa Fe Community College
   Teaching Zoo
3000 North West 83rd Street
Gainesville, FL 32602
904-378-9768

GEORGIA

Atlanta Zoological Park
800 Cherokee Avenue
Atlanta, GA 30315
404-658-7059

Lanier Museum of Natural History
2601 Buford Dam Road
Buford, GA 30518
404-945-3543

Oatland Island Education Center
711 Sandtown Road
Savannah, GA 31410
912-897-3773

HAWAII

Honolulu Zoo
151 Kapahulu Avenue
Honolulu, HI 96815
808-923-4772

ILLINOIS

Chicago Zoological Park
   (Brookfield Zoo)
8400 West 31st Street
Brookfield, IL 60513
312-485-0263

Glen Oak Zoo
2218 North Prospect Road
Peoria, IL 61603
309-682-9669

Lincoln Park Zoo
2200 North Cannon Drive
Chicago, IL 60614
312-294-4660

Wildlife Prairie Park
R.R. #2 Taylor Road
Hanna City, IL 61536
309-676-0998

INDIANA

Columbian Park Zoo
1915 Scott Street
Lafayette, IN 47904
317-447-0133

Indianapolis Zoo
3120 East 30th Street

Indianapolis, IN 46218
317-547-3577

Mesker Park Zoo
Bement Avenue
Evansville, IN 47712
812-426-5610

Potowatomi Zoo
500 South Greenlawn Avenue
South Bend, IN 46615
219-284-9800

Washington Park Zoological
  Gardens
Lakefront
Michigan City, IN 46360
219-872-8628

IOWA

Fejervary Zoo
Fejervary Park
12th and Wikes Streets
Davenport, IA 52803
319-326-7812

KANSAS

Emporia Zoo
P.O. Box 928
Emporia, KS 66801
316-342-7306

Finnup Park and Lee Richardson
  Zoo
Box 499
Finnup Park
Garden City, KS 67846
316-276-2800

Topeka Zoological Park
635 Gage Boulevard
Topeka, KS 66606
913-272-5821

KENTUCKY

Game Farm
Number 1 Game Farm Road
Frankfort, KY 40601
502-223-8211

Louisville Zoological Garden
1100 Trevilian Way
Louisville, KY 40213
502-459-2181

LOUISIANA

Audubon Park and Zoological
  Garden
6500 Magazine Street
New Orleans, LA 70178
504-861-2537

Greater Baton Rouge Zoo
P.O. Box 60
Baker, LA 70714
504-775-3877

MARYLAND

Baltimore Zoo
Druid Hill Park
Baltimore, MD 21217
301-396-7102

Catoctin Mountain Zoological Park
13019 Catoctin Furnace Road
Thurmont, MD 21788
301-271-7488

The Salisbury Zoological
750 South Park Drive
Salisbury, MD 21801
301-742-2123

MASSACHUSETTS

Drumlin Farm Education Center
Lincoln Road
Lincoln, MA 01773
617-259-9807

Walter D. Stone Memorial Zoo
149 Pond Street
Stoneham, MA 02180
617-438-6186

Worcester Science Center
Harrington Way
Worcester, MA 01604
617-791-9211

MICHIGAN

Binder Park Zoo
7400 Division Drive
Battle Creek, MI 49017
616-979-1351

Detroit Zoological Park
8450 West 10 Mile Road
Royal Oak, MI 48068
313-398-0903

John Ball Zoological Gardens
West Fulton at Valley
Grand Rapids, MI 49504
616-456-3809

Saginaw Children's Zoo
1730 South Washington
Saginaw, MI 48601
517-776-1657

MINNESOTA

Minnesota Zoological Garden
12101 Johnny Cake Ridge Road
Apple Valley, MN 55124
612-432-9010

St. Paul's Como Zoo
Midway Parkway and Kaufman
 Drive
St. Paul, MN 55103
612-488-5572

MISSISSIPPI

Jackson Zoological Park
2918 West Capitol Street
Jackson, MS 39209
601-960-1575

MISSOURI

Dickerson Park Zoo
3043 North Fort
Springfield, MO 65803
417-833-1570

Kansas City Zoological Gardens
Swope Park
Kansas City, MO 64132
816-333-7406

St. Louis Zoological Park
Forest Park
St. Louis, MO 63110
314-781-0900

MONTANA

Red Lodge Zoo
Box 820
Red Lodge, MT 59068
406-446-2022

NEBRASKA

Folsom Children's Zoo and
 Botanical Gardens
2800 A Street
Lincoln, NE 68502
402-475-6741

Henry Doorly Zoo
River View Park
Omaha, NE 68107
402-733-8401

NEW JERSEY

The Newark Museum
49 Washington Street
Newark, NJ 07101
201-733-6600

Turtle Back Zoo
560 Northfield Avenue
West Orange, NJ 07052
201-731-5800

Van Saun Park Zoo
Forest Avenue
Paramus, NJ 07652
201-262-3771

NEW MEXICO

Alameda Park Zoo
1321 North White Sands
 Boulevard
Alamogordo, NM 88310
505-437-8430

Living Desert State Park
P.O. Box 100
Carlsbad, NM 88220
505-887-5616

Rio Grande Zoological Park
903 Tenth Street South West
Albuquerque, NM 87102
505-843-7413

Spring River Park and Zoo
City Hall
Roswell, NM 88201
505-622-5811

NEW YORK

Buffalo Zoological Gardens
Delaware Park

Buffalo, NY 14214
716-837-3900

Burnet Park Zoo
Burnet Park
Syracuse, NY 13204
315-425-3774

Central Park Children's Zoo
830 Fifth Avenue
New York, NY 10021
212-360-8213

New York Zoological Park
Bronx River Parkway at Fordham
    Road
Bronx, NY 10460
212-367-1010

Prospect Park Zoo
Empire Boulevard and Flatbush
    Avenue
Brooklyn, NY 11225
718-965-6587

Seneca Park Zoo
2222 St. Paul Street
Rochester, NY 14621
716-266-6846

Staten Island Zoo
614 Broadway
Staten Island, NY 10310
212-442-3100

Utica Zoo
Steele Hill Road
Utica, NY 13501
315-797-3280

NORTH CAROLINA

Dan Nicholas Park Nature Center
Route 10
Box 832
Salisbury, NC 28144
704-636-2089

The Natural Science Center of
    Greensboro
4301 Lawndale Drive
Greensboro, NC 27404
919-288-3769

North Carolina Museum of Life
    and Sciences
433 Murray Avenue

Durham, NC 27704
919-477-0431

North Carolina Zoological Park
Route 4
Box 73
Asheboro, NC 27203
919-879-5606

Western North Carolina Nature
    Center
Gashes Creek Road
Asheville, NC 28805
704-298-5600

OHIO

Akron Zoological Park
500 Edgewood Avenue
Akron, OH 44307
216-375-2298

Cleveland Metroparks Zoo
3900 Brookside Drive
Cleveland, OH 44109
216-661-6500

Columbus Zoological Park
9900 Riverside Drive
Powell, OH 43065
614-889-9471

Toledo Zoological Gardens
2700 Broadway
Toledo, OH 43609
419-385-5721

Zoological Society of Cincinnati
3400 Vine Street
Cincinnati, OH 45220
513-281-4701

OKLAHOMA

Oklahoma City Zoo
Eastern Grand Boulevard
Oklahoma City, OK 73111
405-424-3344

Tulsa Zoological Park
5701 East 36th Street
Tulsa, OK 74115
918-835-8471

OREGON

Oregon High Desert Museum
59800 South Highway 97

Bend, OR 97701
503-382-4754

Washington Park Zoo
4001 South West Canyon Road
Portland, OR 97221
503-226-1561

PENNSYLVANIA

Philadelphia Zoological Garden
34th Street and Girard Avenue
Philadelphia, PA 19104
215-243-1100

The Pittsburgh Zoo
Highland Park
Pittsburgh, PA 15206
412-441-6262

Zooamerica at Hershey Park
Route 743
Hershey, PA 17033
717-534-3860

RHODE ISLAND

Roger Williams Park Zoo
Elmwood Avenue
Providence, RI 02905
401-467-9013

SOUTH CAROLINA

Brookgreen Gardens, A Society for
   Southeastern Flora and Fauna
Murrells Inlet, SC 29576
803-237-4218

Charles Towne Landing-1670
1500 Old Town Road
Charleston, SC 29407
803-556-4450

Magnolia Plantation and Gardens
Route 4
Charleston, SC 29407
803-571-1266

Riverbands Zoological Park
500 Wildlife Parkway
Columbia, SC 29210
803-779-8717

SOUTH DAKOTA

Bear City U.S.A.
Box 1110
Keystone Route
Rapid City, SD 57701
605-343-2290

Black Hills Reptile Gardens
P.O. Box 620
Rapid City, SD 57709
605-342-5873

Great Plains Zoo and Museum
15th and Kiwanis Avenue
Sioux Falls, SD 57102
605-339-7059

TENNESSEE

Knoxville Zoological Park
3333 Woodbine Avenue
Knoxville, TN 37914
615-637-5331

Memphis Zoo and Aquarium
2000 Galloway Street
Memphis, TN 38112
901-726-4787

TEXAS

Abilene Zoological Gardens
Highway 36 at Loop 322
Abilene, TX 29604
915-672-9771

Central Texas Zoo
Route 10
Box 173 E
Waco, TX 76708
817-752-9363

Dallas Zoo
621 East Clarendon Drive
Dallas, TX 75203
214-946-5155

El Paso Zoological Park
Evergreen and Paisano
El Paso, TX 79905
915-541-4601

Ellen Trout Zoo
P.O. Drawer 190

Lufkin, TX 75902
409-634-6313

Gladys Porter Zoo
500 Ringold Street
Brownsville, TX 78520
512-546-7187

Houston Zoological Gardens
Hermann Park
1513 Outerhelt Drive
Houston, TX 77030
713-520-3201

San Antonio Zoological Gardens
    and Aquarium
3903 North St. Mary's Street
San Antonio, TX 78212
512-734-7183

The Texas Zoo
110 Memorial Drive
Victoria, TX 77901
512-573-7681

UTAH

Hagle Zoological Garden
2600 East Sunnyside Avenue
Salt Lake City, UT 84108
801-582-1631

WASHINGTON

Woodland Park Zoological
    Gardens
5500 Phinney Avenue

Seattle, WA 98103
206-625-2244

WEST VIRGINIA

French Creek Game Farm
Route 1
Box 210
French Creek, WV 26218

Good Children's Zoo
Oglebay Park
Wheeling, WV 26003
304-242-3000

WISCONSIN

Henry Vilas Park Zoo
702 South Randall Avenue
Madison, WI 53715
608-266-4732

Lincoln Park Zoo
North 8th Street
Manitowoc, WI 54220
414-683-4537

Milwaukee County Zoological
    Gardens
10001 West Bluemound Road
Milwaukee, WI 53226
414-771-3040

Racine Zoological Park
2131 North Main Street
Racine, WI 53402
414-636-9189

Appendix VII

Indian Information

Indian festivals and pow-wows are held all over the country. They provide rich cultural activities and are a lot of fun. Contact the Bureau of Indian Affairs area office to find out when and where festivals are held in your area.

Bureau of Indian Affairs area offices

Dr. Jerry Jaeger
Aberdeen Area Office
Bureau of Indian Affairs
115 4th Avenue, S.E.
Aberdeen, South Dakota 57401
Telephone: 605/225-0250 Ext. 343
(Nebraska, North Dakota, and
    South Dakota)

Vincent Little
Albuquerque Area Office
Bureau of Indian Affairs
5301 Central Avenue, N.E.
P.O. Box 8327
Albuquerque, New Mexico 87108
Telephone: 505/766-3170
(Colorado and New Mexico)

William P. Ragsdale
Anadarko Area Office
Bureau of Indian Affairs
WCD - Office Complex
P.O. Box 368
Anadarko, Oklahoma 73005
Telephone: 405/247-6673
(Kansas and West Oklahoma)

Richard C. Whitesell
Billings Area Office
Bureau of Indian Affairs
316 North 26th Street
Billings, Montana 59101
Telephone: 406/657-6315
(Montana and Wyoming)

William Ott, Acting Director
Eastern Area Office
Bureau of Indian Affairs
1951 Constitution Avenue, N.W.
Washington, D.C. 20245
Telephone: 703/235-2571
(New York, Maine, Louisiana,
    Florida, North Carolina and
    Mississippi)

Jacob Lestenkof
Juneau Area Office
Bureau of Indian Affairs
709 West 9th Street
Federal Building
P.O. Box 3–8000
Juneau, Alaska 99802
Telephone: 907/586-7177
(Alaska)

Earl Barlow
Minneapolis Area Office
Bureau of Indian Affairs
Chamber of Commerce Building
15 South Fifth St. - 6th Floor
Minneapolis, Minnesota 55402
Telephone: 612/349-3383
(Minnesota, Iowa, Michigan, and
    Wisconsin)

Jose A. Zuni
Muskogee Area Office
Bureau of Indian Affairs
Old Federal Building

5th & Oklmulgee Street
Muskogee, Oklahoma 74401
Telephone: 918/687-2295
(East Oklahoma)

Wilson Barber
Navajo Area Office
Bureau of Indian Affairs
P.O. Box M, Box 1
Window Rock, Arizona 86515
Telephone: 602/871-5151 (5111)
(Navajo Reservations only,
    Arizona, Utah, and New
    Mexico)

James Stevens
Phoenix Area Office
Bureau of Indian Affairs
3030 North Central
P.O. Box 7007
Phoenix, Arizona 85011

Telephone: 602/241-2305
(Arizona, Nevada, Utah,
    California, and Idaho)

Stanley Speaks
Portland Area Office
Bureau of Indian Affairs
1425 Irving Street, N.E.
P.O. Box 3785
Portland, Oregon 97208
Telephone: 503/231-6702
(Oregon, Washington, and Idaho)

Maurice Babby
Sacramento Area Office
Bureau of Indian Affairs
Federal Office Building
2800 Cottage Way
Sacramento, California 95825
Telephone: 916/484-4682
(California)

Bibliography

The American Association of Museums. *The Official Museum Directory 1985.* Wilmette, Ill.: National Register Publishing Co., 1985.

Aronoff, Frances Weber. *Music and Young Children.* New York: Turning Wheel Press, 1979.

Auckett, Amelia D. *Baby Massage: Parent-Child Bonding Through Touching.* New York: Newmarket Press, 1981.

Bland, Jane Cooper. *Art of the Young Child.* New York: The Museum of Modern Art, 1968.

Bos, Bev. *Don't Move the Muffin Tins.* Roseville, Calif.: Turn the Page Press, 1978.

Brazelton, T. Berry, M.D. *Toddlers and Parents.* New York: Dell Publishing Company, Inc., 1974.

Briggs, Dorothy Corkille. *Your Child's Self-Esteem.* Garden City, N.Y.: Doubleday & Co., 1975.

Burtt, Kent Garland, and Karen Kalkstein. *Smart Toys for Babies from Birth to Two.* New York: Harper Colophon Books, 1981.

Caplan, Frank. *The First Twelve Months of Life.* New York: Bantam Books, 1973.

Caplan, Frank, ed. *The Parenting Advisor.* Garden City, N.Y.: Doubleday/Anchor Press, 1978.

Caplan, Frank and Theresa. *The Second Twelve Months of Life.* New York: Grosset & Dunlap, 1977.

Cherry, Claire. *Art for the Developing Child.* Belmont, Calif.: Pitman Learning Inc., 1972.

Cline, Dallas. *Homemade Instruments.* New York: Oak Publishers, 1976.

Cole, Ann, Carolyn Haas, Faith Bushnell, and Betty Weinberger. *I Saw a Purple Cow and 100 Other Recipes for Learning.* Boston: Little, Brown and Company, 1972.

Colgin, Mary Louise, ed. *Chants for Children.* Manlius, N.Y.: Colgin Publishing, 1982.

Dodson, Fitzhugh. *I wish I had a computer that makes waffles.* San Diego: Oak Tree Publishers, 1978.

Duncan, Isadora. *My Life.* New York: Liveright Publishing Corp., 1927 and 1955.

Engelmann, Siegfried and Therese. *Give Your Child a Superior Mind.* New York: Cornerstone Library, 1981.

Fraiberg, Selma H. *The Magic Years.* New York: Charles Scribners & Sons, 1959.

Ginott, Haim G., M.D. *Between Parent and Child.* New York: Avon Books, 1965.

Golomb, Claire. *Young Children's Sculpture and Drawing; A Study in Representational Development.* Cambridge, Mass.: Harvard University Press, 1974.

Hagstrom, Julie. *Let's Pretend.* New York: A & W Visual Library, 1982.

Hagstrom, Julie, and Joan Morrill. *Games Babies Play.* New York: A & W Visual Library, 1979.

Haskell, Lendall L. *Art in the Early Childhood Years.* Columbus, Ohio: Charles E. Merrill Publishing Co., 1979.

Hill, Dorothy M. and Jean Berlfein. *Mud, Sand and Water.* Washington D.C.: National Association for the Education of Young Children, 1977.

Hirsch, Elisabeth S. *The Block Book.* Washington, D.C.: National Association for the Education of Young Children, 1974.

Ibuka, Masaru. *Kindergarten Is Too Late!* New York: Simon and Schuster, 1977.

Ilg, Frances. L., M.D., and Louise Bates Ames, Ph.D. *Child Behavior From Birth to Ten.* New York: Harper & Row, 1955.

Jones, Elizabeth. *What Is Music for Young Children?* Washington, D.C.: National Association for the Education of Young Children, 1969.

Kellogg, Rhoda. *Analyzing Children's Art.* Palo Alto, Calif.: Mayfield Publishing Co., 1969.

Kellogg, Rhoda, with Scott O'Dell. *The Psychology of Children's Art.* San Diego: CRM-Random House, 1967.

Kelly, Marguerite, and Elia Parsons. *The Mother's Almanac.* New York: Doubleday & Company, Inc., 1975.

Kelly, Mary Ellen. *Places to Go and Things to Do With the Kids.* Pennsylvania: JK Productions, Inc., 1980.

Kuczen, Barbara, Ph.D. *Childhood Stress.* New York: Delacorte Press, 1982.

Leach, Penelope. *Your Baby and Child.* New York: Alfred A. Knopf, 1978.

LeBoyer, Frederick. *Loving Hands: The Traditional Indian Art of Baby Massage.* New York: Alfred A. Knopf, 1976.

Lewis, Claudia. *The Montessori Method: Education Before Five, A Handbook on Preschool Education.* New York: Bank Street College of Education, 1977.

Lewis, David. *How to Be a Gifted Parent.* New York: Berkley Books, 1979.

Lowenfeld, Viktor, and W. Lambert Brittain. *Creative and Mental Growth,* 6th edition. New York: Macmillan, 1970.

Mandell, Muriel, and Robert E. Wood. *Make Your Own Musical Instruments.* New York: Sterling Publishers, 1957.

Michael, John A., ed. *The Lowenfeld Lectures.* University Park and London: The Pennsylvania State University Press, 1982.

Moore, Raymond and Dorothy. *Home Grown Kids: A Practical Handbook for Teaching Your Children at Home.* Michigan: Hewitt Research Foundation, 1981.

Newson, John and Elizabeth. *Toys & Playthings: A Practical Guide for Parents and Teachers.* New York: Pantheon Books, 1979.

Reed, Herbert. *Education Through Art.* New York: Random House, 1948.

Richards, Mary Helen. *Threshold to Music.* Palo Alto, Calif.: Fearon Publishers, 1964.

Rubin, Judith Aron. *Child Art Therapy.* New York: Van Nostrand Reinhold Company, 1978.

Rubin, Richard R., Ph.D.; John J. Fisher III, M.A.; and Susan G. Doering. *Your Toddler.* New York: Johnson & Johnson, 1980.

Sheehy, Emma D. *Children Discover Music and Dance.* Henry Holt and Co., 1959.

Shilcock, Susan D., and Peter A. Bergson. *Open Connections: The Other Basics.* Bryn Mawr, Pa.: Open Connections, 1980.

Silberstein-Storfer, Muriel, with Mablen Jones. *Doing Art Together*. New York: Simon and Schuster, 1982.

Spock, Benjamin, M.D. *Baby and Child Care*. New York: Pocket Books, 1976.

Stecher, Miriam B., and Dr. Alice S. Kandell. *Max, the Music Maker*. New York: Lothrop, Lee & Shepard Books, 1980.

Thevenin, Tine. *The Family Bed: An Age-Old Concept in Child Rearing*. Minneapolis: T. Thevenin, 1976.

White, Burton L. *The First Three Years of Life*. New York: Avon Books, 1975.

White, Sheldon, and Barbara Notkin White. *Childhood: Pathways of Discovery*. New York: Multimedia Publications, Inc., 1980.

Index

abstract thinking, 86, 125, 156, 261, 324, 342
   see also symbols, symbolization
adaptability, of parents and teachers, 59, 66, 75, 96, 192, 212, 275
adolescence, 32, 209
adults:
   other, influence of, 93–94, 139
   see also models, modeling;
   parents; teachers
age-appropriate activities, 16–23, 76, 140, 216, 222, 268, 275–276, 312
   for art projects, 312, 330–43
   for finger painting, 98, 100
   for group play, 128–29
   for music education, 351–52
   for painting, 183–84, 185
   for reading, 297–98, 315
   for school visits, 234
   for scribbling, 102, 109, 177
   for sports, 116, 348
   toys and, 154, 157, 239–40
alphabet:
   blocks, 157
   scribbling and, 105–6
   toy, 88
American Museum of Natural History, New York, N.Y., 137
amusement parks, visits to, 140
animals, 48, 55, 59, 92, 139, 218
animated characters, on television, 90
Anti-Coloring Book® The (Striker and Kimmel), 107
Anti-Coloring Book® of Masterpieces, The (Striker), 48–49, 107–8, 235, 268
appreciation, of child's performances and reactions, 27–34, 82, 111, 143, 146, 170–71, 174, 178, 190, 192, 255–58, 268, 270–271, 279, 312, 328, 339, 342
   see also praise; respect

approval:
   negative aspects of, 105, 176, 197, 255–56, 268, 308, 330, 341–42, 344
   see also appreciation;
   encouragement; praise
aquariums, 232, 250
art:
   abstract, 230
   adult-directed, 29, 107, 186–87, 234–36, 261–62, 264, 308–12, 314, 321, 329–31, 330–40
   coloring books vs., 107–8, 235, 321, 329, 337–40
   conceptual, 267
   "correctness" and, 154, 235, 265, 269, 311, 329–31
   examples of preschool, 105, 333
   masterpieces of fine art,
     reproductions of, 48, 52, 57–58, 92, 93
     misuse of, 333, 337–38
   subject-motivated, 233, 309, 312, 330–42
   techniques used in, 229–30
   see also drawing; painting;
   pictures; scribbles, scribbling
art classes, 109, 163, 184, 234–37
   how to choose, 234–35, 236
art contests, 344
art education, 321
   beginning in nursery, 47–58, 61, 92
   justifications for, 269–70, 332
   lasting effects of, 47–50, 57–58, 92, 95, 136, 303
   in nursery school, 308, 310–11, 312, 330–39
art experiences:
   at age 0–1, 95–110
   at age 1–2, 169–87
   at age 2–3, 255–74
   at age 3–4, 329–44
   see also books; clay work; colors;

About the Author

Susan Striker taught art in the public schools before opening her own Young at Art® studio, where children age twelve months to twelve years benefit from her unique methods of stimulating creativity through music, movement, art, and play. The author of the best-selling and influential Anti-Coloring Book® series, Striker also holds an M.A. in Fine Arts and is a certified school administrator. She lives in New York City with her husband and her son, Jason.